THE LOST REGION

IOWA AND THE MIDWEST EXPERIENCE

SERIES EDITOR
William B. Friedricks,
Iowa History Center at Simpson College

The University of Iowa Press gratefully acknowledges
Humanities Iowa for its generous support of the Iowa
and the Midwest Experience series.

by Jon K. Lauck

THE LOST REGION

TOWARD A REVIVAL OF MIDWESTERN HISTORY

UNIVERSITY OF IOWA PRESS, *Iowa City*

University of Iowa Press, Iowa City 52242
Copyright © 2013 by the University of
Iowa Press
www.uiowapress.org
Printed in the United States of America

DESIGN BY TERESA W. WINGFIELD

The University of Iowa Press gratefully
acknowledges Humanities Iowa for its
generous support of the Iowa and Midwest
Experience series.

The University of Iowa Press is a
member of Green Press Initiative and
is committed to preserving natural
resources.

Printed on acid-free paper

LIBRARY OF CONGRESS
CATALOGING-IN-PUBLICATION DATA
Lauck, Jon, 1971–
The lost region: toward a revival of Mid-
western history / by Jon K. Lauck.
        pages   cm.—(Iowa and the
Midwest experience)
Includes bibliographical references and
index.
ISBN: 978-1-60938-189-9; 1-60938-189-0
(pbk.)
ISBN: 978-1-60938-216-2; 1-60938-216-1
(e-book)
1. Middle West—History. 2. Regional-
ism—Middle West—History. I. Title.
F351.L33 2013
977—dc23   2013010125

To Amy, Brendtly,
Abigail, Henry, and Jack,
midwesterners all

There is a charm in restoring the past, in compelling the procession of leaders of human thought and action again to traverse the stage of human consciousness, in rescuing from oblivion what is worth the memory of the present day. The events of past years, the institutions that have passed away, the life and manners of societies that are gone, are a precious heritage, not to be wantonly ignored in the heat and bustle of the day.

—FREDERICK JACKSON TURNER

CONTENTS

THE LOST REGION

INTRODUCTION

IN NOVEMBER 2010, I had a meeting with A. G. Sulzberger, the then twenty-eight-year-old son of Arthur Sulzberger Jr., owner of the *New York Times*. A. G. was the heir apparent to one of the nation's largest media organizations and cultural arbiters and was pursuing his journalistic bona fides. After a stint covering the city beat in New York, A. G. was sent to the Kansas City bureau, where he was told to cover Missouri, Nebraska, Iowa, Kansas, North Dakota, and South Dakota. That November, A. G. had come north to Sioux Falls, South Dakota, to look for news stories. He was on the hunt for local color—I pointed to the ongoing harvest, the culmination of the football season, the pheasant-hunting "opener," a recent deer-hunting experiment inside the city of Sioux Falls, news about a developing global wheat crisis, the growth of the wind energy industry, the proposed renovations to the Corn Palace in Mitchell, how some rodeo injuries are ignored by the injured riders so they do not delay the rodeo (if the single ambulance leaves a rural rodeo to tend to an injured rider, the event has to stop), the beginning of high school debate season (the activity originated in South Dakota)—and he settled on a story about the extremes of South Dakota's weather over the course of the previous year.[1]

Sulzberger was eager, sharp, and earnest, and he wrote a fine story, which appeared in the popular Sunday edition of the *Times*. The story's lead focused on a rancher who had preserved a record-setting hailstone the size of a cantaloupe in his freezer. The story depicted an element of life in the center of the country by generalizing from some timely news hooks about violent weather and demonstrated that Sulzberger was diligently earning his stripes. But Sulzberger's sojourn to South Dakota was premised, to a considerable extent, on questing after "interesting local color" and developing oddball themes. His trip had the air of adventure, an attempt to locate and translate the exotic Other, the people in the mostly red states of "flyover country," for the newspaper's largely urban and coastal audience. He conceded that the *Times*'s coverage of the region would continue to be sporadic. Few resources would be devoted to the vast expanse occupied by Missouri, Nebraska, Iowa, Kansas, and the Dakotas. This area would continue to serve mainly as a source of eccentric stories on an intermittent basis for the nation's "newspaper of record," whose correspondents sent to the region, seemingly so removed from its interior rhythms, would, as one University of Iowa English professor once noted, continue to "write like foreign correspondents."[2] The area would be an afterthought. It would function as an attic or old tool-shed from which to periodically pluck a random or antique or period piece, not as a critical region of the republic to be taken seriously on a sustained basis.

These revelations about the coverage decisions of the *New York Times* were not shocking. The main currents of American cultural and political life do not focus on the prairie Midwest very much. Hollywood happenings, new cultural trends, political wrangling in Washington, and international emergencies all consume much of the media's and thus the nation's collective attention. Even country music, a large economic sector that is culturally attuned to the American heartland, neglects the Midwest. The big questions and debates in the American historical profession, which once included a strong contingent of midwestern historians, also fail to focus on the Midwest. The United States is a large and bustling and energetic nation containing multitudes, as Whitman said, and its many regions and activities and cultural and political impulses naturally dilute attention to any one region. But the Midwest receives less attention than other regions, and less than it should in general. This book is designed to draw more eyes and ears to the story of the Midwest, a "ghost among regions" that has been lost to the popular and historical imagination.[3]

In the past, the general neglect of the Midwest has not gone unnoticed. Soon after settlement, efforts were made to give the region a voice. Local leaders began asserting themselves against eastern cultural, political, and economic dominance early on and developing what was then considered a "western" identity. Frederick Jackson Turner, a son of Portage, Wisconsin, was frustrated with the European and eastern focus of the history profession when attending graduate school at Johns Hopkins and began an effort to include the significance of the prairie frontier in the broader narrative of American history. In the early twentieth century, other historians in the Midwest would follow Turner and form a new association to give greater attention to the region and lessen the dominance of the easterners. Other writers and artists would similarly embrace the midwestern cause. Grant Wood, the Iowa artist, would become the best-known representative of this advocacy of a distinctive regionalism and the cause of subverting the cultural colonialism of the East and of Europe.

Beginning in the early twentieth century, in addition to the cultural dominance of the East, midwesterners also had to contend with the outright hostility of some writers and cultural critics and to endure what the historian Christopher Lasch called an "unremitting onslaught against bourgeois culture."[4] Some intellectuals found little to love in the civic life and small town and agrarian culture of the Midwest and thought of themselves as "being suffocated between the Rotarian and the peasant."[5] On the literary front, Sinclair Lewis won fame for this purported assault on the midwestern small town. H. L. Mencken further popularized a dismissive attitude. Mencken said of Willa Cather: "I don't care how well she writes, I don't give a damn what happens in Nebraska."[6] Cutting against the slowly accreting works of historians out on the midwestern prairie, the historical profession also began to denigrate rural and small town life.[7] Some critics even attacked Grant Wood as a fascist for advancing midwestern themes in his artwork.[8] This attitude persists. Some people who are prominently placed in the American cultural hierarchy simply do not think much of the rural Midwest, if they think of it at all. One typical Sunday morning when writing this book I opened the *New York Times Book Review* to find a long book review written by Princeton professor Joyce Carol Oates in which she smugly accepts— without even a shrug—some writer's depiction of "zombie Midwesterners."[9] Arguing for more attention to the history of the prairie Midwest, in short, means swimming against some strong cultural currents.

Although not as successful as the highly organized efforts of the early twentieth century, there have been a few attempts to draw attention to the history of the Midwest in recent decades. The field of social history, which blossomed beginning in the 1960s, produced some important studies set in the Midwest, but not particularly focused on the Midwest as a region. In 1986, the former *Great Lakes Review*, which focused on both history and literature, became the *Michigan Historical Review* and solely devoted to history, and it remains amenable to publishing articles about the Great Lakes region, especially if they relate to historical developments in Michigan.[10] Andrew Cayton has published some authoritative books on the Midwest and even edited a massive encyclopedia about the region.[11] Some of Cayton's books were published by Indiana University Press, whose Midwestern History and Culture series included a number of impressive works about the Midwest, including the collection *Heartland*, edited by James Madison.[12] The early 1990s also saw the release of William Cronon's environmental history of Chicago and its economic hinterlands.[13] The long-running *Wisconsin Magazine of History* does, at times, publish articles more generally about the Midwest, and several impressive state-based history journals continue to publish works about individual midwestern states.[14] More recently, David Brown drew attention to some prominent historians from the Midwest who were once influential but whose prominence declined in the postwar era.[15]

While there is much to recommend this body of work, other longer-term trends indicate great difficulty for the field of midwestern history. The historian John D. Hicks, a successor to Turner at the University of Wisconsin, began making plans for a history of the Midwest in the 1930s, but abandoned the effort when he moved to California in the 1940s, an early sign that the once strong tradition of midwestern history was fading.[16] The Newberry Library in Chicago offered fellowships in midwestern studies funded by the Rockefeller Foundation starting in 1944, but the program ended by 1952.[17] Knopf's planned series of regional histories of the United States, which bore some fruit in the 1960s, never resulted in a history of the Midwest.[18] The greatest blow to the field of midwestern history came in the 1960s, when the once midwestern-oriented *Mississippi Valley Historical Review* transformed itself into the more general *Journal of American History*. This decision left the Midwest without a regional journal such as those enjoyed by the South, the West, New England, and even the allegedly understudied Great Plains.[19]

More recent developments point to continuing neglect of the region. In the 1970s and early 1980s, Richard Jensen directed the Family and Community History Center at the Newberry Library in Chicago, which focused on state and local history and quantification, but the effort was not focused solely on the Midwest, and it ceased by the mid-1980s.[20] A National Endowment for the Humanities (NEH) initiative in the late 1990s designed to promote the creation of various centers for the study of regionalism also yielded much less than was anticipated in the Midwest.[21] One book on the nation's regions published in the 1990s completely ignored the Midwest.[22] A study of this era found that courses in midwestern history were rare and that courses in the history of the West, South, Southwest, Great Plains, New England, and the Pacific Northwest were much greater in number.[23] Despite sporadic exceptions, Carl

Ubbelohde's assessment published in the 1990s revealed a "near dearth of Midwest historical studies," a declining number of dissertations written about the region, and reduced efforts by midwestern historical societies, leading him to conclude that the midwestern historical "landscape is quite barren."[24] Because of such trends, Susan Gray could justifiably say that the Midwest "remains the most understudied region in the United States."[25] One recent treatment concluded that the "Midwest is a classic example of a nonexistent region."[26]

Some journals that seem, at first glance, to be focused on the Midwest either pursue a broader agenda or have ceased publication altogether. *Midwest Quarterly*, started in 1959 at Pittsburg State University in Kansas, is a "Journal of Contemporary Thought" that publishes across multiple disciplines and does not focus on the Midwest.[27] In 1918, the Illinois Catholic Historical Society commenced publishing the *Illinois Catholic Historical Review* in an attempt to create an outlet for articles about Catholic history in the Midwest. In the 1930s, the journal was taken over by Loyola University of Chicago and the name changed to *Mid-America: An Historical Review*. For at least two decades *Mid-America* focused on Catholic and midwestern history, but by the 1960s the journal had become a general history journal. In the 1980s, one adviser advocated refocusing the journal on midwestern history, as its name implies, but the idea was voted down.[28] In 1975, *The Midwest Review: A Journal of the History and Culture of the Mississippi Valley* was launched at Wayne State College in Nebraska and was Midwest-oriented but also published articles on a variety of topics.[29] In 1991, unfortunately, *The Midwest Review* ceased publication, and in 2002 *Mid-America* folded. In 1975, Miami University in Ohio began publishing the journal *The Old Northwest: A Journal of Regional Life and Letters*, but it closed up shop in 1992.[30] In 1978, Western Illinois University started publishing *Western Illinois Regional Studies*, which focused on midwestern history and literature, but it was terminated in 1992 due to budget constraints.[31] In 1981, the University of Minnesota–Duluth started publishing the journal *Upper Midwest History* in order to bring more attention to the region, but it had failed by 1985 due to administrative changes at the university.[32] In the 1990s, Marv Bergman, the editor of *Annals of Iowa*, suggested transforming *Annals* into a midwestern-focused journal of history, but found little support.[33] In another telltale sign of the declining fortunes of midwestern history, the large history department at the University of Minnesota does not even offer a Minnesota history course (the history department at the University of Georgia, by way of regional contrast, employs nine southern historians).[34] The Indiana University Press's series about midwestern history also encountered a production slowdown in recent years and finally became inactive.[35] Iowa State University Press and the University of South Dakota Press, both of which published books about the Midwest, were sold or shut down.[36] By 2010, Ohio State University Press had made the decision to stop publishing works of history altogether.[37] In 2012, the Rural and Regional Studies Program at Southwest Minnesota State University, which once focused on midwestern history, was dismantled, in part due to a failure to understand midwestern regionalism.[38] A new survey of the fields of American history, published in recognition of the 100th anniversary of the Organization of American Historians (OAH), which was founded as a midwestern history organization, ironically ignored midwestern history altogether.[39] As this project was being finalized, the University of Missouri Press, which published many titles about the Midwest, was fighting for its life.[40]

These indicia of decline are not difficult to explain. Scarce resources, of course, are a factor, but resource deployment is a function of priorities, and promoting the study of midwestern history is not high on the academic agenda at present. An older generation of historians, who were often products of small towns and farms in the Midwest, were more committed to this area of study in past decades, and the passing of their leadership necessarily meant less academic and administrative energy would be devoted to the Midwest.[41] This loss of focus is related to a larger diminution of regionalist attachments in an increasingly "placeless" electronic and homogenous world.[42] The fluid borders of the Midwest make it an additionally difficult place to study, especially in comparison to New England or the Old South, and its internal diversity complicates the delineation of unifying characteristics. Without a rigid regional boundary, the Midwest both begets more localism and, because it is seen as a "microcosm of the national macrocosm," more nationalism, and as a result yields less regional history.[43] Historians are also drawn to defining moments and great calamities and civil crises, which, in comparison to other regions, are in short supply in the Midwest.[44] The main currents of life in the American Midwest during its first century were also derived from farming and small town life, which are not a primary focus of historians at the moment. Historians, Andrew Cayton notes, are not now oriented to "territoriality," or regions that were the creations of "European males," and are instead focused on environmentalism and categories of analysis related to race, class, and gender.[45] The most recent study of Grant Wood, for example, focused on whether he was gay, not on his vision of the Midwest as a unique historical or geographical space.[46] Wood's work remains tainted as "corny backwater art . . . stagnating out there in the boondocks."[47] The history of the Midwest, in short, is not especially compatible with the main trends in historical research in recent decades. Noting the Midwest's image of innocent agrarianism, one historian observed that to "put it mildly, neither innocence nor pastoralism were topics highly regarded by historians who came to their careers in the 1960's and 1970's."[48] The consequence of these trends and the failure of recent generations of historians to see the Midwest as historically significant is that the region has become a foreign country, seldom visited or discussed while serving as a periodic source of exotica, but largely off the main map of American historiography and lost to the main channels of historical inquiry.

To end the neglect of their region, midwestern historians will need to explain why the Midwest matters to the broader course of American history. The Midwest deserves greater attention from historians, in short, because the region played a central role in American development by helping spark the American Revolution, stabilizing the young American republic, making it economically strong, giving it an agricultural heartland, and helping the North win the Civil War. The Midwest replicated the republican institutions created by the American Founders, and its settler populism made them more democratic. It fostered the growth of a regional identity and thereby weakened the cultural dominance of the urban East. Attention to land markets on the prairie also deepened the American embrace of capitalist institutions and attitudes. These various foundational dynamics of the Midwest are explored in chapter 1, "Why the Midwest Matters."

Although obscured and neglected now, an impressive group of historians—and still a few today, to be sure—once focused on the history of the Midwest. The much-maligned Frederick Jackson Turner, of course, drew attention to the prairie frontier, but lesser-known regional- and state-oriented historians also helped to develop several state historical societies in the Midwest and began building a body of work to help preserve the region's history. After a Nebraska man took the lead in organizing the regionally oriented Mississippi Valley Historical Association (MVHA), a network of historians and institutions made rapid advances in the study of the Midwest. This body of knowledge, now largely unknown to popular audiences and even to many historians, is the subject of chapter 2, "The Prairie Historians and the Foundations of Midwestern History."

While the Prairie Historians had their weaknesses and neglected some topics, they also wrote foundational books, covered more ground than might be expected by the present generation of historians, and embraced a workable form of history that can serve as a model for future research in an era when many historians are frustrated with the direction of their field. The strengths and weaknesses of the Prairie Historians are considered in chapter 3, "The Case for Midwestern History." The need to move the cause of midwestern history forward is addressed in chapter 4, "Toward a Revival of Midwestern History."

These chapters, I hope, collectively demonstrate the importance of the Midwest, the depth of historical work once performed on the region, the continuing insights that can be gleaned from this body of knowledge, and the lessons that can be learned from some prominent historians that will bolster future attempts to revive the study of the American Midwest. The long-term goal is to contribute to the development of a robust historiography of the Midwest, a project in which the newly created University of Iowa Press's Iowa and the Midwest Experience series will play an essential leadership role.

At the outset of any book about the Midwest, it is wise to discuss what area the term encompasses. The parameters of the Midwest have always given historians and social scientists fits—a definitional problem that has surely inhibited studies of the region—so it is important to designate what version of the Midwest serves as the background for this book. Like so many who have written about the Midwest, I follow Turner. In a 1901 essay entitled "The Middle West," Turner used the census designation of the "North Central" region as his basis for including Iowa, Minnesota, Kansas, Nebraska, South Dakota, North Dakota, Missouri, Wisconsin, Illinois, Michigan, Indiana, and Ohio in the region, a grouping that, as Carl Ubbelohde notes, has "proved durable."[49] According to the geographer James Shortridge, it became the "consensus opinion" that Turner's twelve states constituted the "Middle West."[50] I recognize, of course, that the borders of this Midwest are porous, and the proper perimeter of the Midwest has been and will be debated many times, but I resist the tendency to allow definitional complexity to stifle attempts to study the region.[51]

For the purposes of this book and in order to provide added coherence, I focus on the *prairie* Midwest, as opposed to the areas of the Midwest more connected with the forests and heavy industry around the Great Lakes.[52] The historian Paul Gates explained that western settlers first encountered "small prairies" in Ohio and Michigan, but that it was "not until they penetrated into northern Indiana, central Illinois, Missouri, Iowa, and eastern Kansas and Nebraska did they see the great prairies that stretched to the horizon."[53] These "great prairies" were generally flat or rolling, treeless, and covered in bluestem, featuring soils made rich by the glaciers, which were especially "good to the prairies of Illinois and Iowa."[54] The prairie Midwest is not homogenous and self-contained, of course. Its topography and people vary, and it was influenced by less agrarian components of the Midwest and by other regions and was not immune to national trends, but it also has its own unities and serves as a useful basis of study. There is a reason that the parameters for the Midwest set forth by Turner "had become universal" by the early twentieth century.[55]

IN THE COURSE OF WRITING THIS BOOK, I have incurred many debts. For their help with the research necessary to tell this story and to make my arguments, I want to thank Becky Folkerts and Ronelle Thompson of Augustana College; Harry Thompson of the Center for Western Studies; Rosemary Switzer, Lori Birell, and Nancy Martin of the University of Rochester Special Collections; Martha Briggs of the Newberry Library; David Kessler and Maria Brandt of the Bancroft Library; Bonnie Coles and Patrick Kerwin of the National Archives; Jessy Randall of Colorado College; Ana Guimaraes of Cornell University Special Collections; Steve Ross of Yale University Library Manuscripts and Archives; Peter Blodgett and Jennifer Goldman of the Huntington Library; Bernard Bailyn and Emily Lebaron of the International Seminar on the History of the Atlantic World, 1500–1825, at Harvard University; Timothy Driscoll of Harvard University Archives; James B. M. Schick of Pittsburg State University; Joshua Caster of the University of Nebraska Archives; Elizabeth Sullivan of the Miami University Library; Patricia Nelson Limerick and Amanda Hardman of the Center for the West at the University of Colorado–Boulder; James Potter and Andrea Faling of the Nebraska State Historical Society; Hampton Smith and Tracey Baker of the Minnesota Historical Society; Erin George of the University of Minnesota Archives; Romie Minor of the Detroit Public Library; Erin Gobel of the Indiana Historical Society; Sabrina Riley of the Union College Archives; John Skarstad of the University of California–Davis Archives; Mary Bennett of the State Historical Society of Iowa; Curt Hanson of the University of North Dakota Archives; Kimberly Harper of the State Historical Society of Missouri; David Frasier of the Lilly Library at Indiana University; Dan Daily of the University of South Dakota Archives; Virgil Dean and Sara Keckeisen of the Kansas Historical Society; Harry Miller of the Wisconsin Historical Society; Jean Karlen of Wayne State College; George Toth and Colleen Kelley of the University of Iowa Archives; Neil Storch of the University of Minnesota–Duluth; Ainsley Powell of the University of Mississippi Archives and Special Collections; and Crystal Gamradt and the many librarians of Siouxland Libraries.

For reading parts of the early manuscript or providing comments and research advice along the way, I also want to thank David Anderson, Peter Argersinger, Annette Atkins, Edwin Barber, Marv Bergman, Peter Blodgett, John Porter Bloom, Allan Bogue, David Brown, Joan Catapano, Andrew Cayton, Bob Cherny, Dave Danbom, Robert Dykstra, Dave Emmons, Nicole Etcheson, Gilbert Fite, Mark Friedberger, Susan Gray, Gene Gressley, Paul Hass, Ellis Hawley, Don Hickey, Doug Hurt, Richard Jensen, Ted Karamanski, Dick Kirkendall, Lori Lahlum, Howard Lamar, Bill Lass, James Leary, Dick Lowitt, Fred Luebke, David Macleod, James Madison, Stephen Meats, Frederick Merk III, Eric Miller, John E. Miller, Ron Naugle, Paula Nelson, Marcia Noe, Walter Nugent, Pat O'Brien, Robert Ostergren, David Pichaske, Earl Rogers, Malcolm Rohrbough, John Schacht, James B. M. Schick, James Shortridge, Bob Swierenga, Robert Utley, and John Wunder.

Variations of certain sections of this book have been published elsewhere in different forms as: "The 'Interior Tradition' in American History," *Annals of Iowa* (Winter 2010); "The Prairie Historians and the Foundations of Midwestern History," *Annals of Iowa* (Spring 2012); and "Why the Midwest Matters," *Midwest Quarterly* (Winter 2013). Marv Bergman, the editor of *Annals of Iowa* and also a midwesterner, deserves particular thanks for his support of and contributions to the early component parts of this book and great praise for his dedication to the history of the midwestern historical enterprise.

It is difficult to pinpoint the precise origins of this book. I have been breathing this air for a long time, and the thoughts expressed here have been congealing for many years. Born to a farm family living near Madison, South Dakota, I am descended from an Irishman who emigrated to Nebraska during the famine of the 1840s and then moved to Iowa to farm and a German who emigrated directly from Mecklenberg in the 1880s to South Dakota to become a prairie farmer. I went to college at South Dakota State University, where the farm kids in South Dakota tend to go to college, and to graduate school at the University of Iowa, where there once was a strong tradition of studying midwestern history, and wrote my dissertation on farming and farm politics in the "Grain Belt," or the twelve states that Frederick Jackson Turner designated as the Midwest. I went to law school at the University of Minnesota, where courses in agricultural law were offered, and I later taught agricultural law while in private practice. I also taught history at South Dakota State University, including a class on South Dakota history. In the course of this work and these studies, I was constantly driving around the heart of the prairie Midwest, and, when working on my dissertation and other projects, I developed a deeper sense of the Midwest by working in archives in Iowa, Wisconsin, Minnesota, South Dakota, North Dakota, Kansas, Illinois, and Indiana. In graduate school, I started giving papers at conferences such as the Missouri River Valley History Conference, the Great Lakes History Conference, the Northern Great Plains History Conference, and the Dakota Conference, and I still make a concerted effort to attend these gatherings. Thinking about midwestern history, in short, is not a recent experience, and thus the precise origins of this book are hard to locate.

While I have absorbed the rhythms of the prairie Midwest since birth, my awareness of the region did not take an academic turn until I encountered some serious-minded scholars. At South Dakota State University, I was blessed by the presence of John E. Miller, a product of small towns in Kansas, Minnesota, Missouri, and Illinois and a Wisconsin history Ph.D. who has given voice to the history of the small town Midwest. When I was writing this book, Miller was writing a collective biography of small town boys from the Midwest, and we shared a great deal of research and mutual encouragement.[56] In graduate school at Iowa, I was fortunate to work with Ellis Hawley, who hails from rural Kansas and became an expert on the political economy of the New Deal and provided a model for my dissertation research on competition issues in midwestern farm markets. My dissertation director was Deirdre McCloskey, whose sweeping view of economic history holds a special place for the market towns of the Midwest. Although not a native, McCloskey genuinely appreciated the Midwest, and her accounts of "Bourgeois Virtue" have done much to counter the attacks on middle-class small town life leveled by intellectuals in the United States during the early twentieth century. Professors Miller, Hawley, and McCloskey have been providing me guidance for many years, and I want to thank them, once again, for all their kindnesses and advice.

A great many thanks are also due to Catherine Cocks of the University of Iowa Press and Bill Friedricks, the editor of the Iowa and the Midwest Experience series for the University of Iowa Press. Catherine and Bill maintained a strong interest in this book and deserve high praise and thanks for their advice and support.

Most important, I want to thank my family. My parents grew up on farms near Winfred and Junius, South Dakota, and they continue to embody that social and civic spirit that makes the Midwest a humane and special place. My wife, Amy, is that classic midwestern figure, a Norwegian Lutheran, and she shares my interest in the Midwest, even though she would strongly prefer milder winters and more beaches. For entertainment, my family goes to Minnesota Viking games and watches the Jackrabbits, Coyotes, Bison, Cornhuskers, Hawkeyes, Gophers, and Cyclones, and for family vacations we go to Cedar Rapids, Alexandria, Duluth, Devil's Lake, Forest City, Chicago, Detroit Lakes, Grand Rapids, Branson, Lake Poinsett, Lake Oahe, Lake Madison, Lake Melissa, Lake Kampeska, Oxford (Iowa), Bayfield, Minneapolis, Ponca, Nisswa, Gull Lake, Pierre, Sault Ste. Marie, Mackinac Island, Lansing, Wisconsin Dells, and Fargo. Just after completing the first draft of this book in 2011, we took a family vacation to Quebec to see the site of General Wolfe's victory on the Plains of Abraham, which led to British and then American control of the Midwest. Just after completing the second draft of this book in 2012, we took a family vacation that included an obligatory visit to see the Kensington Runestone, which apparently proves that the Vikings were in western Minnesota during the 1300s. My family, in short, understands why the Midwest matters and, I am sure, would prefer that I tell someone else for a change.

One

WHY THE MIDWEST MATTERS

THE HISTORIAN FREDERICK JACKSON TURNER concentrated his work on forces and moments that mattered in the American past, and his focus yielded essays on the "significance" of the western frontier, the nation's varied regions, the advancement of democratic institutions and attitudes, the influence of the pioneer heritage, and even the evolution of historical writing itself.[1] In an age of cascading data and detailed micro-histories, Turner's breadth of vision provides a welcome respite and offers a rare sense of perspective to a world drowning in information but parched of its relevance.[2] Even a critic such as Richard Hofstadter admired Turner because he "eschewed" the monograph "with its minute investigation of details and its massing of footnotes" and because he spoke to the big questions about the nation's history.[3] Turner's successor at the University of Wisconsin, Frederic Logan Paxson, maintained this tradition, counseling historians to transcend the arcane and "to come to some conclusions" about the nation's past and to "make an attempt at synthesis, however tentative and inexact."[4] In the 1920s, when Paxson announced that the "time is ripe for [a] synthesis" of western history and he tasked himself with writing a sweeping account of the region, his efforts were rewarded with a Pulitzer Prize.[5] Turner's successor at Harvard, Frederick Merk, similarly emphasized "the *longue durée* or long view of events" and sought to explain why they mattered.[6]

While Turner, Paxson, and Merk supported research on the smaller component parts of American history and fully understood how critical these efforts were to their work, they never lost sight of the bigger picture and the need to explain to a broader audience the significance of their studies. For a revival of midwestern history to be possible, the approach of Turner, Paxson, and Merk must be embraced—historians must first explain why this history matters on the broader canvas of human affairs. If they embrace this mission, they will have much to report. The Midwest matters, in short, because it helps explain the course of foundational events in North America, the origins of the American Revolution, the political and social foundations of the American republic, the outcome of the Civil War, and the emergence of the United States as a world power that shaped global events. The Midwest reveals the evolution of interior resistance to the coastal dominance of politics and culture, which begat forms of populism that still persist and resonate in American political culture, and explains the history of capitalism in the United States, over which the debate will long endure. American Indians, who were deeply involved in the formative military clashes of the early Midwest, were pushed farther west by pioneer settlers, and African Americans who sought an escape from the South increasingly chose the Midwest as their home beginning in the twentieth century.

The Midwest's influence on the course of American and global history began in the colonial American backcountry.[7] By the middle of the eighteenth century, New France controlled Canada, Louisiana, and the Mississippi Valley and dominated the Great Lakes region while British colonies lined the east coast of what is now the United States. When the French began to fortify their holdings and British traders and settlers started moving into the interior backcountry, or the future site of the American Midwest, frictions along the frontier border of the French and British empires followed.[8] In 1754, worried about French encroachment on its western flank, the colony of Virginia dispatched twenty-one-year-old Major George Washington to establish a fort on the Ohio River and to signal to the French that the colony would defend its frontier. Washington returned in defeat, but his failed expedition set in motion the train of events that would lead to a global conflict between France and England, which included a "war for the American backcountry," or the Midwest.[9] By sparking what Winston Churchill called "the first world war," frontier settlers in the Midwest served as the proximate cause of the liquidation of France's New World empire, Britain's acquisition of the Midwest, and the later birth of the American republic.[10] As two historians quipped about George Washington's trek into the colonial backcountry, if "Washington was the father of his country, then here was the moment of conception."[11]

After the war, the British made preparations to govern their new western lands, including the deployment of 10,000 troops to the region, a costly plan that, along with the debts from the war with France, led to new taxes and restrictions on their American colonies, which caused colonial grumbling and ultimately chatter of rebellion. Clarence Alvord explained the midwestern origins of these tensions in the colonies, noting that the new imperial taxation plans "arose out of the conditions existing in the Mississippi Valley."[12] The British also made plans to divide the interior region into new colonies, which further angered landholders in colonial Virginia, including Governor Patrick Henry, who maintained claims to the lands to the west. The British decision to assign administrative control over the backcountry to their newly acquired colony of Quebec caused more strife.[13] These British imperial designs and bureaucratic machinations and the resulting conflicts over the future of western lands caused many Virginians to support the growing colonial sentiment in favor of rebelling against the British Crown.[14] Had the British cabinet pursued different policies in what would become the Midwest, as some ministers counseled, they "might have saved the British Empire."[15] Although overshadowed in histories of the American Revolution by the rebelliousness of Bostonians and coastal merchants, Alvord emphasizes that the "roots" of the American revolt were "not confined within the narrow limits of the tidewater region," but "stretched far back into the hinterland and found sustenance even beneath the primeval forests that lined the banks of the rivers Ohio and Mississippi."[16]

Disputes over British managerial control of the lands in the West intensified with the development of an interior political consciousness. Backcountry settlers increasingly resisted the dominance of coastal areas, which tended to control the colonies. By the time of the Revolution, Kim M. Gruenwald explains, the "friction between the backcountry and the eastern seaboard had been seething for a generation."[17] In social affairs, backcountry settlers became less deferential toward colonial elites and more egalitarian and democratic. They also sought a stronger voice in colonial politics.[18] Because of these developing regional sentiments, the controls and diktats of the British imperial system were a recipe for insurrection in the colonial backcountry, which would strongly support the revolt against the Crown.[19] When war came, the American revolutionaries were quick to act in the backcountry. Virginia sent forth George Rogers Clark to secure the western lands and established the future American claim to the Midwest, which was recognized in the Treaty of Paris of 1783.[20]

After the Revolution, more settlers moved west, and the new American nation extended its experiment in republican government beyond the narrow confines of the Atlantic rim. During the 1790s, one New York newspaper deemed this migration a "rage for removing into the back parts."[21] When these settlers arrived in the future Midwest, they "cloned," to employ James Belich's genetic metaphor, the republican and constitutional achievements of the original thirteen colonies.[22] This cloning was formalized by the Northwest Ordinance, which institutionalized a process of state-making for the western lands.[23] Instead of allowing the original colonies to claim the lands to the west and absorb them into the nation's existing political subunits, the young American government created new territories and eventually new states in the West and mandated that they adopt the republican practices and institutions that had prevailed with the American Revolution. The western territories would then become, as Jefferson foresaw, central pillars of the American "empire of liberty."[24]

The republicanism of the American Revolution moved west with the settlers and, as Belich explains, was bolstered by "two pairs of Anglophone institutions."[25] The first pair, representative assemblies and the common law, were products of the original English settlements in America. The second pair, a broad franchise for citizens and the continuation of political decentralization or the "cloning" of republican institutions in the western territories, are less directly products of Britain and are instead "neo-British," or the products of the American Revolution and the movement of Americans westward.[26] Thus the heritage of English and colonial republicanism, along with the critical decisions of American political leaders, especially the adoption of the Northwest Ordinance, promoted democratic development in the West.[27] In the early 1800s, western states entered the Union with "constitutions that were ultra democratic by prevailing standards."[28] As a result, voting and civic participation in the Midwest were much higher than in Britain, where, in 1800, only 3 percent of Englishmen could vote. The decision about what political institutions to plant in the West "did matter," Belich explains, and led to strong democratic traditions in the region.[29] Because of the Northwest Ordinance, according to the historian James Madison, the republicanism of the Revolution and "basic American freedoms extended Westward."[30]

The Midwest's fate was further determined by Napoleon's abandonment of his plans to revive the French empire in North America and by the region's tilt toward the American North. Jefferson's hopes for an "empire of liberty" that also included western lands beyond the Mississippi River were realized with Napoleon's sale of the Louisiana Territory to the United States in 1803, which added millions more acres of prairies and plains to the public domain.[31] Gordon Wood emphasizes that "empire" in Jefferson's mind "did not mean the coercive domination of alien peoples; instead, it meant a nation of citizens spread over vast tracts of land."[32] It also meant the long-run stability of the American republic. In the agrarian territories and states of the West, Jefferson believed, the republican principles and practices of the Revolution would be renewed: "By enlarging the empire of liberty, we multiply its auxiliaries, and provide new sources of renovation, should its principles at any time degenerate in those portions of our country which gave them birth."[33] More western lands also meant more citizen farmers. By the time of Jefferson's election to the presidency in 1800, half of white American men owned land, compared to 10 percent in England.[34]

The nature of midwestern settlement also determined the destiny of the nation. Wood explains that the settlement of the Old Northwest and the new lands of the Louisiana Purchase, which Belich and others see as decisive to American political development, could have shifted American history in a different direction if it had bolstered the strength of the southern section of the new American republic. But the "swarming numbers of anti-slave Yankees from New England" into Ohio and beyond ensured a northern orientation to the Midwest, despite a few sporadic efforts to plant a southern culture and economy in the region.[35] In the prairie Midwest, small farms and small towns were the norm, newspapers thrived, civic life blossomed, and political participation was strong.[36] As a result, the prairies were "more democratic and egalitarian" than the Southeast, where life was shaped by slavery and plantations, and "without snobbishness," like the East.[37] The Midwest became, said the historian Henry Clyde Hubbart, a "turbulent, youthful, rampant democracy."[38]

Jefferson's plans for the West were not universally embraced. Some early American leaders feared that their republican experiment would stumble over the social, economic, and racial diversity in the West. Fisher Ames saw Louisiana, for example, as a "Gallo-Hispano-Indian omnium gatherum of savages and adventurers" that could not be "expected to sustain and glorify our republic."[39] Still others worried that the delicate new experiment in representative government would not work over an extended territory, but Jefferson remained confident that the republic could be effectively expanded.[40] Conservative easterners, who at first feared that republican commitments and religious devotion would erode in the West, came to see the frontier and the resulting prairie states as bulwarks of American republicanism.[41]

In the territories of the Midwest, American settlers embraced the principles of the Revolution, fought for their right to form self-governing states, opposed what they saw as the arbitrary and aristocratic power of federal appointees, and did so in the tradition and language of republicanism.[42] This powerful republican sentiment in the Midwest vexed the appointed territorial governors of the region as settlers clamored for self-government and statehood.[43] The settlers understood that "republics were known to fall prey to ambitious and tyrannical men," and the American republic remained alone in a world of monarchies, so their periodic hyperbole about the danger of aristocratic control is entirely forgivable.[44] The republican impulses in territorial Ohio, where the Midwest began, created a "political atmosphere" where a "large majority of the adult male settlers would vote, in which legislators and governors would change office frequently, and in which the power of the governor would be circumscribed."[45] This commitment to republicanism would "dominate" the political culture of the midwestern states.[46]

Whether the seeds of the American Revolution would take root and flower in the West was no small question. Joyce Appleby notes how reformers and dissenters in monarchical Europe were closely observing the republican experiment in the new United States and praying it would survive and explains how its success led to the wider belief in American exceptionalism, especially among backcountry settlers, and the inculcation of the view that the European monarchical tradition could be escaped.[47] "By construing their own liberty as liberation from historic institutions," Appleby explains, "the enthusiasts of democracy made the United States the pilot society for the world."[48] "We should not take lightly this accomplishment," Appleby wisely cautions, noting the role of frontier settlers in "rooting out the pervasive colonial residues of hierarchy and privilege."[49] As democracy appeared to succeed in the United States, the influence of its revolutionary model and democratic charter grew proportionally. By the 1820s, American-style declarations of independence had been proclaimed in twenty different nations.[50] On Washington's birthday, reformers in England began toasting the United States as settlers moved west—"may her republican institutions be imitated all over the world."[51] In the American backcountry, where Washington led the first mission that made the future "valley of democracy" in the Midwest possible, settlers shared in his veneration.[52] They named the new city of Cincinnati, the "Queen City" of the West, for the society created to honor Washington and his generalship during the Revolution.[53]

If the successful expansion of the republican experiment in the Midwest gave hope to democratic reformers stifled by European monarchies and their colonial regimes, it also pushed the American republic closer to its own ideals. When the cultural and economic conflicts between the yeoman republicanism of the North and the plantation aristocracy of the South finally triggered the American Civil War, the Midwest determined which political and economic system would prevail and thus the course of American history. The states of the Old Northwest grew from a quarter million people in 1810 to over seven million people by the eve of the Civil War, "perhaps the highest rate of growth in human history."[54] Minnesota, which straddled the western edge of the original Northwest Territory, grew twenty-eight-fold in the 1850s, and in 1861 the First Minnesota Volunteer Infantry Regiment became the first unit in the nation to answer President Abraham Lincoln's call for troops.[55] Indiana sent 57 percent of its military-aged men to join the Union army and ranked first in the contribution of soldiers. Illinois ranked second, Ohio fourth, Iowa fifth, Michigan sixth, and Wisconsin seventh, all ahead of older eastern states such as New York. The soldier quotas of the prairie states were "greatly oversubscribed" while there was "bare compliance or actual failure in the East."[56] Whitman said the "tan-faced prairie-boy" had come "to the rescue"—"out of the land of the prairies," he sang, had come the Midwest's "plenteous offspring" with "their trusty rifles on the shoulders to save the young republic.[57]

Historians believe the Midwest made Union victory possible. Midwestern soldiers outperformed their eastern counterparts on the battlefield, and, Belich explains, the Midwest enhanced the Union's military and economic power by 50 percent, which was "probably a decisive contribution" to Union victory.[58] The social and economic integration of the American North and the American Midwest helped to "determine history—in this case Northern victory in the American Civil War."[59] Frederick Merk concluded that the states of the Midwest "joined their young strength to that of the Northeast and together saved the Union."[60] Andrew Cayton explains that at "Shiloh, Vicksburg, Chattanooga, and dozens of other places, tens of thousands of men from the Old Northwest, led by generals from the Old Northwest, directed by a president from the Old Northwest, demonstrated the power of the nation-state with a devastating effectiveness" that the American founders had never contemplated.[61] Carlyle Buley once noted that the Midwest "not only bore the brunt of supplying and feeding the armies which saved the Union but furnished the leadership as well. Grant, Sherman, Sheridan all were its sons; only this section could have produced a man with the outlook of a Lincoln."[62]

Lincoln also personified the elongation of the Midwest and the full incorporation of the western prairies into the republic. The descendants of the first backcountry settlers who crossed the Ohio River and planted the republican tradition in the Old Northwest continued westward and opened the prairies of Illinois that sent Lincoln to Congress, launching the political career of the rail-splitter and country lawyer who became an icon of western democracy. Lincoln's family moved from Kentucky to Indiana when he was seven because of slavery and the problem of disorganized land titles in Kentucky, and thus, Kenneth Winkle notes, his arrival in the Midwest was a direct product of the Northwest Ordinance, which banned slavery and developed an efficient land system.[63] Lincoln was propelled to the presidency by battles over extending Northern-oriented agrarian republicanism and checking the influence of the Slave Power in future states such as Kansas and Nebraska. During Lincoln's presidency, the midwestern political model was also extended into Dakota Territory, rounding out the northwest corner of the Midwest, which began to form with the first settlements in Ohio.[64] Those first Ohio pioneers had "laid the foundations of a distinct section, the Middle West," and had "set a pattern for later settlements across the Mississippi in the American advance toward the setting sun."[65] Lincoln understood what his region had accomplished. He saw it as the "great interior region" and the "great body of the republic" that was capable of saving the Union and of uniting the North and South after the Civil War.[66] Midwesterners appreciated Lincoln's faith in the region and honored his legacy. Two-thirds of the places named after Lincoln in the United States are located in the Midwest.[67]

The Midwest made Northern victory in the Civil War possible and, more generally, made the United States economically and militarily strong and, in a related but less direct way, aided the British Empire, against which the United States once rebelled. The settlers of the Midwest, who provided a settlement model the British could use in other parts of the world, thereby shaped world history. Belich explains that the large-scale settlement efforts of the nineteenth century "gave the Anglos vast 'Wests'" and "allowed the Anglo oldlands to integrate with these Wests, so boosting the bulk and power of the United States and 'Greater Britain,'" which made the United States "a superpower and gave Britain an extra half-century of that status."[68] The prairie Midwest helps explain the coming of the American Century, in other words, and its attendant triumphs and burdens. What Belich calls the "settler revolution" on the prairie and other frontiers made the United States larger and stronger and determined the course of its political development. In addition to extending and deepening the republican tradition, the vast interior prairies became the "most fruitful granary of earth" and, when their population grew, supplied armies for decisive wars.[69]

A half-century after the Civil War, the Midwest again helped tip the balance in conflicts that determined the course of global affairs. During World War I, when the conflict between the Western democracies and the authoritarian Central Powers reached a stalemate, the troops of the American and British Wests proved to be crucial. American soldiers, many from the prairie, made Allied victory in World War I possible in the final decisive battles in France. The Indianan Meredith Nicholson described the "quiet, dogged attitude of the sons of the West" who marched off to war to fight for the "English tradition of democracy," which had been transplanted to the Midwest.[70] The British Wests also bolstered the Allied cause by adding 20 percent more soldiers to the British army and boosting British gross domestic product (GDP) by 40 percent.[71] Canada manufactured one-third of the shells fired by British artillery units in France, and Canadian wheat fed Britain during the war.[72] Two decades later, during World War II, the British Wests contributed 2.4 million soldiers to the Allied cause, including nearly half of Bomber Command's pilots.[73] In addition to the millions of American troops mobilized for the war, the historian Milo Quaife said the food supplied by the Midwest, the "richest agricultural region of the world," along with its vast quantities of iron and steel, "made possible the winning of World War II."[74] The "special relationship" between the United States and Britain that developed during these world wars, which was rooted in the eighteenth-century backcountry that became the Midwest, continues down to the present.[75]

In addition to its critical role in the Civil War and the two world wars, the Midwest altered American politics. The republicanism of the prairie, as first Frederick Jackson Turner and then other historians noted, was not static. It produced its own variations and emphases. Belich and Wood have explained, for example, that the franchise broadened in the West, more citizens became involved in government, and popular participation in civic and community affairs was common. While these trends explain the once-popular views of Turner about the influence of the frontier democratic tradition on American politics, the work of Belich and Wood also underscores that Turner tended to downplay the American political system's debts to English republicanism and parliamentary tradition.[76] But Turner had a point about democratic adaptations in the West and the erosion of gentility. In the course of promoting self-government, people on the midwestern prairie often voiced their frustration with their economic overdependence upon the East and the political and cultural dominance of eastern metropolitan centers. This "settler populism" was "a political creed that proved to be a brake on, and sometimes rival of, elite rule throughout the Anglo-world and throughout the nineteenth century," and it produced political leaders who brought sectional balance and a midwestern voice to American politics.[77] These interior impulses also undergirded the farmer activism and Populist movement of the late nineteenth century. This interior populism, in various forms, remains a mainstay in American politics.

A variant of political populism was settler resistance to the cultural domination of the East. Although the Midwest boasted a strong tradition of independent western newspapering and book production in the early years of the region's development, this independence declined with the coming of the telegraph and railroad.[78] By 1850, New York had gained an "informational hegemony" that only grew in subsequent decades.[79] Belich notes that "some Westerners deeply resented this, and some resent its vestiges, such as the scholarly denigration of Western history, to the present."[80] These frustrations helped precipitate midwestern regionalism, or midwestern variations in art, literature, and other cultural forms, which the Iowan Ruth Suckow described as efforts designed to cut through the "alien haze that belittles and distorts" local and regional culture.[81] Westerners pursued an "intellectual independence" by building their own cultural institutions such as libraries, museums, theaters, schools, and colleges and organizing debating and discussion clubs.[82] Merle Curti noted that the wonder was not that the "agencies of intellectual life were so meager [in the West], but that they were relatively so ample."[83] The study of history was a prominent component of regionalism and was first given shape by midwestern historical societies. In his recent survey of midwestern regionalism, Terry Barnhart pointed to the Midwest's "new conception of the function of a historical society in a republic—that of making history serve a democratic role in the development of community culture."[84] This tradition of supporting midwestern history aided the efforts of Frederick Jackson Turner and others who sought to explain the uniqueness of midwestern history and to lessen the grip of eastern historians who emphasized the history of the Northeast and United States' connections to Europe.[85]

In his study of midwestern regional culture, Edward Watts seeks "to recover one more obscured and nearly erased dimension of our history" and provides an important angle of vision on midwestern *and* world history.[86] Watts explains how the successful republican experiments on the prairie gave rise to the popular image of stable normality in the Midwest, but he also emphasizes the internal complexity of the Midwest that helped generate midwestern regionalism. Watts offers another reason why the Midwest matters by linking the rise of its regional culture to the vast and growing literature known as "postcolonial studies." When exposing the history of the prairie Midwest to this model of interpretation, it should be remembered that the tools of postcolonial studies can be blunt instruments, forged by cultural analysts for use in examining truly brutal colonial regimes. Use of these insights must account for the unique nature of prairie settlement and, following Belich and Wood, recognize the deliberate "cloning" of eastern political institutions and the pride with which settlers viewed the republicanism that emanated from the American Revolution.[87] As Terry Barnhart has noted, "in the minds of westerners the westward movement and the American Revolution were clearly connected. The organization and settlement of the West had extended the blessings of liberty and further institutionalized the gains of the American Revolution in the Western states."[88] One of the founders of the Illinois State Historical Society saw the settlers of the Mississippi Valley as part of "a living stream of freedom" that directly flowed from the Revolution.[89] Postcolonial studies, which often emphasize extreme political oppression and racial conflict, can benefit from more subtle examples such as midwestern resistance to eastern cultural domination, which highlight the wide variance among methods and episodes of settlement. Understanding the unique history of the prairie Midwest, in other words, can bring needed complexity to the large enterprise that is postcolonial studies and its efforts to understand the unwinding of the imperial world from which the American republic emerged.

While regionalism served to unify the Midwest, regional identity remained stronger in the South, New England, and the Far West, which explains the Midwest's role in the development of American nationalism. Regionalism is relatively weaker in the Midwest, Andrew Cayton has explained, because of the perception that the region lacks a dramatic history and that its denizens are not expressive, because it has not experienced intense debates over regional meanings, and because of the persistence of midwestern "localism," or the "pride in family, town, and state," which mitigates against a "coherent regional identity."[90] The midwestern "premium" on politeness also encourages a focus on the "vague and unthreatening universal rather than on the unfamiliar and dangerous particular."[91] Midwesterners, Cayton thinks, are generally "uncomfortable with the whole idea of being distinctive."[92] More important, the weaker strand of regionalism in the Midwest is linked to the popular view of the Midwest as representative of the nation as a whole and as the heartland of its most basic traditions stemming from the Revolution. The Midwest became the "exemplar of an emerging national culture" and, as a result, did not develop a "sense of regional isolation" in the same way as other regions.[93] It did not suffer from alienation because the "Midwest was at the heart of the nation-state."[94] The centrality of the Midwest to the United States' perception of itself as a nation again underscores why the origins and settlement of the region matter. But the softer form of midwestern regionalism also highlights a localist sentiment favoring a benign sense of rootedness and civic obligation and disfavoring disruptive blood-and-soil emotionalism, which can lend itself to Balkanization and secession.[95]

Regionalism is weaker in the Midwest in part due to its mixed heritage. While the influence of the North was strong in the Midwest, upland southerners were also influential, causing the Midwest to be a composite of regional cultures, albeit one that tilted toward the North, and a large influx of foreign-born immigrants added still more diversity to the region.[96] By the end of the nineteenth century, James Madison notes, the "Midwest was one of the most ethnically diverse regions on the face of the earth."[97] Because of this unique mixing of cultures, what Carlyle Buley called the "mingling and mellowing processes incidental to the association of peoples from different sections and countries," the Midwest began to identify itself less as northern or southern, but as western. Midwesterners drew on their republican commitments and "forged a new identity" by defining "themselves as citizens of the republic, as members of political parties, and as Westerners."[98] The southern settlers in the Midwest were less loyal to the Old South because they were upcountry farmers and products of the backcountry and divorced from the interests of the slaveholding planter class and tidewater elites. When the South seceded, most of the upcountry southerners who settled in the Midwest rallied to the cause of preserving the Union.[99] As Nicole Etcheson concluded, most midwesterners, despite the large number from the upcountry South, "marched off to fight for Uncle Abe and the Union."[100] Their time in the Midwest, where their western identity grew, had made them less southern, more nationalistic, and therefore more willing to fight to preserve the Union.[101] In the Midwest after the Civil War, Etcheson explains, an "emerging sense of Westernness increasingly subsumed sectional identities, encompassing them within a Western identity," and "this Western, or Midwestern identity, became the nation's identity."[102]

The prairie Midwest thus played a crucial role in refocusing the American perspective westward. Although the midwestern prairie was "the West" for a time, it soon became the "Middle West" as settlers pushed on to California.[103] While the region was intricately linked to "Atlantic civilization" and English antecedents in the early decades of midwestern history, as Belich and Wood and others have explained, prairie settlers were also moving farther west and farther from Europe, creating a partial American orientation toward the Pacific and Asia. Bruce Cumings's work has focused on a United States that "from its founding 'looked away' from Europe, that turned to face West, unrolling a *novus ordo seclorum* (a new order for the ages, see it on your dollar bill) on a vast continent, an exceptional nation that would negate Europe's monarchies, its despotisms, its landlords and peasants, its wars of nation and class."[104] On the prairie looking west, the legacy of Europe's feudal traditions and aristocratic rule and the radical rebellions against them mattered less and the conditions in the United States mattered more. "Europe extends to the Alleghenies," said Emerson, "while America lies beyond."[105] The farmers out "on the prairies [were] in the midst of incessant technological innovation," embracing American pragmatism, eschewing ideological extremism, and growing more corn.[106] Cumings embraces Turner's deemphasis on Europe and the "profound directional change that the frontier thesis noticed, reorienting people, getting them to face West—away from Europe and New England in almost every sense—and to take seriously the fact of a continent."[107] The settlement of the prairie—and Turner's rendering of it—mattered because it "created an authentic *American* worldview" that preceded the United States' global engagement.[108]

In addition to entrenching republicanism and fostering its variations such as political and cultural populism and regionalism and opening the path to the farther West, the settlement process promoted new modes of thinking. Settlement booms first required an abandonment of the negative stereotypes that had dulled the image of emigration for centuries. At the beginning the new American republic, many elites continued to sneer at settlers as the unwanted and unwashed and to view emigration as an act of desperation or the province of criminals and vagabonds. But by the beginning of the nineteenth century, pioneering became a sign of progress and advancement, and "settlerism" became a "powerful, even revolutionary, ideology, transforming the concept of emigration and giving the Anglo-world the human capital to rise."[109] Combining settlerism with the spreading notions of the Enlightenment, the idea of progress, self-improvement, individualism, and "self-determined salvation" in Christianity, westerners promoted a view of settlement that was broader than mere economic gain.[110] This unique combination of impulses and beliefs embraced by western settlers directly connects the prairie to the historiography of American exceptionalism, or the view that the political and social development of the United States was unique and a decisive break from Europe.

The prairie settlers' embrace of settler ideology was accompanied by a willing adoption of the routine practices that entrenched the workings of American capitalism. Following the original commercial conflicts over the Ohio country, which were spurred by the pursuit of trading opportunities and the contest over the fur trade, the agrarian settlement process continued a strong market-orientation.[111] Prairie settlement was abetted, for example, by the various aspects of what Belich calls "the progress industry," which included the transportation business that hauled settlers to the frontier, the merchants who sold supplies to the settlers, the creditors who made loans to settlers, and the businesses that provided the materials for the building of frontier towns.[112] John Weaver has explored the even more fundamental processes and institutions that fostered capitalism in the West by explaining how settlers established titles to land, how land titles were allocated, how land was surveyed so that titles would be clear, how the legal descriptions of property were refined, how documents establishing title to land were filed in government land offices and with registers of deeds, and how land was valued and sold.[113] These rudiments of capitalist enterprise also fostered democratic development. The establishment of smallholder farms on the prairie, Weaver notes, was "surely important for world history, not simply for American history," because they developed "in conjunction with democracy" and "promoted the idea that land distribution should be open to all improvers."[114] Because the broad distribution of land and democratic practices "thrived in the mainly congenial territories of eastern North America," other regions and nations around the world had a successful model to follow.[115] The centrality of capitalism to modernity as represented by the progress industry and robust land markets again justifies the study of the Midwest, which is known for its market capitalism. "No region in the world," Andrew Cayton says of the Midwest, "saw a more unfettered and less contested expansion of capitalist enterprise in the nineteenth and twentieth centuries."[116] James Madison calls the Midwest "one of the greatest monuments to capitalism the world has ever seen."[117]

The Midwest also became a site of the great nineteenth-century evolution of American capitalism. The dominance of small farm and small town capitalism of the prairie was later diminished by the rise of big business and urban centers. Iron ore from the northern Midwest met coal from the southeastern edges of the Midwest, and the midwestern steel industry came to life. Chicago became a center of the grain trade and the meatpacking industry, and the city became an icon of midwestern urbanism and a symbol that the prairies would not be solely rural. Jefferson, the architect of the rural West, would have regretted the rise of industrialism and urbanism on the prairie, despite the maintenance of an "interior mentality" in midwestern cities.[118] Chicago, Bruce Cumings notes, became the "starkest example of Jefferson's rapacious urban monster operating at a white heat, chewing up the prairies as an early Los Angeles of the Middle Border."[119] Turner also lamented the changes wrought by the "great forces of modern capitalism" and feared that with the passing of the agrarian prairie, the "material forces that gave vitality to Western democracy [were] passing away."[120] The growth of cities and the power of big business helped spawn prairie political movements such as the Grange, Populism, and Progressivism, the goals and spirit of which still exert a force in national politics.[121] The friction generated by the transition away from an Anglo-American Jeffersonian rural world and toward an urban, multiethnic, and industrial future constitutes one of the central themes of American history, and the Midwest provides perhaps the best vantage point for viewing this conflict and the subsequent rise of organized labor, the long-term fate of the American manufacturing sector, and the coming of the "Rust Belt," which culminated in the final implosion of Detroit.[122]

The Midwest also provides a window on the history of Native Americans and African Americans. The Seven Years' War was fought not only by the English and the French but also by various Indian tribes who maintained shifting alliances with both empires. After a major Iroquois offensive drove the Algonquin tribes west into the central Great Lakes region during the 1600s, the French orchestrated a cooperative alliance with the Algonquin based on much diplomacy and numerous cultural interchanges that initially served as an effective bulwark against the British.[123] This arrangement ultimately proved unstable, however, especially in the Ohio region, and slowly eroded in the face of British military victories in the late 1750s.[124] After the Seven Years' War, conflict between Indians and the British and later the Americans continued and finally gave way to American control and agrarian settlement. While Indians were pushed westward by pioneer settlers and defeated in battle by American armies, they also continued to be recognized by way of treaty-making and land purchases.[125] The Northwest Ordinance, following British practice, "called for the rule of law in dealing with Indians."[126]

The Midwest also includes important elements of African American history. The small number of blacks in the early Midwest faced racism and attempts at legal exclusion, but also benefited from the prohibition on slavery included in the Northwest Ordinance, the prevalence of free labor ideology, and the growth of abolitionist sentiment in the Midwest, which led to the creation of the midwestern-based antislavery Republican Party in the 1850s.[127] Many midwesterners fought to keep slavery illegal in the region prior to the Civil War, and some historians believe that the "main credit of the abolitionist crusade should go to the Middle

West rather than to New England."[128] In the early twentieth century, many blacks moved to northern cities such as Chicago and Detroit to escape Jim Crow segregation in the South.[129]

Despite the relative neglect of the Midwest and its history, the region matters on multiple levels. In the 1750s, backcountry traders and settlers in the Midwest helped spark a global war that reconfigured North America, and in the 1770s they helped fuel a revolution that produced the world's first successful republic. The Midwest then proved to those who were skeptical that this republic could expand and that republican commitments could persist and intensify. The settlement of the prairie Midwest explains how the United States grew large, rich, and powerful and, by derivation and deliberate modeling, how it contributed to the maintenance of the British Empire. The Midwest tipped the scales in the Civil War, preventing the early demise of the American republic that skeptics had anticipated, and proved essential to the Anglo-American cooperation that stanched the spread of appalling forms of twentieth-century tyranny. The prairie states would also generate newer and modified political and cultural forms that would underscore American pluralism and highlight interior resistance to metropolitan culture and urban economic dominance. The economic strength of the Midwest was derived from its relatively unfettered capitalist development, which gave rise to the nation's agro-industrial core, and the region became a site of contestation over the proper extent of the market. Recounting these reasons that the Midwest mattered to the course of historical events is not an exercise in assembling "Washington Slept Here"–style factoids or in regional chauvinism, but an exercise aimed at broadening our sense of the nation's component parts, and demonstrating why, in particular, one understudied region deserves more consideration from historians and how this region's history can help us see the totality of our national past. There once was a time when a group of historians understood why the Midwest mattered and studied its history with a seriousness of purpose equal to the significance of the region.

Two

THE PRAIRIE HISTORIANS
AND THE FOUNDATIONS
OF MIDWESTERN HISTORY

FROM THE EARLIEST DAYS of the American republic, New England received considerable attention from historians. The American South also produced many men of letters and later historians dedicated to understanding its traditions and peculiar institution. At the same time, the American "West," a line of demarcation that steadily moved throughout the nineteenth century, was given short shrift in the main channels of American historiography. By the beginning of the twentieth century, however, historians in the Midwest were beginning to assert themselves in the form of published works, increasingly active state historical societies, and new scholarly journals. From the late nineteenth century extending several decades into the twentieth, a cadre of midwestern historians busily chronicled their region. These "Prairie Historians," as I call them, made a substantial contribution to the historical profession and wrote the foundational histories of the prairie Midwest, but they are seldom thought of today. The history profession is still interested in New England and the American South, and in recent decades the American Far West has developed into a major field of study that dwarfs the midwestern history enterprise. Even the few brave souls who now work on midwestern history pay little attention to the Prairie Historians. This once-proud band, however, devoted much of their lives to the region, and the body of work they left behind deserves to be remembered both on its own terms and for what it can do to inspire a revival of midwestern history.

Grouping intellectuals, including the Prairie Historians, is always difficult. The Romantics, the Southern Agrarians, the New York Intellectuals, and the British Marxist historians, for example, all defy tidy categories, yet the thrust of their work and attitudes has at times been successfully captured by their chroniclers.[1] The "main currents" of their thought and their collective "mind" can be mapped and described while due consideration is given to the nuances, intricacies, and contradictions within their work. The characteristics that unite the Prairie Historians do not apply to all of them all of the time, of course, but the unifying elements are reasonably strong. Many of the Prairie Historians were born in the prairie Midwest, and many of them were born on midwestern farms and were particularly inclined toward the study of their home region. They supported local history, state historical societies, and regional journals focused on the prairie Midwest. They admired Frederick Jackson Turner, studied the political and economic development of the Midwest and its international context, and embraced democracy as a central theme in their histories, and, more particularly, they focused on law, farming, Populism, land and geography, and social history. This collective effort yielded a raft of major books and several Pulitzer Prizes.

I proceed with this analysis of the Prairie Historians fully realizing that the vast corpus of their works simply cannot be added to the already burgeoning reading lists of most historians and general readers during an age when the rate of production of historical works blurs the eyes.[2] I think a substantive, chapter-long look at the work of the Prairie Historians is, however, a useful tool for those seeking a gateway into and a roadmap of this world but who cannot commit to a long excursion. Perhaps this probe into an old and generally forgotten world will cause readers to launch a deeper exploration and to arrange an extended stay. I hope so, but I realize before booking a ticket it is good to know that the sights are worth seeing.

In a recent book, the historian David Brown opened a door onto this world, intelligently connected the works of some well-known historians from the Midwest, and offered a wonderfully rendered portrait of one strain of the midwestern historical mind.[3] It was a bracing and well-executed encore to his first book on the intellectual development and output of the New York–oriented historian Richard Hofstadter, who provides the perfect foil to the sentiments of some midwestern historians.[4] Historians from the Midwest, as Brown explained, reflected the rhythms of their section and forged an "interior tradition" in American historical writing.[5] Unlike aristocratic New England and the hierarchical and racially polarized South, the Midwest was more democratic and egalitarian, more attuned to agrarian populism, and less enthused about the exertion of federal power and the launching of foreign adventures. In the Midwest, the old "Anglo/rural folkways" persisted as they weakened in the East.[6] While the states of the Midwest each had their own unique elements, they "shared a territorial past and a sense of regional identity outside of eastern cosmopolitanism and southern exclusivity."[7] Brown chose his midwestern historians based on their larger impact on the profession and their proven ability to shape the broader historical debate, and one cannot quibble with his choices. Brown's book, however, is best seen as an account of a prominent midwestern tradition of leftist historical writing. It reveals, in other words, *a* midwestern historical tradition, not *the* midwestern historical tradition. While Brown masterfully analyzes the historians he chose to include and examines the happenings at the University of Wisconsin in particular detail, there was another tradition carried on by the Prairie Historians, especially in the first half of the twentieth century, which also brought a genuinely midwestern voice to history.

Although he does not fit the general pattern of criticism carried on by the other historians he analyzes, Brown begins his discussion, as any discussion of midwestern history must, with Frederick Jackson Turner.[8] Turner was a ninth-generation American descended from the Puritan founders; the son of a Wisconsin newspaperman and GOP activist; a devotee of fishing, camping, and hiking; a natural public speaker; and a witness to the passing of the midwestern frontier. When Turner began his study of history in the 1880s, Curtis Nettels noted, the "writing of history was almost a monopoly of the Atlantic seaboard."[9] In a great break with eastern historians, who saw midwestern culture and institutions as derivative and imitative and who largely ignored happenings beyond the Hudson River, Turner argued that midwestern settlers advanced American democratic practices on the frontier and begat a tradition of historical writing about and from the Midwest. Turner said he saw his famous frontier thesis as "a protest against eastern neglect."[10] The Prairie Historians took cues from Turner and developed a pattern of thought and a network of personalities, affiliations, and institutions that congealed into an early twentieth-century movement to advance the cause of studying the history of the prairie Midwest.

In keeping with Turner's call for greater attention to the Midwest, the Prairie Historians sought an outlet for the region's history. The secretary of the Nebraska State Historical Society, Clarence Paine, a Minnesotan living in Iowa who caught the eye of former Nebraska territorial governor and U.S. Secretary of Agriculture J. Sterling Morton, led the charge.[11] Paine convened a meeting of representatives of midwestern historical societies in Lincoln, Nebraska, in 1907, and they debated a constitution for a new organization called the Mississippi Valley Historical Association (MVHA), which would be premised on the "realization that the history of the Middle West is marked by a unity of development which justifies an organized and unified study."[12] The eastern-dominated American Historical Association (AHA) opposed the new organization, but the MVHA's leaders refused to compromise their plans, continually noting that the AHA devalued the history of the West.[13] At the meeting of the AHA in Madison, Wisconsin, in December 1907, the leaders of the new MVHA adopted a constitution, which declared that the "object of the Association shall be to promote historical study and research and to secure cooperation between the historical societies and the departments of history of the Mississippi Valley."[14] The new organization set the first meeting of the MVHA for Lake Minnetonka, Minnesota, in June 1908. The AHA continued to refuse to work with the MVHA, so the budding organization subsequently met on its own in St. Louis and Iowa City, Iowa, and again in Lincoln.[15] Throughout the years between 1910 and 1920, despite midwesterners' attempt to assert a stronger voice, the "domination" of the profession by the easterners "continued unabated, as did resentment in the outback."[16] In 1915, the MVHA president signed a circular on MVHA letterhead lending support to "reformers" within the AHA who wanted to break the eastern clique that dominated the AHA.[17] The MVHA found an audience by drawing on this midwestern regionalist impulse and grew from its seven original members in 1907 to 840 members by 1923.[18]

Among the founders of the MVHA were Clarence W. Alvord of the University of Illinois and Benjamin F. Shambaugh of the University of Iowa. Alvord took over the presidency of the MVHA during its first year when the original president, from Alabama, complained about the first meeting being held too far north in Minnesota and lost interest.[19] Alvord was a strong proponent of maintaining the regional distinctiveness of the MVHA and fought the co-optation efforts of the AHA, which, he argued, was too focused on the East and which, he noted, was mounting "a good deal of opposition" to the new MVHA.[20] Alvord thought that the "development of the Northeast, particularly of New England, [had] usurped too prominent a place in the annals of America" and that eastern historians were prone to erroneous "blunders" about western history.[21] In addition to leading the MVHA, Alvord also collected, edited, and published many records from early Illinois history, served as the editor of *Illinois Historical Collections*, led the Illinois Historical Survey, and wrote books about the history of Illinois.[22] The historian Frederic Logan Paxson, who sympathized with the effort to break the "northern tide-water point of view," wrote in the 1920s that the "sound scholarship of Alvord and his host of associates has cleared the ground" for the development of western history.[23]

Shambaugh was a native Iowan born on a farm in Clinton County and, although formally a political scientist, served as the superintendent and editor of the publications of the State Historical Society of Iowa in Iowa City from 1907 to 1940.[24] Shambaugh aided the budding MVHA by editing its *Proceedings* and publishing the MVHA's conference papers until Alvord secured funding from the University of Illinois for the permanent publication of the association's new journal, the *Mississippi Valley Historical Review (MVHR)*.[25] Alvord became the first editor of the *MVHR* and served until 1923.[26] The *MVHR* was "primarily interested in the history of the Mississippi Valley," but was open to other articles bearing on the development of the region.[27] Alvord promised that the *MVHR* would be "more closely connected with the historical societies in the country than the *American Historical Review* is."[28] Shambaugh, in keeping with the antieastern posture, populist spirit, and public orientation of the MVHA, placed great importance on reaching a general audience, bringing high school teachers into the association, and generating a "commonwealth" history usable to the citizenry by studying subjects such as constitutional development.[29] Shambaugh praised the MVHA for the "absence of that smugness which too often finds its way into historical societies."[30] Alvord sought to make the *MVHR* serve the "great public" instead of being limited to "specialists" and to publish articles that were "clear" and "self-explanatory" [sic], which he said was "not contrary to scientific work."[31] Shambaugh agreed that there was "no reason why readability, accuracy, and scholarship cannot be combined in the same article."[32] The *MVHR* became the "organ of the Westerners."[33]

The new MVHA, midwestern-oriented and ably led by Alvord and Shambaugh, was aided by other members of the founding generation of Prairie Historians. Following Alvord's leadership at the University of Illinois was Theodore Calvin Pease, born in Cassopolis, Michigan, who earned a B.A. from Illinois and a Ph.D. from the University of Chicago and went on to author detailed histories of Illinois and assist the state's historical society.[34] Following Shambaugh's lead at the University of Iowa was Louis Pelzer, who grew up on an Iowa farm, earned his Ph.D. at Iowa, and went on to write several works of Iowa history.[35] Orin G. Libby, who was born on a farm in Wisconsin and earned a Wisconsin Ph.D. under Turner and was originally scheduled to speak in Turner's famous slot at the Chicago World's Fair, taught at the University of North Dakota from 1906 to 1945.[36] Solon Justus Buck, who also grew up in Wisconsin, earned his B.A. from Wisconsin and his Ph.D. from Harvard under Turner, and went on to teach at Indiana, Illinois, and Minnesota, where he revived the Minnesota Historical Society.[37] John D. Barnhart, born in

Decatur, Illinois, took his B.A. from Illinois Wesleyan and, after several teaching stints, earned his Ph.D. in 1930 from Harvard, where he studied with Turner. Barnhart mostly taught at Indiana but also in Nebraska and Minnesota, edited the *Indiana Magazine of History* from 1941 to 1955, and wrote several books about the Midwest.[38] Frederic Logan Paxson was born in Pennsylvania and earned his Ph.D. from Pennsylvania, but quickly turned to studying the West after teaching at Colorado and Michigan, and, in 1910, he replaced Turner at Wisconsin.[39]

This founding generation of Prairie Historians was assisted by a budding institution in the Midwest, the state historical society. Beginning in Wisconsin in the 1850s with the work of Lyman Draper, the State Historical Society of Wisconsin became a model for other midwestern states.[40] Reuben Gold Thwaites, of Oshkosh, Wisconsin, became secretary at the State Historical Society of Wisconsin in 1887 and abetted Turner's efforts to craft a regional historical consciousness.[41] Milo Quaife, born near Nashua, Iowa, went to Grinnell College in Iowa, earned a Ph.D. from the University of Chicago, and succeeded Thwaites as superintendent of the State Historical Society of Wisconsin when Thwaites died in 1913.[42] Quaife launched the *Wisconsin Magazine of History*, served as president of the MVHA, edited the *MVHR*, and is remembered for his opposition to "Eastern bias" in American history.[43] Quaife was replaced at the State Historical Society of Wisconsin by Joseph Schafer, born in Grantsburg, Wisconsin, who earned a Ph.D. under Turner at Wisconsin and led the Society until his death in 1941.[44] More than a dozen Society leaders and Wisconsin-connected scholars went on to become president of the MVHA.[45] Although not as well known as the Wisconsin figures, others diligently advanced the cause of midwestern state historical societies, including George W. Martin and William Connelley in Kansas, Clarence and Clara Paine and Addison Sheldon in Nebraska, Doane Robinson in South Dakota, and Warren Upham in Minnesota.[46] They all worked diligently to collect and publish as many materials about the Midwest as they could find.

Building on the foundation laid by the first generation of Prairie Historians and their allies in midwestern historical societies, several scholars carried on in this tradition in subsequent years. Frederick Merk, born in Milwaukee, earned his B.A. at Wisconsin, worked at the State Historical Society of Wisconsin for five years, and then followed Turner to Harvard, where he earned his Ph.D.[47] Merk maintained his allegiance to the Midwest (always rooting for the "tough Westerners" against the "effete Easterners") but would assume Turner's courses in western history at Harvard and train such students as Paul Gates, who became an expert on western land policy.[48] John D. Hicks, born in small town Missouri, earned his Ph.D. at Wisconsin under Paxson, taught at Nebraska, then replaced Paxson at Wisconsin in 1932.[49] When teaching at Nebraska, Hicks helped Everett Dick, who was born on a Kansas farm, win entry into Wisconsin, where Dick became a Paxson student.[50] While at Wisconsin, Paxson also trained the Indiana-born historian R. Carlyle Buley, who went on to teach at Indiana and won the Pulitzer Prize in 1951 for his two-volume history *The Old Northwest*.[51] Prominent Prairie Historians also emerged from outside the immediate orbit of Wisconsin. Allan Bogue, born on a farm in Ontario, earned his Ph.D. under Gates at Cornell and went on to teach at Iowa and then Wisconsin, where he became the Frederick Jackson Turner Professor of History. At Iowa, Pelzer trained Vernon Carstensen, who was born on an Iowa farm and went on to teach at Wisconsin and Washington, and Elmer Ellis, who was from North Dakota and who went on to teach at Missouri.[52] At Kansas, Frank Hodder, who was from Aurora, Illinois, trained James Malin, who was originally from North Dakota and earned the first doctorate in history granted by Kansas.[53]

In addition to organizing the MVHA to promote midwestern history, the Prairie Historians were strongly committed to aiding the state historical societies of the Midwest, which flourished during the late nineteenth and early twentieth centuries.[54] In 1916, in an emblematic moment, Shambaugh and Buck talked until 2:00 A.M. at a history conference about Buck's speech "The Functions of a State Historical Society."[55] As president of the MVHA, Paxson gave Alvord the chairmanship of the association's committee on "The Relation of Historical Societies and Departments of History."[56] Alvord was a good choice, having collected a massive amount of materials for the Illinois Historical Survey and having turned the *Illinois Historical Collections* he had created into a "veritable laboratory of state history."[57] The Illinois Centennial Commission named Alvord as the editor and organizer of a multivolume history of Illinois, which was "generally recognized as setting a new standard for state histories."[58] Working as a graduate assistant with Alvord at Illinois, Pease cowrote "Archives of the State of Illinois" with Alvord. As a professor at Illinois, Pease took over as editor of the *Illinois Historical Collections* in 1920, when Alvord moved to Minnesota, and edited it until 1939. Pease also traveled throughout Europe collecting materials relating to early Illinois from European archives, making copies before some were destroyed in World War II.[59] Pease edited many other collections, and, in a measure of his dedication to saving the remnants of the past, he became the editor of the newly formed journal *American Archivist* in the

1930s.[60] Pease was a member of the Illinois State Historical Society for thirty-nine years and also served as its president.[61]

In addition to the frenetic activity in Illinois and the long-standing work of the State Historical Society of Wisconsin, the Prairie Historians actively aided the historical societies in other midwestern states. Shambaugh and Pelzer remained committed to supporting the State Historical Society of Iowa. Solon Buck "rebuilt" the Minnesota Historical Society, became its superintendent, launched its quarterly journal, edited a four-volume history of Minnesota, encouraged the organization of county historical societies, and generally "proceeded to reorganize and revolutionize the institution."[62] In North Dakota, Libby started "reorganizing the moribund State Historical Society," served as its secretary for four decades, planned six state parks, started publishing the *Collections*, and launched the *North Dakota Historical Quarterly* in 1926.[63] For all of his work, Libby became known as the "father of North Dakota history."[64] In addition to assisting state historical societies and publishing in the *MVHR*, the Prairie Historians actively used the pages of state history journals to publish their research and urged journal editors to reach out to professional historians.[65]

The Prairie Historians' dedication to state historical societies was complemented by an intense commitment to state and local history. In his 1923 presidential address to the MVHA, Solon Buck lauded the increasingly "scientific" work of the "historical societies of the Mississippi valley" but also noted the growing interest among the region's historians in state and local history.[66] Buck's speech signaled the Prairie Historians' professed devotion to local studies.[67] Solon Buck's student Theodore Blegen, who earned a Minnesota Ph.D. and followed Buck as superintendent of the Minnesota Historical Society, denounced the "inverted provincialism" of "urbane and cosmopolitan" scholars who "rejected the near-at-hand as local and insignificant" and dismissed "regionalists."[68] Buck praised Blegen's work on Minnesota history, and Frederick Merk pointed to James Malin's study of prairie locales as setting "a pattern for local history that much needs to be followed."[69] Throughout his career, Allan Bogue would honor Malin's "admonition that the good historian should master both local and national history."[70] John Hicks echoed Malin's point, arguing that the historian "should be able to weave into the national story the complicated contributions of localities, states, and sections, and yet not lose himself in insignificant detail."[71] Only on the basis of strong local histories, the Prairie Historians argued, could larger interpretations properly be made.[72] They found it frustrating that other historians failed to see the larger importance of local history and that they continued to treat it as "provincial."[73] Malin noted that local history had been in "disrepute" and lamented the "virtual elimination of local history from the scene."[74] In place of historical writing "from the top down," Malin argued for a "bottom up" history and a "recognition of the basic fact that all history of human activity must necessarily start from the individual at a particular time and place—locality."[75]

The energy expended organizing the MVHA, aiding state historical societies, and advocating state and local history underscored the regionalist sensibility of the Prairie Historians and their tilt toward studies of midwestern history. The *MVHR* was purposely geared toward the history of what Shambaugh called "the Great Valley."[76] Alvord said the *MVHR* "belongs to all the historians and historical organizations of the Mississippi Valley," and the journal featured reports on "historical activities" in regions designated as the "Old Northwest and Canada" and the "Trans-Mississippi Northwest."[77] The original organizers of the MVHA worked diligently to attract historians at regional universities such as Minnesota, Kansas, Nebraska, Michigan, Missouri, Iowa, Cincinnati, and Chicago.[78] The Prairie Historians also tried to keep the presidency of the MVHA in the hands of scholars who focused on western history.[79] Alvord thought the MVHA would become a "laughing stock" by going "so far afield as to elect a modern history scholar for our president."[80] In keeping with its regional focus, the MVHA often met in cities such as Lincoln, Lake Minnetonka, Iowa City, Bloomington, Omaha, Grand Forks, St. Paul, Madison, Des Moines, Vincennes, Columbia, Indianapolis, Milwaukee, Cedar Rapids, Columbus, Rock Island, and Cincinnati.[81]

This dedication to the regional dimension of midwestern history stemmed from the leadership of Turner. Since Turner first challenged the dominance of the East and promoted the study of the Midwest, regionalism was thought to be "synonymous with Frederick Jackson Turner."[82] Turner, after all, was a "son of the Prairies," and his writings were "in fact predicated largely upon the unique conditions of the Prairie West and became the basis of a historical school that had its center in that region."[83] As early as 1887 Turner said he would focus "chiefly upon the Northwest and more generally upon the Mississippi Valley" and those "peopling the prairie."[84] Turner remained attuned to "state resistance to the nationalizing process" and to regional "resistance to national homogeneity."[85] Michael Steiner argues that the "furor" over the frontier thesis has "blinded" historians to "Turner's more persistent concern" with regionalism, which led him to win the Pulitzer Prize.[86] The "rallying cry" for regional history, Fulmer Mood once reminded historians, "came from Turner, at Madison."[87] Turner would provide the leadership at Wisconsin for the promotion of regional history, and, he said, "our earnest western boys will supply the best sort of material."[88]

Turner's midwestern focus shaped the work of the Prairie Historians, who often recognized his influence and admired his growing prominence in the historical profession at large. Clarence Paine, the organizing force behind the MVHA, called Turner one of the "big guns" of American history.[89] Paxson said that all American historians had "reshaped their views of the meaning of our history" in the wake of Turner's focus on the West.[90] Hicks taught the History of the West course at Nebraska and then tried to "maintain the reputation" established for the course at Wisconsin, where Turner and Paxson had led the effort (a succession that triggered discussion of the "Turner-Paxson-Hicks overemphasis on Western history").[91] Before he began his long tenure teaching western history at Harvard, Merk began his career with "five very happy years of editing and writing" at the State Historical Society of Wisconsin, but then went on to graduate school at Harvard to be with Turner, and "that was the culmination of all good things."[92] Shambaugh, Pease, and Barnhart also took cues from Turner.[93] In a measure of Turner's long influence, the history department at Wisconsin was still receiving letters for Frederick Jackson Turner in the 1970s.[94]

While amenable to Turner's regionalist ethos and his emphasis upon the role of the Midwest in American history, the Prairie Historians were certainly willing to modify his findings.[95] If Turner and some Prairie Historians had emphasized the rapid Americanization of immigrant settlers in the Midwest, others were closely attuned to ethnic persistence.[96] Theodore Blegen, for example, who became a professor at Minnesota, always advocated more work on the "immigrant factor."[97] If Turner had emphasized the uniqueness of the frontier democracy too much and had not adequately accounted for European and eastern precedents, the Prairie Historians accepted the critics' points.[98] If Turner saw the frontier as a social "safety valve" for the nation, the Prairie Historians recognized that the frontier did less to relieve pressure on the body politic than Turner thought. Paxson rather enjoyed the "good row" during the 1930s over Turner's "'safety valve' idea."[99]

While certainly willing to accept modifications to Turner's writings, the Prairie Historians also cautioned others about the use of Turner as a straw man. Paxson called attention to the "difference between [Turner's] ideas and those of over-ardent disciples" and issued a warning about treating the Turner frontier theory as "revelation."[100] Merk praised an essay by Merle Curti about Turner but also worried that Curti was conceding too much to Turner's critics, who had "set up a target" to shoot at.[101] Despite the claims of critics, for example, Turner was well aware of immigrant diversity and the persistence of immigrant culture in the Midwest and was not a simplistic advocate of melting-pot theory.[102] While Turner generally thought the frontier was a major force in American development, he also often explained that no single factor determined American history.[103] Even a critic such as Richard Hofstadter conceded Turner's recognition of the "polylateral character of historical development."[104]

A number of the Prairie Historians carried on Turner's emphasis upon the prairie Midwest as a unique meeting ground where diverse peoples and cultures successfully mixed and which gave rise to a more egalitarian social order. The distinctions between the North and South were more pronounced in the East, Alvord said, but in the West there was more "friendly intercourse" among peoples.[105] Paxson described the mixing of colonial settlers and German and Scotch-Irish immigrants in the backcountry and explained how their "divergent and contradictory traits" were brought into the "melting pot of the interior valleys" and "speedily submerged in the common nationality."[106] Carlyle Buley noted the "dual heritage" of paternalistic New England Puritanism and "Scotch-Irish frontier individualism" in the Midwest.[107] John Barnhart described the many "racial and national strains" in the Midwest, including the important role of southern immigrants.[108] Because of this great diversity, Libby said that midwestern history was "amply continental, never petty or sectional."[109] While recognizing cultural persistence among these groups, the Prairie Historians also sought to understand the "solvent power" of the American experience relative to a divided and Balkanized Europe.[110]

The social and ethnic mixing in the Midwest, the Prairie Historians thought, was accompanied by a greater degree of egalitarianism in the region. Shambaugh said the "frontier was a great leveler" that "fostered the sympathetic attitude" and made "men plain, common, unpretentious" and "really democratic."[111] Most settlers were small landholders, and thus, Barnhart said, the Midwest was a "poor man's home" where people participated in civic affairs and the "pretensions of the aristocrats" were shunned.[112] Buley found that on the midwestern frontier, egalitarianism was the norm: "Equality was not a theory or creed; it was merely a natural circumstance."[113] The midwesterner thought he could "serve in any political capacity from assistant dog catcher or fence viewer to governor or even president."[114] Buley pointed to nineteenth-century travelers who also noted this egalitarianism and the "American's tendency to profanity, tobacco chewing, and leaning back on the hind legs of a chair, his devotion to newspapers."[115]

While often focused on the unique mingling of peoples in the Midwest and more generally on the development of the region, the Prairie Historians did not neglect the international context of these events. Indeed, Turner himself often discussed the broader implications of the settlement of the Midwest and its relationship to global affairs, a theme carried forward in recent histories of the Atlantic world.[116] Francois Furstenberg notes that Turner wrote widely about the international context and implications of the frontier and "set the action of the Mississippi Valley amid vast forces of European empires clashing against land-hungry American settlers and nascent nation-builders in a grand panorama of what we today might call *histoires croisees*."[117] Furstenberg says that "Turner and his generation first raised the question"—this "generation" being the Prairie Historians—that "should be humbling to currently triumphant Atlanticists."[118] The "historians of the past keenly sensed," Furstenberg says, that the history of the Midwest shaped the lives of peoples and empires in the region but also shaped "modern world history itself."[119] Despite recent calls for historians "to become more imperial," or to recognize the intersection of empires that shaped the development of regions such as the Midwest, the Prairie Historians had done this long ago.[120]

While promoting the history of the Midwest, Turner said that this "local history must be read as part of world history," and the Prairie Historians paid heed.[121] In 1922, for example, Alvord went north to Duluth to deliver a talk to the Minnesota Historical Society on the global dimensions of midwestern history.[122] Alvord also wrote the prize-winning book *The Mississippi Valley in British Politics*.[123] One reviewer said when discussing Alvord's work on the early Midwest that Alvord was never "content to deal with that history apart from its European background."[124] Alvord died in Italy in 1928 while working on a general history of the role of the Midwest in the American Revolution.[125] Paxson, whose dissertation had focused on the rebellions in South America against Spain, explained how the Midwest took "shape in the final years of the century of colonial wars" and placed the story in the broad context of the French, British, Spanish, and native rivalries that shaped the Midwest.[126] Merk's 1960 presidential address to the MVHA explored the complex conflict with Britain over the Oregon Country.[127] While admitting to the pursuit of the "red-haired Muse of diplomatic history" during a time of "indiscretion," Merk also pointed out that his "first love" was western history.[128] While the history of the West remained their "first love," the Prairie Historians' attention to the international dimension of this history does much to dispel the charge of midwestern parochialism. Turner's own support of the League of Nations, which he thought would be bolstered by his writings on regionalism, underscores the point.[129]

By broadly focusing on the global dimensions of early midwestern history and more narrowly on the mixture of settlers who moved to the Midwest and the region's political development, the Prairie Historians were writing the history of the colonial backcountry and underscoring the wider implications of this history. Most prominently, they explained how the egalitarian norms of the midwestern backcountry led to constant friction with Crown officials and the wealthy colonials along the coast and ultimately helped trigger the American Revolution.[130] Barnhart argued that Americans moved to the backcountry to escape the domination of the planter class on the coast and to "establish a more democratic social, political, and economic order."[131] As they moved toward the western frontier, these backcountry settlers sparked conflicts with the French empire that ignited the Seven Years' War. Westerners served with the British army during the war, and this experience promoted a "self-consciousness and solidarity" among the colonists that made tighter British control of the colonies after the war impossible.[132] The Prairie Historians convincingly explained how conflicts between midwestern settlers and British imperial administrators and the entrenchment of democratic practices in the West then fueled the American Revolution.[133] After the Revolution, American diplomats argued in favor of acquiring the future American Midwest from Britain on the basis of obviating future conflicts over the backcountry. Franklin argued at the Paris peace talks after the war, in Alvord's words, that the "danger of disagreement would always come from the back countries, where dwelt lawless pioneers, whose disputes would be a constant source of international bickerings."[134]

Alvord was alluding to budding regional impulses in the backcountry and the development of a midwestern identity. The backcountry settlers living beyond the Appalachian Mountains, Barnhart explained, were seizing the "opportunity for the formation of a new sectional culture in the interior."[135] While the colonial holdings near the East Coast were best "examined as European frontiers in America," Paxson argued, in the West was an "American frontier to be studied in contrast to the East," or as an emerging American region.[136] After the American Revolution, backcountry settlers realized that the arguments in favor of the war against the British Empire also bolstered their complaints about the political and economic dominance of coastal elites.[137] The western regions of the new American states chafed at coastal power just as the colonies had chafed at the Crown's control.[138] As time passed, these western settlements began to produce local leaders who "had begun to grow on local roots, and frontier points of view had gained coherent spokes-men."[139] Paxson says "frontier thought" developed in the "isolation and distance, which bred self-confidence, equality, and distrust of the absen-tee."[140] In 1925, Paxson won the Pulitzer Prize for his book *History of the American Frontier, 1763–1893*, which explored many of these themes.

By highlighting the growth of democratic practices in the midwestern backcountry, the Prairie Historians were tracing what they saw as the exceptional nature of American democracy. This focus on what has come to be called American exceptionalism is often traced to Turner.[141] The Prairie Historians continued this tradition by frequently noting distinc-tions between midwestern democratic progress and reactionary regres-sions in Europe. The states and provinces of the vast interior region of the United States were unique, Libby wrote, especially in comparison to Europe, where a "state of tension exists, resulting from centuries of conflict and rivalry."[142] The people of the Midwest had "never shed each other's blood and . . . have never desired to do so."[143] Barnhart empha-sized that the settlers of the Midwest "remembered the injustice that was Ireland as well as the stories of want and cruelty in Germany during and after the Thirty Years' War."[144] The Prairie Historians also noted how democratic reformers in other countries borrowed American ideals. Pease explained how the "stirrings of revolution and liberty in Europe and South America" took place "under the influence and example of republican America."[145] Merk praised Merle Curti, who was a product of Pappillion, Nebraska, and who studied with Turner at Harvard, for explaining the role of American democratic ideas in the reform efforts of mid-nineteenth-century Germany and German reformers' embrace of the American model of framing a constitution for a new Germany.[146] Merk also enjoyed Curti's article outlining European fears of American democracy during the early nineteenth century.[147] Curti had emphasized the extent of anti-Americanism among European conservatives, who saw the new American republic as "dangerous to the established order of the Old World."[148] The study of American history and political institu-tions was banned in all European universities (except in Switzerland); a professor was banned from the Sorbonne for planning a lecture on the American Constitution; European authorities banned the circulation of the *North American Review* and *Rip Van Winkle*.[149] From Turner to Curti at Wisconsin, where Curti replaced Hicks, and among the Prairie Historians generally, the nation's unique heritage was a given. Indeed, Wisconsin's history department and the State Historical Society of Wis-consin, Curtis Nettels noted, "fostered writings" that explained "why the United States [was] a distinctive nation."[150]

The most important component of the exceptionalist story for the Prairie Historians was the development of American democracy on the midwestern frontier, which constituted a dominant and unifying theme in their writing. Turner set the tone for this emphasis in his 1893 address in which he said that the "most important effect of the frontier has been in the promotion of democracy here and in Europe."[151] In his presidential address to the MVHA in 1952, Curti stressed how Turner brought the "democratic theme" into American historical discourse.[152] Hicks praised Curti's speech for its attention to the "essentials of democracy" and recounted his own efforts to capture and communicate the "various ingredients of the American concept of democracy" to broader audiences.[153] In 1943, Hicks himself had written *A Short History of American Democracy*.[154] In Curti's *The Growth of American Thought*, which won the Pulitzer Prize in 1944 and was dedicated to the memory of Turner, Curti also emphasized the rise of democratic modes of thought in the West.[155]

The year after Curti's presidential address, Barnhart published *The Valley of Democracy*, which encapsulated many of the democratic themes embraced by the Prairie Historians and summarized much of their work. In the book, Barnhart thanked Turner, Alvord, and Buck for sparking his interest in western history and thanked Pease for his help with sources.[156] Barnhart saw his book as a "testing" of Turner's democratic emphasis in which he found Turner's argument generally sound, but also in need of correction in certain areas.[157] Barnhart noted the important role of the civic and legal heritage of England and the East, but concluded that "something else was added in the New World."[158] As a result of democratic reforms in the region and the recognition of the "worth of the common man," American democracy won "significant victories" in the Midwest, where the "aristocracy inherited from colonial days" was destroyed.[159] The focus on the ingredients of workable democracy by Turner, Barnhart, and the other Prairie Historians constituted an early form of the historiography of republicanism, which would emerge in the latter half of the twentieth century.[160]

Recognizing the advancement of democratic practices in the Midwest should not be confused with the claim that the frontier created American democracy. Following Barnhart in *The Valley of Democracy*, Buley said the Americans did not "invent" democracy in the Midwest, but they improved it.[161] On the debate over Turner and the development of democracy on the frontier, Bogue said that "it seems much more important that America was a democracy than that Americans enjoyed a unique kind of democracy."[162] Whatever its origins or level of uniqueness, the Prairie Historians were proud of the Midwest's democratic heritage and its broader influence. Pelzer, Malcolm Rohrbough said, thought that the force of democracy "pulsed from the ordinary frontier farmers of the legislatures—in the territories, in the states, and eventually into the Congress of the United States."[163] If anyone tried a "putsch on the Italian or the German model," Joseph Schafer said, the "entire West" would rise against them given how entrenched was the democratic tradition in the region.[164] Merk thought the future depended on the preservation of the democratic ideals of the frontier.[165]

For the Prairie Historians, a focus on the development of American democracy involved close attention to law and constitutionalism.[166] Working under Turner at Wisconsin, for example, Libby closely analyzed the bases of support for the ratification of the federal Constitution.[167] Because of its fundamental importance to the legal foundations of the Midwest, the Prairie Historians also extensively studied the Northwest Ordinance. Pease said the members of the MVHA considered it "secondary only to the Constitution."[168] Pease had received his Ph.D. at the University of Chicago by studying with the constitutional historian Andrew McLaughlin, who was born in Beardstown, Illinois, and served as the fifth president of the MVHA.[169] Pease turned his dissertation into his first book, in which he connected English Leveller ideology to the development of American constitutionalism, and he edited the *Laws of the Northwest Territory*.[170] Paxson succeeded McLaughlin at Michigan when McLaughlin moved to Chicago, took over his Constitutional Law and Political Institutions class, and developed a strong interest in western constitutions.[171] After moving to Wisconsin, Paxson also pushed his advisee John Hicks to study western constitutions and "brushed aside" Hicks's initial plan to study Populism.[172] Hicks discussed his work on constitutional history with Barnhart, who also focused on the constitutional development of the Midwest.[173] Shambaugh wrote *The Constitutions of Iowa*, and, when he moved to the National Archives, Buck published works on the ratification of the Constitution and the first ten amendments.[174] When focusing on the constitutional development of the West, Pease, along with others, noted the westerners' debts to the East and England, providing another qualification to Turner's overemphasis on the uniqueness of frontier conditions.[175]

In addition to seeing constitutionalism as a core component of the American democratic tradition, the Prairie Historians paid particular attention to the popular assertion of democratic rights in campaigns and elections. Most prominently, the Prairie Historians saw democratic passions and the influence of backcountry and frontier norms at work in the Populist rebellion of the late nineteenth century, and their resulting research gave birth to Populist historiography. Turner called attention to farmer activism, and his more general assertion of the importance of western history served as a "historiographic counterpart of the farmer's revolt."[176] Turner's student Solon Buck began the tradition of focused studies of farmer activism with his book *The Granger Movement*, which provided the "scholarly foundation" for studying Populism and "opened the way to scores of books and articles" about Populism.[177] Paxson praised Buck's book in the first issue of the *MVHR* and linked the democratic energy of farmer movements to the Midwest's frontier heritage of democracy.[178] Paxson saw the frontier's political culture "undergoing transmutation into agrarian influence."[179] Buck followed *The Granger Movement* with the publication of *The Agrarian Crusade* in 1920.[180]

John Barnhart and John Hicks followed in this tradition. Barnhart consulted with Turner when he pursued his graduate work on Nebraska Populism, and his first two published articles were about Populism.[181] His first, published in 1925, noted that the "significance of Populism is being increasingly recognized" and cited Buck's books and a number of new articles in the *MVHR*, the *Indiana Magazine of History*, and the *Iowa Journal of History and Politics*.[182] During the 1920s, while teaching at Nebraska, Hicks also turned to the study of Populism. Paxson, who had earlier vetoed Hicks's plan to study Populism in graduate school at Wisconsin, was enthused with Hicks's Populism research and also urged him to study agrarian activism past 1900 and even to compare American Populism with French "debtor psychology" and opposition to paying war debts after World War I.[183] Hicks and Buck discussed Hicks's new work on Populism.[184] Hicks and Barnhart also worked well together and collaborated on studies of Populism during these years.[185] Hicks's work resulted in the publication of *The Populist Revolt*, which was written "in the context of the Turner thesis."[186] Merk was enthusiastic about the "sympathetic yet shrewd judgments" in Hicks's book, which he called the "definitive book on Populism."[187] Merk similarly saw Populism as a product of the settlement of the West.[188] Hicks later gave himself the "task of finding out what had happened to the farmers of the Middle West after Populism."[189] He put his research assistant Theodore Saloutos to work on the project, and, Hicks admitted, Saloutos largely wrote the resulting book with himself as "silent partner in the enterprise."[190]

To study Populism is to study farming, and the Prairie Historians, many of them products of midwestern farms, were intense about this enterprise. The midwestern democracy that Turner chronicled had its "economic basis," Barnhart noted, in the small farm, and thus Turner actively promoted the study of agricultural history.[191] Malin thought that Turner's frontier thesis was essentially an "agricultural interpreta-tion of American history."[192] The Prairie Historians followed this course of study by actively promoting the creation of the Agricultural History Society (AHS) in 1919, which, like the MVHA, was also resisted by the AHA.[193] Supporting and advocating the study of farming was a natural fit for historians focused on the Midwest.[194] In 1934, Iowa State University historian Louis Bernard Schmidt, born in Belle Plaine, Iowa, gave his presidential address to the AHS and underscored the centrality of family farming to the region.[195] An "ardent admirer" of Turner and a proud "son of the Middle Border," Schmidt explained the development of farming in the prairie Midwest and the distribution of land, which had created 6.5 million farms in the region by 1920.[196] The prairies, he noted, gener-ated over 60 percent of the nation's farm income and gave the nation its secretaries of agriculture.[197] Several Prairie Historians were active in and served as president of the AHS and published articles in and served as editors for its journal, *Agricultural History*, which was launched in 1927.[198] The teaching of courses of agricultural history was also common at land-grant institutions in the Midwest, which the Prairie Historians also studied and held in high regard.[199] When he died, Paxson was work-ing on a history of land-grant universities.[200] Paxson was half finished with the book when he told administrators he could not finish and left his study, went to the hospital, and died.[201]

The agricultural history genre included Allan Bogue's classic treat-ment of midwestern farming, *From Prairie to Corn Belt*.[202] Bogue was raised on a farm in Ontario, and, when he considered graduate school, he wrote to the president of the AHS and asked for advice on where to study.[203] Bogue decided to study at Cornell with Merk's student Paul Gates, who introduced Bogue to Malin.[204] In *From Prairie to Corn Belt*, Bogue thanked Malin for his help, and, revealing his own agrarian roots, he argued that such works of history were needed because "city-reared and urban-oriented historians [had] come increasingly to dominate our profession."[205] Bogue's book chronicled the agrarian settlement of the Iowa and Illinois prairie and sought to focus on "the man with dirt on his hands and dung on his boots."[206] Bogue discussed the settlers' reaction to the prairie experience; where they settled; how they acquired land; where they were from in the states to the East and in Europe; how they built houses and barns; how they plowed, raised livestock, used machinery, and innovated; how they consumed farm newspapers and attended agri-cultural fairs; and how they dealt with the costs of farming such as credit, taxes, and shipping. Bogue concluded that the "achievements had been striking" for the prairie farmer, and that by the end of the nineteenth century the farmer could look back and think it "was good to have pioneered here, to have been an 'old settler,' and made virgin prairie 'productive' by stocking it with fine animals and raising bountiful crops."[207]

Bogue thought prairie farmers had a "strong commercial orientation" and, along with other Prairie Historians, devoted significant attention to the brass tacks of farm economics.[208] Bogue's first book, which began as a dissertation under Gates and was made possible by time studying with Malin in Kansas, examined the intricacies of farm mortgages in the Midwest.[209] Bogue's work followed in a tradition that traced back to Turner, who placed great emphasis on economic history, as did subsequent Prairie Historians.[210] Bogue and other Prairie Historians expanded on this tradition of economic history by promoting the broader use of statistical and quantitative methods.[211] Bogue said statistics were "like drug addiction. I realize that I am hooked, regret it periodically, but keep coming back."[212] Beyond economics and statistics, Bogue more generally advocated that historians use insights from the social sciences.[213]

When studying the economic details of agriculture and the broader story of midwestern farming, the Prairie Historians closely examined land distribution and geography. Bogue's mentor, Paul Gates, a student of Frederick Merk, Turner's replacement at Harvard, devoted the bulk of his career to studying land distribution and believed that no other issue so consumed the federal government in the century after the Revolution.[214] Merk thought that Gates was the scholar who had "most effectively modified the Turner hypothesis" by explaining how the distribution of land had been disrupted by speculators through Gates's "intensive borings in manuscript collections," but he also thought that Gates had "pushed his ideas rather hard."[215] Merk, Paxson, and Vernon Carstensen all wrote extensively and often critically about federal land policy, and the Prairie Historians called for others to study land policies.[216] In tandem with their studies of land distribution, Turner and the Prairie Historians all took geography and the role of weather, soils, and vegetation in the settlement process seriously.[217] Malin was particularly interested in what would now be considered environmental history, asking, "How much has man modified the ecological setting of history in America?"[218] But Malin thought that there had been "less fundamental change than is usually assumed by conservation propagandists" and resisted, along with Merk and Bogue, what he considered the misuse of environmental data to promote natural resource policies during the New Deal era.[219]

The role of geography and economics in the development of the Midwest brought the Prairie Historians into debates over historical determinism, or the question of what was the major force or forces that determined the course of American development. The issue of determinism had been broached very early by Turner, who rejected the "germ theory" of American development in favor of a greater emphasis on the influence of the frontier, which included a focus on the role of geography and economics as social forces.[220] When he launched History 17 at Harvard, his class on the West, Turner said "there is no key to American history" but added that he thought the "most important thing in our nation's history, and that which most nearly approaches the long sought key, is the westward movement."[221] Turner's emphasis upon the frontier sparked a rich debate beginning in the 1930s led by historians who instead argued that England and the eastern United States played a major role in western development. The Prairie Historians worked within this larger debate and gave Turner's critics their due, but tended to favor the significance of the frontier. Turner did not reject European influences, but, Barnhart said, he "did insist upon the greater importance of American factors."[222] Paxson noted the English language and the "institutions of British life" brought by the colonists and said the "British origins survive[d] to mould" the life of the frontier, "but its destiny and its spirit have become American."[223]

The Prairie Historians also continued to note the environmental adaptations made by western settlers. In the 1890s, Turner had called for the study of the "physiographic basis" of American history and for the historian to work "hand in hand" with "the geologist, the meteorologist, then biologist."[224] The Prairie Historians followed these suggestions and discussed soils, grasses, and geographic formations extensively.[225] James Malin was particularly focused on linking ecology and the natural sciences to historical development. Merk told Malin he had a "genius for tying in the sciences, and especially the more rapidly developing sciences, with history," and said "no other American historian writes as you do the insights of science and history."[226] Merk read Malin's *The Grassland of North America* and said he had "not often in recent years read a work as filled as this with new information, ideas, and approaches" and said the "book represents a new plateau in our knowledge of western America which historians of the future will have to ascend before they begin their own work."[227] Hicks wished he knew as much about agriculture as Malin and said Malin's work was "as important as anything that is going on in the historical world."[228] Bogue also praised Malin's work and applied Malin's insights in his own research.[229] While giving great attention to environmental forces, Malin also fought against overly deterministic modes of thought and rejected "all forms of single- or limited-factor interpretations" as a "fragmentation of knowledge, with its resultant distortion of facts."[230] Turner's and Malin's differing forms of emphasis on the role of the natural environment shaped the work of the Prairie Historians. In an address to the AHS a few weeks after Pearl Harbor, for example, Everett Dick set forth a broad range of environmental adaptations and developments that frontier farmers endured and promoted, much as he did in several books.[231] Carstensen continued this focus. Richard White noted that Carstensen went beyond "farms and farming" and remained "endlessly fascinated by how the natural world responded to human attempts to control it and by the odd results those attempts sometimes yielded."[232]

The work of Malin, who emphasized the importance of writing history from the "bottom up," also underscores the Prairie Historians' attention to early forms of social history.[233] In keeping with a focus on frontier democracy, farming, and economic history, however, there was naturally a political and economic spine to the corpus of works produced by the Prairie Historians. Paxson said he "found the political framework, among other conventional frameworks, indispensible [sic] in telling a general story," as did Pease.[234] Hicks taught American Social History at Wisconsin and tried to squeeze out all mentions of "political and economic" factors, but agreed with Paxson that this was like "trying to nail jelly to the wall."[235] Hicks said that "political and economic history weave together readily and provide an almost essential background for every other kind of history."[236] Without them, a "reliable scheme of organization is hard to find."[237] Hicks tried to organize the course around "cross sections of American life and thought," but believed this only worked if the "students already knew their political and economic history."[238]

Despite these obstacles, the Prairie Historians were keen to examine social history, again following Turner, who first revolted against a history profession focused solely on the East, elites, and formal politics and diplomacy.[239] Michael Steiner calls Turner "perhaps our first self-conscious social historian."[240] Alvord, Pease, Buck, Pelzer, Paxson, Merk, Gates, Blegen, Buley, and Dick followed suit, and all advocated and wrote social history.[241] Alvord called for a "real history" that went beyond governors' messages and treasury accountings and that exhibited a "far greater knowledge of the life of the people."[242] Pelzer was seen as "primarily a social historian" because he was "interested in people, in what they thought and did and how they lived," and focused on their "social customs and manners."[243] Blegen condemned elite-oriented history and what he called the "arrogance of inverted provincialism," which "masked an ignorance of, and disinterest in, the actualities of the common life."[244] Everett Dick's books about the settlement of the prairie and plains were thick with the details of social history.[245] Carlyle Buley's massive two-volume treatment of early life in the Midwest, which won the Pulitzer Prize in 1951, was also replete with the details of social life.[246] The book was so massively detailed and lengthy that Buley struggled for years to find a publisher.[247] Buley, a son of Indiana who studied with Turner, Paxson, and Schafer and earned his Ph.D. from Wisconsin, had taught midwestern history for decades at Indiana, and his book, which he had been planning since 1923, represented the culmination of much of the work of the Prairie Historians.[248] At his award ceremony, Buley called on midwesterners to maintain an "esprit de locale" that other regions in the country enjoyed.[249] He also joked that he probably won the Pulitzer because "there was some midwesterner on the committee."[250]

If a sympathetic midwesterner on the Pulitzer committee gave Buley a boost, it would have been part of a strong midwestern regionalist sentiment that united the Prairie Historians during the early decades of the twentieth century. The Prairie Historians brought to the study of history personal experiences, often on farms or in small towns in the Midwest, that shaped their views and provided a regionalist ethos that unified their work. In their revolt against eastern condescension and neglect, the Prairie Historians gave birth to an intellectual movement organized around the study of the democratic, economic, and social development of the Midwest, which was supported by regional research institutions and scholarly journals. While maintaining scholarly norms, they also understood that by compensating for eastern historians' ignorance of the "great interior of North America," they could, as Libby said, generate histories from an "altogether different viewpoint."[251] In the course of their work, the Prairie Historians sought to maintain their movement's regional grounding. When deciding on meeting locations for the MVHA, they sought out "different points in the west" and were guided by the principle of "locality."[252] When seeking a new director for the State Historical Society of Wisconsin, they praised a candidate for completing research "in the Middle Western field," rejected one for his "lack of a western connection," and ruled out a southerner because of "his lack of experience with Middle Western mores and his lack of knowledge of Middle Western history."[253] They praised the University of Minnesota for providing fellowships for writers to study the region.[254] In a measure of the Prairie Historians' regional consciousness, Bogue rejected the idea of living in the urban East, and Hicks turned down an offer from Harvard because he said he "could never fit comfortably into an Eastern environment."[255] Some devotees of the midwestern cause resented Turner for "deserting the West" and moving to Harvard, but he insisted, "I am still a western man in all but my place of residence."[256] These commitments were part of the persisting belief that professors "should be spiritually attuned to the region" where they worked and contributed to the "continued regionalism" within the American historical profession, which, as Peter Novick explained, constituted one of the barriers to the "scholarly norm of universalism" within the discipline.[257] As Novick intimates, however, the regionalist ethos of the Prairie Historians would ultimately give way to broader pressures and national modes of thought.

By about the time of World War II, the Prairie Historians' project began to fall apart.[258] In the 1930s, critics had already started to assail Turner, and the assault accelerated after the war. Prominent intellectuals began to "disavow" the values of the frontier as an aspect of the nation's "detrimental" and "useless past" in keeping with a "larger revolt against what was considered to be the Midwestern domination of American life and values."[259] In 1947, in a sign of its drift away from its original mission, the MVHA terminated its "Teachers' Section" and soon dropped its effort to promote history in high schools.[260] By the 1950s, the MVHA was moving beyond its "regional beginnings," its "old guard" had lost clout, and its transition into a national organization "was never in doubt."[261] By the 1960s, the once midwestern-oriented *MVHR* became the generalized and nationally focused *Journal of American History*.[262] Populism, which had been treated as a positive democratic force by the Prairie Historians, was attacked as backward and provincial in the 1950s, and regionalism, a sentiment that had united the Prairie Historians since Turner, "was largely scorned as an irrelevant force in American life."[263] Hicks, who had been planning to write a history of the Midwest when he was teaching at Wisconsin in the 1930s, moved to Berkeley in the 1940s, following Paxson, who left a decade earlier.[264] Beyond the confines of midwestern history departments, the increasingly "liberated, widely traveled, and mobile Midwestern citizen" with access to radio, television, and movies also transcended the "physical contours of his old region" and contributed to the erosion of midwestern identity.[265]

With certain important exceptions, the energies and organizational principles of the Prairie Historians' project have largely dissipated. While in subsequent decades younger generations of historians have explored much that they failed to see and rightly corrected their various failings, the Prairie Historians deserve to be remembered for what they did accomplish and for what they anticipated, including the need to amend Turner, the importance of studying the international context of history in combination with local analyses, and the value of studying Populism, social history, and the environment. When Carlyle Buley was researching an earlier group of midwestern historians, he noted that they had been "more or less forgotten, unknown to any except specialists in the field," but that they were "too important to be permitted to pass into oblivion."[266] So, too, the Prairie Historians, who called attention to the Midwest, toiled to make the region's historical institutions functional and productive, won Pulitzers, and focused on our democratic heritage and prospects, points of emphasis that can help us all. A strong case can be made for returning to the Prairie Historians' mode of history.

Three

THE CASE FOR MIDWESTERN HISTORY

WHEN THE PRAIRIE HISTORIANS lost their organizational focus in the 1950s, midwestern history suffered. Historians' attention to the Midwest has declined ever since. The historical vision of the Prairie Historians was, of course, limited, and subsequent generations of historians would rightly incorporate additional perspectives and insights in order to provide more complete accounts of the past, but it should be remembered that the Prairie Historians had created and built the subfield of midwestern history, included many more facets of the past in their work than is often remembered, and brought an insightful regional dimension to historical writing. Through the course of their work, they also developed a mode of thought that constituted a strong argument in favor of the writing of history, one that helps resolve the crisis of confidence that has enveloped the discipline of history in recent decades.

Before discussing the contributions of the Prairie Historians and what they can still offer us, a reckoning with their limitations is in order. The Prairie Historians had obvious blind spots and flaws, which have often been noted—mostly in the form of a generalized and too casual dismissal—by succeeding generations of historians. Some groups simply did not figure prominently in the Prairie Historians' work. Although in the 1890s Turner called for more studies of African Americans, American Indians, workers, immigrants, women, and cities, he did not pursue these topics in any detail.[1] The study of groups previously on the margins of American history—including those who were not part of the general narrative of midwestern history—was taken up by successor generations in a much more detailed and sophisticated manner than the Prairie Historians ever employed, a change in direction that has added meaningful diversity to our accounts of American history.

The Prairie Historians, for example, failed to devote significant attention to the study of the history of women, which was a common shortcoming in many fields of history during their era of active work. They were, however, more advanced than other fields on this front and did support the pioneering work of some female historians. Turner trained women Ph.D.s; Louise Kellogg of the State Historical Society of Wisconsin was elected president of the MVHA in 1930; and Shambaugh, Merk, Gates, Paxson, Buck, Hicks, Malin, and Bogue all welcomed female graduate students into their seminars and praised their work.[2] Although she was not a historian, Clara Paine also managed the MVHA for decades (thus the "Nebraska matriarchy"), and the MVHA executives relied heavily on her skills. But the supportive sentiments toward women were not universal. Hicks once said that he personally liked a female graduate student and wished her well but discouraged her from continuing because she was "still very juvenile in her mental processes," and he thought she "should find her a boy and get married."[3] On other occasions, however, Hicks praised a woman's impressive talents.[4] Hicks, while at Nebraska, once sent two female graduate students to Wisconsin, and Paxson praised their abilities and informed Hicks that "your two girls are functioning smoothly in their proper levels."[5] Bogue was proud of the many scholarly accomplishments of his wife, Margaret Beattie Bogue, whom he met in Gates's seminar.[6] Lillian Cowdell Gates, who met her husband in graduate school, also published widely.[7]

As white men of primarily agrarian backgrounds, the Prairie Historians also failed to examine African American or labor history in the Midwest in great detail. But there were prominent exceptions. Louis Pelzer's first work was a long treatment of the history of African Americans in Iowa; Theodore Pease discussed slavery and African Americans in Illinois extensively and noted the state's "savage black code"; Fred Shannon wrote about African American soldiers in the Union army; and, more generally, the Prairie Historians often wrote about the Civil War and conflicts over slavery.[8] Bogue's student Robert Dykstra would also write a book about the politics surrounding African Americans in Iowa.[9] The Prairie Historians did study midwestern ethnic groups, and in the 1940s, via committee, they advocated more work on "ethnic and minority groups."[10] But some of the Prairie Historians were not enthused about studies of African Americans, made racist comments, and engaged in racial stereotyping. In 1926, Milo Quaife found it "appalling" that when assessing the "negro contribution to civilization," some historians were promoting the "idea that all the races of mankind occupy one common level of mediocrity."[11] Quaife and Orin Libby also used the derogatory term "darkies."[12]

Hicks said that African Americans possibly preferred cotton agriculture because "their characteristic shiftlessness was less damaging to cotton than it might have been to other crops."[13] At the same time, however, Carlyle Buley called "backwoods" whites "shiftless," indicating that the term was applied across racial groups.[14] Buley also sided with those within the MVHA who failed to be moved to direct action by the early civil rights movement. Buley thought the MVHA should stay out of the segregation issue and that historians should address the issue on an individual level, not in an organized fashion, while Gates, Curti, and others pushed the MVHA to discontinue meetings in segregated cities.[15]

Labor history was also secondary for the Prairie Historians, who focused on land and farming, but this neglect should not be exaggerated. Turner's focus on economic history was fully compatible with studies of factories and workers. Turner also brought Richard T. Ely to Wisconsin, and Ely and his student John Commons created the American Bureau of Industrial Research, which focused on labor issues and was housed at the State Historical Society of Wisconsin and aided by Reuben Thwaites.[16] Early in his career, when working at the State Historical Society of Wisconsin, Merk wrote *The Labor Movement in Wisconsin during the Civil War.*[17] Shambaugh also advocated and published labor history from his earliest years at the State Historical Society of Iowa.[18] Fred Shannon, when both at Kansas and Illinois, advocated labor history.[19] The study of farmers, moreover, is a form of labor history. Gates explained that many farmers were first farm laborers.[20] But since the Prairie Historians were mostly farm boys, not sons of factory workers, it is not shocking that formal labor history was not a primary focus of their work. At the same time, their rural and often humble origins made them much closer in social orientation to future labor historians than to the pedigreed sons of privilege in Ivy League history departments who focused on social and political elites in their research.

Despite recent claims that the field of American Indian history was historically neglected, the Prairie Historians were quite active in this area of research.[21] At the first the meeting of the MVHA at Lake Minnetonka, Minnesota, Libby gave a presentation about the Mandans and generally argued that Indians had been "exploited, cheated, and exterminated" and said that "all lovers of humanity" would appreciate Indian culture and support political reforms designed to aid Indians.[22] When he arrived at the University of North Dakota, Libby went west to the Missouri River and began recording Mandan and Hidatsa legends, and, based on his historical research, the Mandans called the tall professor the "Long-man-who-gets-things-right."[23] Libby also studied Custer's

Last Stand and interviewed Arikaras who had served as scouts in the battle.[24] Alvord sought a "representative of the science of Indian ethnology" to serve on the board of editors of the *MVHR* in its early years, and the MVHA urged Congress to allocate money to preserve American Indian languages.[25] Merk started his major work on western history with two chapters about Indian history, and on the first page of his opus Paxson discusses the "native races that were dispossessed" and describes the "conquest of the continent" by white settlers.[26] Gates worked a great deal on the "efforts of Indian tribes to obtain recompense for inadequate treaty compensation," and his efforts contributed to the passage of new federal legislation designed to accomplish this goal.[27] Malin's dissertation focused on Indian policy, and he questioned the "discovery" of America, deeming such a view "egocentric" and asking, "To whom was it new?"[28] Paxson and Buck praised Malin's book *Indian Policy and Westward Expansion* and called for similar research in the future.[29] A committee of Prairie Historians concurred and called for more study of Indian history and the treatment of Indians by the government and settlers.[30] The third most studied topic in the first decades of the MVHA was "the Indian," behind "Settlement" and "Politics and Government."[31] While the Prairie Historians work on Indian history surely had its flaws, it is far from correct to say that the topic was neglected.[32]

In addition to their limited attention to certain historical topics, anti-Semitism within the history profession persisted during the years when the Prairie Historians were most active.[33] In his book on midwestern history, David Brown describes Turner's "soft anti-Semitism" and his doubts about the effect of eastern and southern Europeans on his Anglo-American rural Midwest, but also notes that one of Turner's Jewish and socialist students recognized his democratic egalitarianism and said that Turner embraced a "nationalism with the 'welcome sign' out to all who were capable of being infected with his own inspiring enthusiasm for America."[34] Selig Perlman, for example, studied with Turner and earned his Ph.D. in economics from Wisconsin in 1915 and did much to advance the cause of labor history.[35] But other examples indicate lingering prejudice. Hicks delayed the appointment of one Jewish professor at Berkeley, whom he worried might have "ultra left wing tendencies so common to the New York Jewish intelligentsia," until he was sure that the professor was not opposed to American foreign policy in the late 1940s.[36] One professor saw Hicks as anti-Semitic.[37] One of Hicks's Jewish graduate students, however, praised his mentor, and Hicks worked with and "greatly admired" Perlman when he was at Wisconsin.[38] While Perlman worked with Turner and was friends with Hicks, he also warned Jewish graduate students at Wisconsin that "history belongs to the Anglo-Saxons. You belong in economics or sociology."[39] Perlman's warning underscored the continuing barriers faced by Jewish historians. Merk worried about Bert Loewenberg running "into the stone wall of anti-Semitism," and he and several other Prairie Historians tried to help him find a position, which he finally secured at the University of South Dakota.[40] As late as 1957, Bogue was a "bit sick" at the thought of a new Ph.D. being rejected by an "eastern institution" for being Jewish and worried about this still being a problem in the Midwest.[41]

In 1956, the Wisconsin history department hired its first Jewish faculty member and was becoming known as a welcoming and supportive environment for Jewish graduate students.[42] During the 1950s, Wisconsin drew a large number of Jewish students from the East who were attracted to the progressive history and political activities of Madison. The history of dissent and the embrace of progressive causes at Wisconsin made it an "inviting location for Jewish students eager to join in a kind of heartland radicalism."[43] Several young Jewish students at Wisconsin founded the journal *Studies on the Left* in 1959. "*Studies* was pretty much Jewish," recalled its only "Gentile editor," but it made common cause with other like-minded Wisconsin students, including those who were critical of American foreign policy during the early Cold War.[44]

During the 1950s, the question of anti-Semitism also burst into the historiography of Populism. In 1955, Richard Hofstadter, who was Jewish, published *The Age of Reform*, which argued that the Populist movement, the study of which had been pioneered by Solon Buck, John Barnhart, Hicks, and other Prairie Historians, was grounded in reactionary agrarian politics and laced through with anti-Semitism.[45] Hicks and others defended the Populists.[46] Hicks wrote to his student Theodore Saloutos that Hofstadter could understand urban America, but found "his background . . . quite inadequate for any reasonable understanding of Populism."[47] It was Jewish scholars, with the exception of the radical historian Norman Pollack, who found the Populists anti-Semitic, while the Populists were generally defended by Gentiles, but this dimension of the debate was rarely discussed openly.[48] Bogue was asked to organize and chair a panel on Populism in 1961 that included Pollack, and he asked Hofstadter to participate, but Bogue said Hofstadter declined because he "had no wish to break lances with Pollack in public."[49] Bogue also asked Saloutos to participate to bring in the "old Hicks approach" to Populist history.[50] Pollack, who defended the Populists, was also a young Marxist who represented an early form of New Left scholarship and remembered the panel on Populism as a "disaster."[51] Despite all the energy and passion poured into this debate, Hofstadter later admitted privately that he had purposely exaggerated the anti-Semitism of the Populists for effect.[52]

Perhaps the most important lesson to be gleaned from the debate over anti-Semitism and the Populists is the differing worldviews and personal experiences that historians brought to the discussion. In his account of the historical profession's struggle over objectivity, Peter Novick explains the skepticism of the Populists among some Jews: "they were only one generation removed from the Eastern European *shtetl*, where insurgent gentile peasants spelled pogrom."[53] Daniel Bell noted in 1978 that Hofstadter's interpretation was linked to a "particularly Jewish fear" of "mass action, a fear of passions let loose. . . . When man doesn't have halacha, the law, he becomes chia, an animal."[54] The Prairie Historians, on the other hand, tended to see the Populists as agrarian reformers, often in the form of their grandfathers, engaging in civic action in Turner's democratic Midwest. Curti said that Hofstadter's "position [was] as biased by his urban background and [his reaction to] the new conservatism as the work of older historians was biased by their rural background and traditional agrarian sympathies."[55]

The problem of anti-Semitism and the small number of women in the discipline of history is surely linked to the sometimes intimate and clubby nature of the profession in the early twentieth century. The Prairie Historians often wrote personal letters to one another, shared their research findings and recent publications, met at conferences for socializing, and associated with other academic and professional men in the college towns where they lived.[56] Libby was a Lion, a Mason (worshipful master and grand historian), and a member of the SAE fraternity, the Fortnightly Club, and the Franklin Club, and he devoted much of his time to such groups.[57] Pelzer was a thirty-five-year member of the Triangle Club, a "social center for University faculty men" at the University of Iowa.[58] Quaife founded the Algonquin Club in Detroit in 1934.[59] Barnhart was a longtime member of the Bloomington Rotary Club.[60] Gates liked "smokers," which were popular at MVHA meetings.[61] Blegen liked the "Cosmos Club" in Washington, D.C.[62] Hicks was active in the "Town and Gown Club."[63] When he arrived at Wisconsin to join the faculty, Hicks enjoyed "floozy dinners" and "much informal entertaining" with other scholars.[64] He even enjoyed a welcoming dinner party attended by Wisconsin governor Phil LaFollette.[65]

Membership in fraternal clubs, frequent dinner parties, and informal socializing could foster solidarity, conversation, and friendly communal networks. The Prairie Historians said they could "sit by our firesides and smoke and argue in the best of good humor" with people who disagreed with them.[66] The cozy relationships among these men was conducive to detailed discussions of who was considering an offer at a different university, salaries and leave time, who the newly minted Ph.D.s would be, and where the job openings were. In contrast to the complex hiring procedures, diversity requirements, and promotion and tenure processes of recent decades, such critical decisions could be informal or controlled by a few men in earlier years. Hicks was simply hired at Berkeley by the department head without any consultation of the faculty, a decision that in later years, Peter Novick notes, would be "unthinkable."[67] The Prairie Historians' interest in civic groups and socializing was mostly driven by public interestedness and fun and the old American tradition of joining, which was especially strong in the Midwest, but it could also lead to feelings of alienation among those who were not included or those who chose a more private path.

While their activities were not generally motivated by a desire to exclude and were mostly a product of the social practices of their times, the Prairie Historians certainly were, one might say, "old school." As Peter Novick once noted of another group of older historians, the Prairie Historians were "culturally very 'straight.'"[68] They were, for example, involved with Christian churches to varying degrees. Some were active members while others were more passive, but they were generally not hostile to organized religion. Turner was nominally a Unitarian, while Libby was a "devout Episcopalian" and served as senior warden of St. Paul's Church in Grand Forks, North Dakota.[69] Paxson was a Quaker and his family used the formal "thee," and he went to great lengths to keep his daughters away from strange men.[70] Hicks planned to attend the seminary and become a Methodist minister after completing his degree at Northwestern, but could not go through with his decision in the end, so he went to graduate school in history instead.[71] When the Congregational minister and a "legion" of other pastors attempted to persuade Hicks to join their church in Madison, Hicks demurred by saying, "I'm a retired Methodist."[72] The Prairie Historians often came from religious families. Hicks's father was a Methodist minister; Gates was the son of a "New England Baptist preacher"; and Blegen's father was a Norwegian Lutheran minister.[73] Everett Dick was an Adventist who was planning to go to Iowa for graduate training, but his plans changed when the Adventists instead decided to send him to the Philippines to manage a school. When that plan was delayed due to the coming of war in the Pacific, he went to Wisconsin, where he said the training was "much more valuable than that given at Iowa City," but he remained active in the church when he became a professor at Union College in Nebraska.[74]

While often amenable to religion, the Prairie Historians also favored the trappings of the cultivated intellectual. Libby was absorbed with ornithology, which Turner thought consumed too much of his time, and he became known as the "Birdman" when he was at Wisconsin (he also liked movies and "automobiling").[75] Pease was drawn to English museums and London streets, excelled at fencing, and loved playing bridge, hiking, and growing flowers.[76] Paxson liked to play golf and enjoyed "the usual spring kick out of the garden."[77] Many of the Prairie Historians, perhaps to compensate for leaving the farm, embraced gardening. Buley preferred his azaleas and rhododendrons (he also tended to stray birds).[78] Hicks's father, who grew up on a farm near Red Wing, Minnesota, kept his son active in the garden.[79] When Bogue toured the Kansas countryside with Malin, they had a picnic lunch with the University Botany Club overlooking a stream, and then adjourned to the Malin home to see the flowerbeds and enjoy coffee and piano.[80] Gardening was a quiet pursuit, conducive to writing, and comported with the Prairie Historians' general demand for conditions and surroundings that fostered scholarly productivity. When he arrived in Berkeley, Paxson bragged to Hicks that his "study in the library would turn you green with envy. It is big and quiet, with French windows to a balcony from which bay and mountains are much in evidence."[81]

As intellectuals consumed with writing and the details of publishing, the Prairie Historians had their professorial quirks, as indicated by their debates over printing. Benjamin Shambaugh, Clarence Alvord, and Paxson discussed at length the color of the cover of the *MVHR*, whether to list the contents on the cover (Alvord hoped to include nothing which "offends the asthetic [sic] taste") and trim the covers (Shambaugh thought trimming gave a "very undignified appearance"), the costs of printing, and capitalization rules.[82] Paxson thought Shambaugh's printing of the early *Proceedings* was "too fancy" and that the *MVHR* should resemble "books of sober scientific merit."[83] Alvord and Clarence Paine always worried about the costs of the "finer sort of printing" and sought a "good enough" approach.[84] The Prairie Historians also spent a great part of their lives in the archives, and they often fussed about conditions for research. Bogue even worried about the contents of archival boxes "settling" and wondered if the contents should be subject to periodic "reshuffling" to prevent it.[85] The quirks were not limited to scholarship. They often discussed their health in their letters (Bogue informed Malin of his "good old fashioned spastic colon attack").[86] Vernon Carstensen and Merle Curti discussed eggplant, and Bogue and Malin discussed animal vitamins.[87] They were always trying to arrange places to stay during research trips and to sell the houses in the towns they were leaving. Louis Pelzer stayed at the "Hicks ranch" in Lincoln during one summer (Pelzer asked, "Shall we bring our electric fan or is there one in the place?").[88] Paxson negotiated with Turner about buying Turner's house in Madison (Paxson wanted to know what to do with the bicycles Turner left behind) and then tried to sell the house to Hicks.[89] Hicks later tried to sell Curti his house in Madison ("There is a good oil burner in the house, and we keep comfortably warm in the coldest weather"), but Curti was stuck with a house that would not sell (even though it included "four fireplaces etc etc!").[90] In the midst of the varied federal policy responses to the Great Depression, Paxson joked about creating a "Federal-Migrant-College-Professors-Corporation to take over all realty belonging to those who move, and to guarantee to dispose of it at a happy profit for cash money."[91]

Despite their tweed coats and pipes and their appreciation of the traditional ways of the academy, the Prairie Historians were generally not conservative in the contemporary sense of the term. Although "culturally straight," their politics was mostly liberal and supportive of the New Deal. Turner was a progressive, and Wisconsin was a center of progressivism where the class-based analyses of Charles Beard were popular. Libby "championed" the Nonpartisan League in North Dakota and, because of his support, "escaped dismissal by a hair's breadth."[92] Libby's analysis of the ratification vote on the Constitution prefigured Charles Beard's class-based critique of the Constitution and was later embraced by the New Left.[93] Gates praised Beard's books and argued that Beard's liberalism "made easier the role of the teacher in attempting to instill liberalism in the minds of a young generation of complacent Americans."[94] Gates was remembered as an "old radical" who worked for the Henry Wallace campaign for president in 1948 and who believed that liberals needed a "great and effective leader" or to "mass such strength in Congress that they can overwhelm the combination of southern reactionary Democrats and northern Republicans."[95] Hicks sympathized with the Populists and noted that "many" of his colleagues at Wisconsin were "extremely sympathetic with the efforts of the New Deal to care for the needy and to get the national economy moving again."[96] Curti sought to give a "socialistic if not Marxian interpretation" to history.[97] Carstensen bemoaned the absence of a "strong liberal party" in 1948, saw Truman as part of the "Missouri gang," and despised MacArthur, the "Hearst press," Nixon, and the Central Intelligence Agency (CIA).[98] Fred Shannon was a socialist, and Frederick Merk voted Communist.[99] The Prairie Historians' support for the New Deal and the Left paralleled the more general developments in the historical profession during the 1920s and 1930s, when progressive history and Beard were ascendant and "many historians, almost certainly the majority of younger historians, were either New Dealers or critics of Roosevelt from the left."[100]

The support for liberalism and the New Deal was not uniform among the Prairie Historians, however, and some diversity of political opinion was in evidence. Buley was a critic of the Progressives, whom he saw as a "conglomerate of balmy idealists," and "Willkie one-worldism."[101] Hicks supported American intervention in World War II, which he knew would elicit "screams of rage" from the "Beard worshipers," but he also said he did not like being on the same side as the "Communists and the fellow-travelers" once the Nazis invaded the Soviet Union.[102] Malin objected to the coming of the "welfare state" and the New Deal's pursuit of a "regimented social order," and thought the New Dealers were manipulating Turner's work to advance their political goals.[103] The Prairie Historians' general respect for Turner also caused conflicts with Marxists who were increasingly critical of Turner during the 1930s.[104] The Prairie Historians' recognition of the success of midwestern democratic development also conflicted with the growing number of historians in the profession who targeted the "Philistine, the Pioneer, and the Populist" as the sources of the nation's ills.[105] The liberal historians who participated in the "revolt against what was considered to be the midwestern domination of American life and values" caused obvious tension with the Prairie Historians, who strongly identified with the cultural and political traditions of the Midwest.[106] These eastern liberals saw the rural Midwest as the home of McCarthyism, "ignorant biblical literalists, rednecks, and crypto anti-Semites," fascist and authoritarian undercurrents, and the generally darker aspects of democratic life.[107]

Public conflicts over politics, disputes over historical interpretations, and clashes with eastern historians were accompanied by less visible bureaucratic and personal quarrels. Clarence Paine, who spearheaded the organization of the MVHA, had to fight for his job at the Nebraska State Historical Society.[108] Turner was unhappy with the regents' interference at Wisconsin, which contributed to his decision to depart for Harvard in 1910.[109] Libby felt "handicapped" at Wisconsin by Turner, who recommended him for a post at the University of North Dakota without Libby's knowledge, a maneuver that Libby never forgave.[110] Alvord's work on the Illinois centennial history series caused him a great deal of stress and many tensions with Pease, and Alvord finally had to check into an Indiana sanitarium to "recover his health."[111] Alvord also felt underpaid by Illinois so left for Minnesota in 1920.[112] Quaife, who became director of the State Historical Society of Wisconsin in 1914, was demoted five years later and soon moved to the Detroit Public Library, from which he was "dumped" in 1947.[113] Quaife bitterly denounced the "decadence" of the State Historical Society of Wisconsin under the "[Joseph] Schafer regime" and thought that "professors are for the most part an impractical group of men living in a world of make-believe."[114] Hicks faced strife in the Nebraska history department, and Paxson counseled him to avoid "any alignments with any side among the factions" and urged him to be sure that "negligent" administrators did a "cleansing" of the department, thereby assuming the consequent "odium," before Hicks agreed to become department chairman.[115] Hicks said the "depression has set us back sorely" at Nebraska and noted that when he left for Wisconsin, "My place here will not be filled. So the depression works."[116] Personal spats, power struggles, and conflicts with administrators were not uncommon.[117] Barnhart complained of the "slow work for a young man to break into a long established department composed of older men" and of "struggling with the precedents of the status quo."[118] Carstensen was angered by Buck's review of his history of the University of Wisconsin, written with Curti, and Carstensen and Curti often discussed the "envy and jealousy" of colleagues, the danger of "ulcers and nervous collapse" brought on by serving as department chair, the "bitterness" and "tirades" of colleagues, and the favoritism displayed by university presses.[119] Malin's conflicts with publishers and other scholars and his decision to self-publish limited the accessibility of his work, and he is remembered for being "burdened by his times and embittered in his later years."[120]

The Prairie Historians, in short, were human beings with human flaws and failings and not immune to the pettiness of academic politics, nor were they catholic in their research and writing. In the practice of history, their attention to the role of women, African Americans, and workers in the American past fell below current norms, and their attitude toward civil rights was uneven and, at times, less than enlightened. The Prairie Historians' failings should never be discounted, but neither should the evidence of their openness be overlooked. In the course of this study, I actually anticipated finding more evidence of racism and anti-Semitism and less evidence of the Prairie Historians' willingness to consider new topics and methods of inquiry. Accounts of the Prairie Historians' faithfulness to the cause of history, moreover, should be remembered and counterbalance their flaws. They were often praised for their decency and fairness. Merk's key to success was, in "a single word, integrity."[121] One of his students said, "Fred taught integrity."[122] Pelzer, for another example, was remembered for having a "certain fineness and simplicity of character," for being kind, funny, and charming, and liking to social-ize—he "liked people and they liked him."[123] One historian praised him for his "rugged integrity" and for being a person who, once his friend-ship was earned, was forever loyal, and another said that "integrity was in his very marrow."[124] Another called Pelzer "a gifted son of the Middle Border," a comment that points toward one of the great strengths of the Prairie Historians.[125]

Whatever their personal flaws and the limits of their vision, what separated the Prairie Historians from others in the profession and gave them a unique voice was their roots in and orientation toward the Mid-west. This regionalist ethos was unquestionably related to the personal backgrounds of many of the Prairie Historians. Turner's "affection for his native soil" underpinned his interest in studying the Midwest.[126] Pel-zer's background on an Iowa farm led to his interest in midwestern his-tory and his devotion to the MVHA.[127] One historian recalled that Pelzer "loved the width and breadth of the generous, liberal vision of the great Valley of Democracy."[128] Hicks, who was born in a small Missouri town to a Methodist preacher and had a mother who was born in a frontier log cabin, "reflected many of the values and beliefs of America's heartland."[129] Hicks praised a graduate student who had a similar background, noting that he knew "farm life at first hand" and was "a hard worker and a clear thinker."[130] Dick's background in Kansas and work in Nebraska were major influences on his scholarship.[131] Curti "always retained his sympa-thetic understanding if not invariably his sense of identity with the Mid-dle West."[132] When Curti was exhausted from work, Carstensen urged him to go back to Nebraska to relax and enjoy the prairie spring to renew his strength.[133] Bogue's father wanted him to stay on the family farm, and his rural origins influenced his writing and research.[134] As a young man, Bogue "had seen the auctioneer's gavel separate an indebted neighbor from his farm," and he remembered his "mother's dread of mortgages."[135] When Bogue sought out Malin in Kansas to work with him on agricul-tural history, he emphasized that "I was raised on the farm" and "I found the work very congenial."[136]

In addition to bringing a regional sensibility to their work, the Prai-rie Historians should be credited with more practical accomplishments. While some historians have condescended to the "archive rats" and "fact grubbers" in the profession, especially in an era when analyzing texts is a common project, these efforts are critical to the foundations of histori-cal knowledge. In an address to the Minnesota Historical Society in 1915, Alvord traced the archival urge back to the Irish bards and noted how people's "unconscious longing for information" about their past led to more organized efforts at retaining records.[137] Alvord said the "drudges of the historical fraternity" had to collect and prepare all the necessary material for the "would-be Francis Parkmans" to use.[138] On the dangers of not collecting historical materials as soon as possible, Buck quoted an old English archivist who worked during the reign of Queen Elizabeth and worried about the dangers to documents such as "Fier, Water, Ratts and Myce, Misplaceinge [and] even plaine taking of them away . . . by a Privy Councilor . . . or anie of the Kings learned Counsell."[139] Buck followed his own advice and pushed for an "organization of archivists," which became the Society of American Archivists.[140] Pease was a founding member and became the editor of its journal, the *American Archivist*.[141] After the creation of the National Archives in 1934, Buck became assistant director and then became the second archivist of the United States and later became chief of the Manuscript Division at the Library of Congress. Most of the Prairie Historians worked with archival repositories to gather materials for their collections, and they frequently corresponded about finding people of high stature to lead historical organizations.[142] They took the mechanics of historical research seriously.

In addition to collecting historical materials, the Prairie Historians researched and wrote histories at a time, extending until World War II, when publishing was not common among academic historians.[143] The launching of the *MVHR* to promote publishing among midwestern historians was a milestone and a major accomplishment, as was the creation of the journal *Agricultural History*. Alvord and others prodded historical societies to cooperate, collect materials, and publish historical journals and books.[144] Due to his efforts to collect historical materials and his scholarly productivity, Alvord was said to have run a "History Factory" at the University of Illinois.[145] The Prairie Historians placed a premium on publishing. Hicks praised a student for being "very publicatious" and urged the hiring of another student on the grounds that he was "a research man."[146] To promote publishing, Hicks also organized the University of Wisconsin Press in the mid-1930s and, in so doing, used the University of Minnesota Press as a model.[147] In a common complaint, Gates worried about his effort to publish being undermined by teaching and administrative duties.[148] When leaving the chairmanship of the history department at Iowa, Bogue lamented the "books unread, articles unwritten and intellectual development stunted. My successor is picked and may God have mercy upon his soul."[149]

In addition to collecting historical materials and placing a high priority on publishing, the Prairie Historians pursued readers. In keeping with the early mission of the MVHA, they sought to reach a broad audience with books of history that general readers could understand. David Thelen notes that although the MVHA started from a "deep rooted-ness in a particular place," its founders sought a wide audience, included many nonspecialists in their meetings, and engaged many high school teachers, a set of emphases that stands in contrast to present-day complaints about historians being "narrow and overspecialized" and their tendency "to talk with other specialists."[150] In the 1920s, Buck advanced the MVHA's mission by pushing state historical societies to keep their publications in a form accessible to the "general reader."[151] A committee of Prairie Historians found the old historian who only "lusteth after facts" charming, but also thought historians should pursue topics that have "some significance" and relevance to the "affairs of the world."[152] The committee recognized how history played an "important role in the contemporary world" and how the "sound historian" should promote "readable history that is to the point" lest citizens turn to "unsound historians" for their historical knowledge.[153] Toward this end, Shambaugh advocated "applied history," and others, including Turner, embraced the pursuit of recent American history.[154] Despite these efforts, by the 1960s Bogue confessed to concerns about historical work being "unintelligible to the public for some time."[155]

One unifying quality to their efforts at collecting historical materials and publishing works they hoped would reach beyond the academy was sheer hard work and determination.[156] The extreme exertions of Alvord, Paine, Shambaugh, Libby, Buck, and Paxson during the early years of the MVHA, when its continued existence remained precarious, and their constant fund-raising, searches for quality articles, and solicitation of subscribers are admirable. Paine praised Alvord for his extensive work raising money for the *MVHR*: "You have certainly missed your calling. You ought to be a field agent for a denominational college, bible society or some other good work that needs money."[157] Alvord said the *MVHR* was "my own chick and I am nursing it during this early period of its career," and he sought to "keep it in cotton wool by the fireside and feed it by hand" and keep it out of "fights."[158] Alvord's diligence and "enthusiasm [were] so contagious that a conference with him was a powerful stimulus to more and better work."[159] From his seminar room in Schaeffer Hall at the University of Iowa, Pelzer would instruct graduate students to study the new issues of the *MVHR*, give impressive student presentations a hard-earned "well done," tell students to work hard, and inform them, "You've got to wear out the seat of your pants in the library."[160] Pelzer believed in "rigid technical training," and, according to one account of Pelzer's regimen, the "unenergetic died by the side of the trail."[161] Libby forced students to "work like turks," and he was a "ruthless enemy of the bluffer and idler."[162] Paxson was happy to help students, but he also did not waste time in chitchat, and visitors to his office "could sense the there was much to be done and time was fleeting."[163] As a graduate student at Wisconsin, Hicks stayed away from women in order to remain productive and rarely left the library.[164] Paxson had told Hicks, "You can't get married until after you've taught for five years."[165] Dick proved that one could serve as a professor at a small college with a large teaching load and still publish impressive books.[166] Because of his productivity, Malin was seen as "twins—one man simply couldn't do all that work—maybe it's triplets."[167] Bogue confessed to "mulish exhaustion" and the straining of his "cerebral muscles" from excessive work.[168] He worried about his research and writing being in a "state of arrested animation" due to other duties and was happy when he could teach a class and yet still have "preserved four to six hours a day for research and writing."[169] Bogue skipped a history conference so that he could stay home "and research as hard as possible."[170] After winning the Pulitzer Prize for his book on the Midwest, Buley said it was his "innate stubbornness" and hard work that allowed him to win "one of Uncle Joe's Oscars."[171] In a common theme, Blegen vowed not to "graze in the green pastures of inactivity" during retirement.[172]

The Prairie Historians planted themselves in the archives and worked hard because they generally adhered to the principles of scientific history, which required the continuous pursuit of facts and evidence in order to advance an objective interpretation of the past. In 1901, Turner said historians should try not to take sides in past historical conflicts and called for "cool-headed historical criticism free from 'viewpoints.'"[173] The Prairie Historians generally sought to advance this principle. Alvord informed the editor of *Literary Digest* that the *MVHR* would be "devoted to the scientific study of western history" and said the MVHA would "do its best service by clinging to its ideals of scientific accuracy."[174] In keeping with this goal, Alvord criticized what he saw as myths and exaggerations in past historical accounts.[175] Buck said that Alvord let "no prejudices of race, nationality, section, party, or religion" affect his writing and that he was in essence a "scholar, pursuing truth in history for the sake of knowing it and making it known to others, but with little interest in the practical utility of such knowledge."[176] While based at the State Historical Society of Wisconsin, Quaife wrote in the second issue of the *MVHR* that the historian writing about the Midwest must maintain "unceasing vigilance in the scanning of his materials" in order to attain "even approximate truth."[177] Buley sought to "present a balanced summary of the record, without emphasizing the interesting and dramatic at the expense of the prosaic but important."[178] In order to avoid distortions when presenting history to his readers, Buley said he wanted "to give them the facts."[179] Libby agreed that assembling information and facts was critical, and he criticized those, including Turner, who made conclusions based upon "inadequate research and scanty evidence."[180] Pelzer similarly embraced rigorous standards and tried to avoid the temptation toward sensationalism at the expense of objectivity, and his lectures, according to one of his students, were "restricted to the provable facts of history."[181] Paxson captured the sentiment of many of the Prairie Historians: "Say what one may of historical philosophy, history is a matter of facts; and the establishment of facts, desiccated as they may be, is the chief function of the genuine historian."[182]

While Paxson preached the need to gather facts, he did not embrace "historical absolutism" and was well aware of how bias and incomplete information limited historical interpretation.[183] Recognizing the Prairie Historians' belief in the pursuit of objectivity is not to say that they had foreclosed all doubt about the difficulties of such a project or that they failed to recognize the failings of past historians. Their whole project began, after all, as a rebellion against the easterners who dominated the profession and were biased against the study of regions to the west. They tried to make the MVHA less subject to the control of a few historians and prevent the resulting bias, which they saw as a primary weakness of the American Historical Association.[184] Given the time period of their foundational work, the Prairie Historians were very much aware of the discussions about the "new history" and the problem of relativism, which was clearly articulated in the early twentieth century by Carl Becker, an Iowan, and Charles Beard, an Indianan. Turner certainly understood that each generation would have new interpretations of history and recognized historians' biases.[185] Bias would remain a problem for historians to wrestle with, and the facts, once collected, would always be subject to interpretation. The University of Missouri historian Lewis Atherton, in keeping with the sentiments of the Prairie Historians, adhered to Carl Becker's admonition: "To establish the facts is always in order, and is indeed the first duty of the historian; but to suppose that the facts, once established in all their fullness, will 'speak for themselves' is an illusion."[186]

The Prairie Historians often grappled with the problem of bias in historical interpretation. When Shambaugh promoted "applied history" to bring more historical knowledge to public policy debates, Alvord expressed discomfort with "tendencies" toward presentist bias in the profession and, while supportive of Shambaugh's attempts, also defended the "old fashioned idea of what history is."[187] The Prairie Historians, for an example coincident with their ascendancy, struggled with the propaganda efforts surrounding World War I.[188] Alvord tried to keep the MVHA separated from the war promotion efforts because the "historical scientist cannot take part in a war and remain scientific in spirit."[189] Milo Quaife thought that if the MVHA became involved, the organization would be "swept from its moorings" and become compromised, as had historians in England and Germany.[190] Libby, however, thought that the MVHA could provide an "intelligent direction" to the discussion of the war.[191] In the decade after the war, historians often debated the Beards' major book, *The Rise of American Civilization* (1927), in the context of objectivity. Paxson criticized the Beards because he thought they made their facts "generally incidental to some conclusion that has predetermined their selection and arrangement."[192] During the New Deal years, Malin was often critical of the government's propaganda efforts.[193] When he gave his presidential address to the MVHA, Curti noted the difficulties of objectivity and explained how outside forces influenced historians' work.[194] The Prairie Historians thought objectivity was the proper organizing principle for the discipline and a defense against the political extremism of the age. In the mid-1940s, a committee of Prairie Historians that surveyed the field called for the publication of accurate histories to combat demagogues who "distort the past in order to win adherents to programs which every real historian will recognize as intolerant, shortsighted, vicious in their effect upon the commonweal, and false."[195] In the 1960s, as political passions again intensified, Bogue said he was "uncomfortable" with attempts to use history in the service of politics and said we "must fight the biases that play within us, impelling us to find what we think is best for society rather than what 'is.'" Bogue said that Malin, who thought the growing embrace of "relativist theory" and "presentism" were warping the view of the past, had pointed out this danger "long ago."[196]

The Prairie Historians' focus on collecting evidence and attempting to interpret that evidence as fairly and objectively as possible still constitutes the best organizational model for the discipline of history. By applying these principles, the Prairie Historians proved their value by creating the field of midwestern history and leaving behind a legacy of important books, journals, and institutions. If a revival of interest in the history of the Midwest is to happen, it will rely heavily on this heritage. If new histories of the Midwest incorporate the insights of historians from recent decades who have done much to compensate for what the Prairie

Historians overlooked, the resulting combination will yield important and substantive work.

A greater appreciation of the work of the Prairie Historians could also help historians more generally. In contrast with the pervasive doubts about the impossibility of objective history in recent decades, the Prairie Historians acknowledged the problem of bias and limited information and then moved ahead and attempted to write the most balanced history they could, an approach that fused a recognition of the need for hard work and exhaustive archival digging with a posture of prairie pragmatism toward the obvious limits of objectivity and historical knowledge. This approach can be found at work in the sensible writings of James Kloppenberg. When responding to Peter Novick's grim tale about intellectual chaos in the historical profession caused by the proliferation of different viewpoints and the rise of postmodernism—what Christopher Lasch called "a skepticism so deep that it becomes indistinguishable from nihilism"—Kloppenberg argues that historians "need not choose between the absolute authority of facts and the anarchy of idiosyncratic interpretations."[197] Kloppenberg wisely counsels historians to recognize the "indispensability of the scientific method of verifying facts" *and* the need to interpret these facts, a project he calls "pragmatic hermeneutics."[198] In this age of doubt and indeterminacy when past interpretative paradigms have collapsed, Kloppenberg says, historians can play an important role by insisting on the "indispensability of historical studies as one of the most fruitful forms of inquiry in a world of uncertainty."[199] Kloppenberg is making the case for the Prairie Historians and their practical approach to history. Kloppenberg is echoing the case that John Hicks made to his Wisconsin replacement, Merle Curti, in 1944: with a maximum usage of the factual evidence available and a minimal reliance on the "jargon of the philosophers, or other word-worshippers," historians have the "obligation of going as far as we can in the direction of explaining how things came about" while always realizing the "difficulty in attaining objectivity."[200] "We all know that, being human," Hicks added, "we can never really make that grade, but we have to try" and "do the best we can."[201]

The Prairie Historians' good faith effort to cope with the problem of bias and to fairly interpret the available facts as best they could also makes the point about the need for a variety of experiences and viewpoints among historians. Turner, as a midwesterner, made this point most effectively by changing the focus of American history and drawing attention to untapped themes in American life. He was able to do so by drawing on his own experiences, so much at variance with the dominant figures in the history profession at the time, as a son of rural Wisconsin. So, too, the other Prairie Historians, who could give voice to the history of a region through their experiences on midwestern farms and in small towns, their historical training in the Midwest, their work in and for midwestern archives and history journals, and even their memberships in Christian churches and Rotary clubs. Turner and the Prairie Historians, Hofstadter once noted, "took the writing of history out of the hands of the Brahmins and the satisfied classes."[202] In an age when the study of midwestern history is not popular, when American historians are drawn to other topics, emphases, and regions, and when reviving midwestern history must cut against many cultural currents, Turner's old rebellion is worth remembering. Turner brought the Midwest into the conversation about American history through his resistance to eastern dominance. If Turner favored his own region, his later critics and also those who neglect the study of midwestern history in the present are also limited by their predilections and biases. Avery Craven, who grew up in rural Iowa, said Turner "unquestionably revealed his own midwestern background in his writing," but Craven also warned that the "revisionists who examine Turner's work should be careful that they too do not reveal sectional backgrounds."[203]

The project of the Prairie Historians once made the practice of history in the United States better, more complete, and more balanced. It can do so again. Looking to this project can offer guidance and, dare I say, hope to those frustrated with the apparent chaos in the field. Revisiting the work of the Prairie Historians may inspire new research in the now anemic but once vital field of midwestern history. Insights from their work can help us see the past more clearly and to understand the limitations of more recent historical works that are too far removed from the midwestern historical tradition.

Four

TOWARD A REVIVAL OF
MIDWESTERN HISTORY

THE MIDWEST WAS CRUCIAL to the development of the United States, and a faction of American historians oriented toward the study of the region once articulated this significance to the profession and broader audiences. The histories of the Midwest that these Prairie Historians produced suffered from limitations and were colored by their time, but they were much more advanced than we are accustomed to believing, and they also captured and articulated the Midwest's importance and demonstrated how a formidable movement of intellectuals can successfully rebel against the slighting of their region. Their work serves as a practical model that all historians can still follow, and their discernment and regional sensibility can help us to see the weaknesses and biases of present-day forms of historical scholarship. Their universe can serve as a source of insights and a reservoir of knowledge that can still inform the work of historians, and, more fundamentally, their democratic sensibilities can help us all.

Despite the significance of the Midwest to the nation's development and the Prairie Historians' strong contributions to history in the form of published works about the region and their still useful guidance to historical interpretation, midwestern history is a weak and declining field of study. By the 1950s, the old cohesion of the Prairie Historians had dissolved, and American historians generally focused their energies elsewhere. When the postwar academic boom fizzled and economic pressures began to squeeze history departments beginning in the 1970s, the combined effect of new research agendas, declining budgets, and the retirement of an older generation of historians resulted in fewer professors, courses, and books focused on midwestern history. Several journals of midwestern regional history folded. Despite a few spasms of life at irregular intervals, the field of midwestern history is now comatose, surviving on a life-support system of small state-based historical society journals and sustained by a few close relatives who periodically visit and help stave off the final reckoning by delivering a rare but rejuvenating book about the region.

To resuscitate the field, those mourning its condition must articulate its importance to whoever will listen and not be shy. "Amid the chatter and hum of academic discourse," the late Tony Judt once said, "it sometimes helps to shout if you really want to be heard."[1] Midwesterners, even if it cuts against their grain at times, will need to be personally committed and forceful in advancing their agenda. They should take their region seriously and not consign themselves to absorbing commentary on national happenings and consuming the products of the culture industry on the coasts and instead confidently articulate the case for studying their region.[2] They should, for example, cajole the *New York Times* into writing more than periodic local-color stories about the Midwest. History departments in the Midwest should also make it a priority to teach a course on the region, and, if they fail to do so, administrators, boards of directors, regents, alumni, and midwesterners in general should prod them. This bureaucratic pressure will generate some demand for scholars who study the region and thus cause some young graduate students, who are rightly conscious of the demands of a weak academic job market, to take up midwestern topics in their dissertations, which can provide the bone and sinew of a larger corpus of work about the region. Some entrepreneurial midwesterner should also visit Warren Buffett in Omaha (or another similarly situated party) and ask him to fund a new *Journal of Midwestern History* to serve as a home for historical studies of the region, which have been largely homeless since the rebranding of the *Mississippi Valley Historical Review* in the 1960s. Historians in and of the Midwest will need to take a leadership role and be active in this movement and embrace what Ruth Suckow once called, in a speech to writers gathered at the University of Iowa, a "sharpening cause," which, in an earlier age, "turned a few middle-westerners into fighters" for their region.[3] They will need to engage in what Robert Dorman calls "deliberate reflective acts of recovery" to promote regional studies.[4] They can tap the academic penchant for things "new" or the alternative impulse toward historical restoration or perhaps a potent hybrid of the two. But they must be more productive and helpful to the cause than, for example, the old historian at North Dakota State University whose contribution to the region was a history of the Fargo Rotary Club. The decline of midwestern history was not foreordained by the stars. It was the result of conscious political and bureaucratic decision making and shifting trends within the profession and thus can be reversed.[5] Turner and the Prairie Historians once did this with, relatively speaking, far fewer resources at their disposal, so it can be done again.

These are practical steps that can be taken by pragmatic midwesterners to save their region from the historical abyss and, more generally, serve as a weapon in what the Wisconsinite Joseph Schafer called "man's warfare against oblivion."[6] Many other strategies, I am sure, are possible, and I will leave them to the relevant parties. Whatever recovery plans might be developed, the general goal of reviving midwestern history can be bolstered by several arguments that highlight the benefits of local and regional history, explain the dubious basis of the turn away from the Midwest, justify a new emphasis in historical writing that draws upon the tradition of midwestern history, and affirm a commitment to historical practice and its place in a democracy.

Midwesterners, whose regional history has been comparatively neglected, will benefit from a deeper connection to their home. The historian Dixon Ryan Fox, when discussing the economic advantages of human mobility in the United States, also noted that the transitory nature of American life entailed the "moral sacrifice of good home sentiment."[7] He lamented the erosion of local and regional roots and believed that the "study of the multifarious records of the valley where we come to live must in some degree enrich the associations of the hearthstone so as to make life more interesting and lovely; the tales of a grandfather that set forth its heroic and picturesque traditions are not to be despised by the historian, provided that the touch of truth has marked them."[8] Few people are "called to build great empires or to wield the mighty forces of the world," Fox said, but the "humble occasions of the common life" would be deepened and our lives enriched if we knew "our neighbors and the special heritage we share."[9] The Prairie Historians focused on this heritage and the local histories of the Midwest and their broader meaning with zeal, and Turner, their patron saint, connected the local history of the Midwest to the wider currents of national and global history. Avery Craven, a son of rural Iowa who always meant to write a history of his home county, explained that "Frederick Jackson Turner lifted the story of simple, scattered localities, engaged in the homely tasks of living and living better, into the dignity of world history."[10] The local stories of their region and the "humble occasions of the common life" shared by midwesterners thus simultaneously provide roots *and* a global perspective on history.

The value of a rooted and shared sentiment is the reason why the midwesterner Christopher Lasch fought to sustain regional loyalties against the perils of rootlessness, resisted elite-led demands to adhere to universal norms, and dismissed the charges of parochialism often lobbed at midwesterners.[11] Lasch's penetrating analysis and rebuke of the critics of local and regional traditions is a reminder that their criticism caused a needless detour that ended with many years in the wilderness for midwestern history. It is also a reminder that these critics have been given more credence than they deserve. H. L. Mencken and Sinclair Lewis were foreigners to "midwestern nice" and not well-adjusted people, and their polemics, while mildly amusing and a revealing window onto early twentieth-century intellectual life and worth some attention, are not worthy of the extensive energies that have been expended on them by scholars or the emphases given to them in subsequent accounts of our cultural history, which mostly ignore what they had to say that was positive about the Midwest.[12] One observer of the post–World War I intellectuals who led the condemnation of the Midwest noted that they disliked "almost to the point of hatred and certainly to the point of contempt, the type of people dominant in our present civilization."[13] They recoiled, in particular, at the "midwestern domination of American life and values."[14] We seldom account for the impact of the village rebels' polemics, which were too readily absorbed by other intellectuals and used to make the Midwest "a convenient whipping boy . . . for all that was wrong with American life," on the once-promising enterprise that was midwestern history.[15] The Iowa-born historian Jon Gjerde noted that, contrary to the impression left by these well-remembered and oft-cited critics, midwesterners often recalled their lives in the region with great fondness and appreciation.[16] A greater commitment to midwestern history can help us understand why and perhaps help us recover from what Zachary Michael Jack calls the "staggering loss of heritage" endured by midwesterners in the last half of the twentieth century.[17]

The intellectual attack on the Midwest beginning in the early twentieth century was in part politically motivated and led by those who were less interested in accurately portraying life in the Midwest and more interested in paving the way for a new social order.[18] Richard Hofstadter, no friend of the midwestern agrarian and small town tradition, explained how an emergent American intellectual class began an "assault on national pieties" that "culminated in the unconstrained frontal attack of the 1920s" and included a "war" of "metropolitan minds against the village mind" and against the nation's "pioneer heritage."[19] These intellectuals did not deny the importance of the settlement process or the frontier experience described by Turner, but instead blamed it for the individualism, commercialism, coarseness, and "Puritanism" that, they believed, "seemed to account for the harshness and stringency of American life."[20] They saw American development as exceptional and unique, but agreed that it "was a unique case of pathology," to be cured through the political reforms and cultural liberation they sought.[21] Midwestern history, as it was comprehended by Turner and the Prairie Historians, was not "useful" to their political goals. Many of the assaults on other midwestern regionalists were, similarly, "ideologically biased attacks."[22] If the political basis of the critics' attacks on the Midwest is accounted for and the validity of their criticism thereby diminished, the project of recovering midwestern history gains added moral legitimacy. If the motives of the original turn against the Midwest are suspect, the case for reviving midwestern history rests on a stronger foundation.

A revival of midwestern history, in addition to overcoming the deeply rooted hostility to the region planted during the early twentieth century, will need to contend with some prominent trends in the history profession. Historians in recent decades have been skeptical of what is called the "grand narrative" in American history, in part represented by Turner, which once focused on the growth and progress of American democratic institutions and thought and capitalism and economic growth and how they all combined to create the exceptional nature of American development.[23] Beginning in the 1950s, prominent historians such as Richard Hofstadter and then a subsequent generation of historians instead focused on the "totalitarian potential of American society" and how the American "liberal consensus was not voluntary; it was coerced by the processes of capitalism, bureaucratic rationalization, mass culture, and their ruling elites."[24] A new generation of postmodern theorists also argued that narrative itself was a "coercive category" and that grand narrative had a "coercive hold on the imagination."[25] Historians followed these developments by focusing on dissent and "resistance" to the dominant narrative and developing "counternarratives" that have become, ironically, the main story in American history in recent decades.

In part because of these trends, the broad and enduring historical forces at work in the Midwest are not favored at the moment among many historians, who now tend to scour the past for evidence of the experiences of the marginal, the subaltern, and the Other. Such studies once made sense as a corrective to the neglected aspects of American history, including topics in midwestern history overlooked or understudied by the Prairie Historians, but in recent years the Other has come to dominate the historical imagination. Social analyses at present, David Pichaske notes, "privilege the Other on the margins over the traditional

Self," a privileging that carries consequences.[26] As Pichaske argues in his recent account of midwestern regionalism, "it is good to encounter the Other, but it not good to be absorbed into the Other, to become decentered."[27] Maintaining one's primary history and identity or, simply, one's Self, is difficult when the Other remains the constant focus. Pichaske worries that the academic preoccupation with the Other in recent decades has intensified "to the extent that the Other annihilated the Self."[28] Perhaps no region has suffered more than the allegedly dull, homogenous, and mainstream Midwest as a result of this state of affairs. It helps explain why, as Pichaske says, the "Midwest has lost much of its social, political, and literary clout in the past three decades."[29]

The focus on the Other yielded many insights about the language of dominant groups and their narratives and dissension from them and became part of a massive body of work on "discourses," the "making" of various minority factions, and the "invention" and "imagining" of traditions and modes of thought by ascendant groups and how these were "constructed" and how elites attempted to maintain their "hegemonic" control of the culture.[30] Operating under the banner of "cultural Marxism" and with an eye toward social transformation, a significant part of this large-scale project was focused on "unmasking" and "demythologizing" the past in order to "liberate" us from it.[31] Marxists and progressives were engaged in a conflict with the dominant society over the legitimacy of existing institutions. "To change the world," Myra Jehlen noted, "the insurgents needed to prove that its present order was neither naturally good nor necessary."[32] The agrarian and small town Midwest would not fare well in this interpretive project, if it was afforded much attention at all.

If the limitations of this school of interpretation can be understood, midwestern history and its early practitioners can be more fully appreciated. The "metahistorical commitment" underlying cultural Marxism, as Jack Hexter noted, can result in a "blinkered vision" that "blocks out" important aspects of the past and indeed the main currents of history in regions such as the Midwest.[33] Besides being "equally unreadable and inaccurate," David Hacket Fischer once denounced this form of history as "polemical" and "methodologically reactionary," too resistant to evidence that does not fit the goals of the historian and too resistant to stories that do not fit the counternarrative.[34] It can leave the historian numb to the sins of propaganda, as Linda Gordon's recent biography of Dorothea Lange demonstrates, and blind to particulars and nuance about places such as the Midwest.[35] This approach to history, in general, obscures the complexity of the past.[36] More specifically, for our purposes, it inhibits the study of the Midwest. Regions, including the Midwest, are "not merely imagined or invented," Fischer explains, but possess a "cultural reality."[37] In historians' efforts "to contest the existence of dominant notions of community and to construct alternative ones that cut across and eviscerate national and regional lines" and "to deconstruct and delegitimize the supposed national hegemony of white males," Andrew Cayton notes, the story of the Midwest as a region can be lost.[38] Too much obeisance to theory, too much hostility to state and local history and exceptionalism, too much "fear of heroism," and too much opposition to recognizing the "good consequences" of historical events, says the historian Paula Nelson, a Minnesotan trained in Iowa who teaches in Wisconsin and studies South Dakota, means the sacrifice of the "smaller scales of human existence," where much of midwestern history is located, and the degradation of citizenship.[39]

While recent approaches to history are generally not amenable to the production of works about the main currents of midwestern history, they have also hurt the cause of midwestern history by way of their treatment of Turner, who first articulated the midwestern story. Given the weakness of midwestern history and the minimal level of scholarly activity in the field, the attacks on Turner occurred in other venues, particularly in the history of the American West depicted in the "New Western History." Alan Brinkley has noted how this history often begins with "an obligatory, almost ritualistic repudiation of Frederick Jackson Turner."[40] The influential New Western Historian Patricia Nelson Limerick, Susan Gray notes, launched a "search-and-destroy mission" against Turner.[41] Much of this work, like criticisms launched against the Midwest in the early twentieth century, carries a strong political overtone. The historian Gerald Nash explained that the New Western Historians were "products of the 1960s" and "applying New Left perspectives of that era to the history of the American West."[42] While Turner and the Prairie Historians had their weaknesses, so, too, does the New Western History, cultural Marxism, and other related modes of historical interpretation prominent in recent decades. The Prairie Historians covered far more ground than they are often given credit for, and, at a minimum, they made it possible for a broader audience to understand the significance of the Midwest.

The once-promising enterprise of midwestern history, then, went off track beginning with the attacks on the region in the early twentieth century and then suffered from the passing of the Prairie Historians from the scene, the general trends in the history profession of the mid to late twentieth century, and the more recent attacks on Turner. But hope for a revival of midwestern history is not lost. While these metatrends within the historical profession have not been conducive to the study of the Midwest, these modes of interpretation have not been universal and have been subject to searching criticism. Dissent from this discourse is possible and finds support among historians who are frustrated with the direction of the profession.[43] Dissenters could take heart from the Prairie Historians, who understood the practical limitations of historical interpretation but could still write fine works of history that spoke to a broad audience about topics that mattered. A renewed appreciation of their work might yield more studies of the Midwest and, given the Prairie Historians' dedication to the historical enterprise itself, could also bolster historians' faith in their profession.[44]

This faith might, more generally, elevate the status of history, whose place in American intellectual life has been declining for decades. More than any other discipline, history is capable of helping us understand who we are and where we come from and what we can accomplish. The Prairie Historians' integration of the common life of the Midwest with broader social trends helps us understand what George Mosse called the "forces of history" and how they made our world.[45] As a Jew forced out of Europe by the Nazis, Mosse personally understood the power of the forces of history and took their study seriously, leaving him "intolerant of those historians for whom writing history seemed to be only a profession like any other."[46] Some historians, Mosse says, "could just as well have been accountants."[47] In addition to his resentment toward the passionless plodders in the historical profession, Mosse was not impressed with recent trends in the historical profession, the cult of "victimization," the new "age of sensitivity training," and the rise of "multiculturalism," which leaves a student "without any one solid foundation from which he can extend his knowledge."[48] Grasping our history and honestly making sense of it and ourselves and communicating it to a broad audience could shape our own world and make it better. Mosse liked to quote the Renaissance historian W. K. Ferguson: "what man is only history tells."[49]

Mosse's earnestness about the historical enterprise, his scorn for those who were mere dabblers or slaves to academic fashion, and his doubts about recent trends in the profession have added significance for those who seek to revitalize midwestern history and may be sheepish about the legacy of the Midwest, its limitations, and the peccadilloes of some of the region's historians. Mosse cannot be dismissed as a chauvinistic booster of his home region. He was an uprooted Jewish refugee from Hitler's Europe and a gay socialist who fell in love with the Midwest.

After earning his Ph.D. at Harvard, Mosse decamped to Iowa City and taught at the University of Iowa, where his classes were wildly popular.[50] He "wanted to be considered a true American, naturalized on the western side of the Mississippi, instead of," he quipped, "the effete Eastern side, so close to Europe."[51] Mosse "used to say that any historian who had not passed through Iowa was not worth his salt."[52] He later moved to Wisconsin, where Turner was the "patron saint of the department," and he admired the "anti-establishment thrust" of the work in Madison and its "emphasis on the American heartland."[53] Even though he remained an "eternal emigrant" and personally conflicted about his own uprooting and place in the world, Mosse says, "in the end the settled citizen of the American Middle West was destined to win out."[54] He prized his "years in the heart of the American Middle West."[55]

Mosse's affection for the Midwest was in part based upon its deep democratic tradition, which the Prairie Historians once chronicled and in which Mosse was able to participate. He spoke to dozens of Rotary Clubs, Lions Clubs, civic groups, women's clubs, and high school commencements; served as a delegate to state political conventions; campaigned for Henry Wallace but also admired Robert Taft; hosted a Sunday radio program about politics broadcast from Des Moines; talked hog prices; and admired *Bonanza* (he wanted to be named to the "Cartwright Chair" at Wisconsin).[56] Mosse noted that the midwestern "grassroots politics in which anyone could make a difference were unknown in Europe with its rigid party structures and encrusted political hierarchies."[57] Mosse knew an open democratic tradition when he saw it. He would have appreciated the democratic nature of the Iowa caucuses, for example, the historical significance of which is lost without a broader grounding in midwestern history.[58]

Mosse brought a comparative perspective to his observations about midwestern democracy that is crucial to understanding the democratic development of the region described by Turner and the Prairie Historians. Recognizing these achievements does not mean sanitizing midwestern history. When describing the advancement of democracy in the Midwest, all the region's failures and historical warts should be included, but the comparative success of this advancement must also be placed in context. In their focus on the democratic achievements in the early Midwest, the Prairie Historians and the historical actors they studied understood what Gordon Wood calls a "kind of oppression that has been lost" to many in the current generation of historians. This "comprehensive oppression," as Wood calls it, "involved all common ordinary Americans" in addition to "both slaves and women," who Wood's critics saw as the primary measure of the success of early American democracy.[59] When focusing on the development of democracy and small-scale capitalism in the Midwest and contrasting this development to conditions in Europe, the Prairie Historians were taking notice of the eclipse of what Wood describes as the "age-old humiliation felt by all commoners in the premodern world" where the labors of the common man were treated with derision.[60] Wood says backcountry American settlers led the break from these Old World constraints and thus made the American Revolution and its extension westward "radical."[61] The "claim of equality by all white males" established by the Revolution was "no mean feat since it took a few thousand years of Western history to accomplish," and it allowed for "other claims to equality" to follow "rather rapidly."[62] Indeed, these early claims grew in the Midwest, where the democratic gains of the Revolution were consolidated and extended, where slavery was prohibited, where settlers balked at the continuing power of coastal elites, and where forms of populism sprouted.

The power of comparison, Mosse's emphasis on the "forces of history," the essential democratic thrust of Turner's legacy, and the weaknesses of recent historiography all came together for me when I simultaneously read a book by Timothy Snyder and a speech by Turner in the final stages of this project. In May 1918, in a moment that captured Turner's influence over the Prairie Historians and their work to preserve and chronicle midwestern history, Turner spoke at the dedication of a new building designed to house the Minnesota Historical Society, which he called a new "shrine to Minnesota's historic life."[63] On that occasion, which coincided with the annual meeting of the Mississippi Valley Historical Association, Turner commented that the Midwest was roughly comparable in size to central Europe, noted the old "racial animosities" that European immigrants to the Midwest sometimes carried, and cited a nineteenth-century American aphorism about how the "American laughs at these steerage quarrels."[64] Turner was arguing that the ethnic and cultural blending, the mixing and egalitarianism, and the democratic practices in the Midwest were preferable to the ethnic clumping, chronic tensions, and persistent despotism in Europe. When I read Turner's speech to the Minnesota Historical Society, I also happened to be reading Snyder's *Bloodlands*, which explores in gruesome detail how, two decades after Turner's speech, a region roughly the size of the America Midwest exploded into ethnic rage and bloodshed.[65] It provided the starkest contrast to the development of the American Midwest where, as Turner said in St. Paul, "pioneer ideals" were at work and continued to sustain the American "faith in the destiny of the common man under freedom."[66]

On that occasion in Minnesota, when the first of Europe's twentieth-century global wars raged, Turner prayed that the pioneer ideals of the Midwest, where he thought European hatreds had been submerged, would not become a "lost and tragic story of a futile dream."[67] In Turner's prayer, resting on his and the Prairie Historians' study of the successful planting of a democratic tradition and how it "tied together" the "past and the future" of the American republic, can be found the most important reason why the Midwest matters and why this lost region is worth finding again.[68]

EPILOGUE

FREDERICK JACKSON TURNER'S articulation of the enduring promise of the Midwest's democratic spirit set forth in St. Paul in 1918 would have been understood by Guy Stanton Ford. Born in the town of Liberty Corners in Kenosha County, Wisconsin, in 1873, Ford and his family settled in Plainfield, Iowa. Ford rode horses across unbroken prairie, his hands "as a boy held a plow that broke the virgin sod of Iowa," he played baseball, and he excelled in school, earning an Iowa teaching certificate at age twelve. After several years of teaching in Iowa country schools, Ford headed for the University of Wisconsin in 1892, where Frederick Jackson Turner had recently assumed his duties. Ford completed his undergraduate degree and taught at Wisconsin Rapids, where he launched the school's football team, and then completed a graduate degree in history with Turner in Madison.[1] Ford went on to earn his Ph.D. in history from Columbia and taught at Yale, but he said the "Yale experience convinced me that the future belonged to the state universities, and *I was a Midwesterner.*"[2] He accepted a post in the history department at Illinois, "returning to the comfortable atmosphere of the prairie culture and to a vigorous, young school where he could 'expand.'"[3] At Illinois, Ford hung images of Francis Parkman and Edward Gibbon and an original letter from Leopold Ranke to his publisher on the wall of the history seminar room in Lincoln Hall, and, in 1907, the year that the Mississippi Valley Historical Association (MVHA) was launched, Ford married a young woman from Wisconsin on her family's farm near Bristol in Kenosha County.[4] After seven years of teaching in the Illinois history department and chairing the university's library committee, Ford was hired to serve as the dean of the Graduate School at the University of Minnesota, a position he held for twenty-five years. Over a long career,

Ford embraced the role of intellectual and pipe-smoking history professor; remained humane and curious; sought out scholars of talent; was averse to pettiness, triviality, and wasting time; and possessed a "gentleness which comes from a deep inner, and integrated, strength."[5] In addition to launching the University of Minnesota Press, which published books about the Midwest with enthusiasm, Ford ultimately became the president of the university in 1938.[6]

Ford understood the limitations of life in the prairie Midwest, but he remained rooted in his region: "Yes, I am a Midwesterner! I proclaim it from the treetops!"[7] As a midwesterner by birth, temperament, and proclamation, Ford wanted the Prairie Historians to persist in their regional project, but as World War II drew to a close, he sensed the erosion of the old regional coherence that united their work. During the month that Japan surrendered, Ford wrote a letter to John Hicks, who had recently left Wisconsin for Berkeley, in response to rumors that were circulating about "renaming and reorienting the Mississippi Valley Historical Association." Ford questioned the "advisability" of this "mistaken policy" because the Prairie Historians had "yet to write or stimulate the writing of the whole inland empire that [Clarence] Alvord," Ford's old colleague at Illinois, and the MVHA's "founders opened up to them."[8] Ford cherished, as Benjamin Shambaugh aptly pronounced during the genesis of the MVHA, the "realization that the history of the Middle West is marked by a unity of development which justifies an organized and unified study."[9] He called on Hicks, Frederic Logan Paxson, Theodore Blegen, and other Prairie Historians to preserve their regionalist emphasis and save the field of midwestern history. Ford thought if the Prairie Historians allowed the name of the MVHA to be changed, it would dilute the organization's original mission and undermine its regional orientation. Ford warned that "such a move would rob them of their reason for being and scatter their efforts in futility."[10]

A combination skilled historian, academic administrator, bureaucratic turf defender, and, most important, devoted midwesterner, Ford understood the importance of the unifying power of regionalism for the Prairie Historians and midwestern history and the dangers of its dissipation. Ford was previewing the consequences for the field of the later mission and name change of the *Mississippi Valley Historical Review* (*MVHR*), whose founders had originally declared that the journal was "primarily interested in the history of the Mississippi Valley" but whose inheritors had lost their regional vision.[11] Ford understood the later argument of the Indianan James Madison, who believes that without a topically oriented journal such as the *MVHR*, "there can be no field, no sense of scholarly community around a subject, no us/them, no impetus to think of a genre of scholarship."[12]

Without the MVHA and the *MVHR* to serve as a central organizing force, associated institutions in their orbit also lost focus and direction. The journal *Agricultural History*, which was pioneered by Prairie Historians, once found a home in Iowa and North Dakota, and, as Earle Ross noted, much of its work focused on farming the midwestern prairies.[13] But now *Agricultural History* has moved to Florida, and much of its work is focused on the new social history and international topics.[14] Journals such as *Midwest Review, Mid-America, The Old Northwest, Upper Midwest History*, and *Western Illinois Regional Studies* have collapsed altogether, as have publishers of midwestern history books such as Iowa State University Press and the University of South Dakota Press. The University of Missouri Press has just barely avoided being shuttered.[15] In a contemporary measure of the consequences of these losses of institutional support and their contribution to the decline of midwestern history relative to other regions, a Google search returns 20 times more material about the history of New England compared to the Midwest and nearly 350 times as much material about the history of the American South.[16]

These are all sad developments and indicia of decline and disorganization in and for the field of midwestern history, but all hope is not lost. While histories that focus on the Midwest as a region are now rare, there have still been some impressive works of history published about events, institutions, people, and trends in the Midwest in recent years, and these studies deserve a much broader audience than they have received. In addition to dusting off the older works of the Prairie Historians, these newer works can serve as building blocks for a more integrated history of the Midwest as a region in the future.[17] Future Prairie Historians will not be starting from scratch.

Some direction can be taken from western history, which was born in the Midwest. Turner first began academic history's turn to the Great West, although he mostly focused on the Midwest in his own work.[18] Many other native midwesterners focused on the broader West, however, including Herbert Bolton, Louis Pelzer, Oscar Winther, Allan Bogue, Gene Gressley, and Robert Utley.[19] Several other midwesterners decamped to California, including Turner himself along with Paxson, Hicks, Martin Ridge, Ray Allen Billington, and John Parish, an Iowan who landed at UCLA and founded the *Pacific Historical Review*.[20] Vernon Carstensen, after a long career at Wisconsin, moved to the University of Washington and became one of the founding members of the Western History Association (WHA), served as its president in

1980–1981, and edited the *Pacific Northwest Quarterly*, a transition that highlighted the nexus between an earlier midwestern history and a later, more western-oriented field.[21] Billington, a Michigander who taught in Illinois, agreed to take the horns of the new WHA when it was launched in Santa Fe in 1961 by westerners who recognized the neglect of their region.[22] About the time that the midwestern history project was fizzling, the new western history organization was taking shape, and, as a result, several increasingly homeless midwestern historians ended up in a formally western history organization. In addition to recognizing the midwestern histories and the continuing midwestern sympathies of these midwestern-turned-western historians, there are organizational lessons for future midwestern historians in the westerners' regional emphasis and their resulting scholarly achievements.

There are also lessons to be learned from a still later surge of interest in western history. In the 1980s, sensing ebbing interest in western history and the field's impairment by outdated models, the "New Western Historians" sought to revive and refocus the field. This movement was led by Patricia Nelson Limerick, who served as its primary advocate, spokesperson, and organizer and explicitly set forth the movement's goals.[23] Although the scholarship of the New Western Historians suffered from exaggerated claims to newness (the Prairie Historians pioneered many of their points of emphasis) and from a politicized frame of reference, the organizational achievements and scholarly output of the New Western Historians can serve as models of success, especially in more recent years as the newer forms of western history have become more complex and less laden with the burdens of the ideological and generational warfare of the late 1980s.[24] The New Western Historians, in attempting to dethrone Turner and de-emphasize the frontier process in favor of a focus on the West as a region, triggered an extensive and useful discussion of the nature of regions and what constituted "the West," but they also, unfortunately, tended to exclude the Midwest from their conception of the West, and, as a result, the region did not benefit from the surge of interest in western history.[25]

One prominent historian who was once deemed a member of the "gang of four" historians who led the New Western Historians but who has resisted such a categorization is William Cronon.[26] Unlike other western historians, Cronon has maintained a strong interest in the Midwest in part because of his regional roots. His father taught in the Wisconsin history department, from which so many Prairie Historians took their cues. As an undergraduate at Wisconsin, Cronon's interest in the Midwest and West was sparked by a course taught by the Prairie Historian

Allan Bogue.[27] After a stint teaching at Yale, Cronon returned to Wisconsin and became the Frederick Jackson Turner Professor of History. Bogue's close association with James Malin can be found in the work of Cronon, who focuses on the changes in the natural environment caused by humans, an area of study first formalized by Malin decades earlier.[28] While Cronon is much more sympathetic to studying the American Midwest than others—Cronon says he "has long fought to keep the Middle West within the intellectual boundaries of western history"—he is also more focused on environmental history than he is on the history of the Midwest as a region.[29] In terms of understanding the Midwest, however, few works rival Cronon's enviro-economic study of Chicago and its hinterlands, and Cronon, to his great credit, is exceptional in his open appreciation of Turner, whose work remains critical to the historiography of the Midwest.[30]

The environmental history genre that Cronon does so much to lead includes a number of works set in the Midwest.[31] Theodore Karamanski, for example, has written several impressive works about northern Wisconsin and Michigan and the upper Midwest more generally.[32] Related works of *natural* history set in the Midwest are also available.[33] The impact of the Dust Bowl, especially along the midwestern/Great Plains border, continues to serve as a subject of study with a strong environmental emphasis.[34]

Other recent books that address the Midwest also tend to be organized around categories of analysis other than midwestern history and do not key on the Midwest as a "cultural entity," but are nonetheless valuable volumes.[35] The rise of social history in the 1970s, for example, which had earlier been promoted by Turner and other Prairie Historians, albeit in a different form, has yielded important studies set in the Midwest.[36] But in many of these books, as Andrew Cayton cautions, the Midwest "remains a setting, not a particular constellation of attitudes or behaviors," and not a unique historical "place."[37] Despite the absence of a strong regional focus, these works of social history are of great value. A prominent early example is Don Doyle's treatment of Jacksonville, Illinois.[38] John Mack Faragher's study of frontier settlement in Sangamon County, Illinois, has also inspired much commentary and many works of community history.[39] Jane Marie Pederson's study of a county in western Wisconsin published in the early 1990s has revealed important facets of local life in the Midwest, but it is also oriented toward the broader debates in social history.[40] Other, more recent community studies set in the Midwest have followed in this tradition.[41]

Closely linked to and intertwined with these social histories are studies of gender, which are often associated with the "New Rural History," which has emphasized the history of women and workers in contrast with an older form of "agricultural history" focused more on technology, farmers, and farm politics. Mary Neth, for example, prior to her untimely death, carefully studied the challenges to the family farm tradition and rural community in early twentieth-century Wisconsin, Iowa, and North Dakota and how women, in particular, were affected.[42] Neth's work remains a bright star in a constellation of other impressive works of social history emphasizing the experiences of women and families in midwestern settings. These works seemed to peak in the early to mid-1990s.[43]

Related studies include examinations of the persistence of cultural and ethnic orientations and loyalties among midwestern settlers. Susan Gray's study of New England immigrants' move to Kalamazoo County, Michigan, emphasizes the continuing salience of New England folkways in the Midwest amid strong market participation.[44] Other studies focus on the adjustments of foreign-born immigrants in the Midwest and are often oriented toward the broader history of immigration to the United States.[45] The Iowan Jon Gjerde, prior to his premature passing, authored a study of cultural frictions in the Midwest, which also focuses on the experiences of immigrants and stands as a major contribution to the field of immigration studies while also addressing the Midwest as a region.[46] In recent years, some scholars of race have also focused on the issue of slavery in the Midwest and race relations in midwestern cities.[47]

The emphasis on social history and cultural conflict has also fueled the great interest in Native American history in recent decades, which has included studies of midwestern Indian tribes. Richard White, whose adviser was the Iowan and longtime Wisconsin history professor Vernon Carstensen, generated a great surge in interest in Indian history with his treatment of the relations between various tribes and French and English colonists around the Great Lakes during the colonial era.[48] White started writing his prize-winning book while he was living in the Midwest and serving as a professor of history at Michigan State University.[49] A number of books have followed White's lead and focus on Indian tribes in the colonial backcountry in the era of the American Revolution.[50]

Studies of the colonial era and the American Revolution have also resulted in books relating to the early Midwest that feature a strong political and imperial emphasis.[51] The burst of scholarship associated with Gordon Wood and the study of the American ideology of republicanism, for example, has yielded important insights about midwestern states. Andrew Cayton, who has actively sought to promote the study of the

Midwest, was a student of Wood who first turned his scholarly focus to early states in the Midwest such as Ohio and Indiana.[52] In a similar vein, Nicole Etcheson has focused on the political culture of the early Midwest and how it influenced the region's role in the Civil War.[53] Books about the later settlement period have also focused on political culture and noted the persistence of early midwestern republicanism in parts of the western Midwest such as Dakota Territory.[54] More recent works set in the region have also used political culture as an organizational tool.[55] Studies of the politics of Populism, which tend to highlight the Great Plains or farther west, have also included important works set in the Midwest.[56] The politics of the Great Depression along the seam of the Midwest and Great Plains also draws continuing interest.[57]

Studies of Populism and the Great Depression are often framed by economic issues, and this orientation can be found in several histories related to the Midwest. These include studies of midwestern agriculture, which remains a dominant economic force in the region.[58] Other books focus on prominent midwestern businesses.[59] David Blanke has also studied the impact of consumer culture and higher degrees of market participation on the rural Midwest.[60] Labor history, another variation of economic history focused less on business enterprise and more on workers, has also led to books about the midwestern working class and union organizing efforts.[61] Some of this work is related to the leadership of the University of Iowa labor historian Shelton Stromquist and the emphasis on labor history—often with a racial dimension—at the University of Illinois and the University of Illinois Press.[62] Generally related to labor history and the development of commercial centers in the Midwest are a number of works of urban history set in the Midwest.[63]

Future historians of the Midwest, then, will have available to them significant raw materials from which to draw. While much of this material is related to and shaped by debates in other subfields, some of it is more refined and consciously organized to contribute to a regional history. Most important, Andrew Cayton has written, cowritten, and coedited important books on the region.[64] Cayton's work with Susan Gray resulted in perhaps the leading volume of essays about the region.[65] James Madison also edited an impressive volume of essays about individual midwestern states, which was published in 1988.[66] David Brown has more recently examined one strain of early midwestern history, and Michael Steiner has thoroughly explored Turner's devotion to midwestern regionalism.[67] From their outpost in southwestern Minnesota, Joe Amato and David Pichaske have valiantly carried the flag for regional and local studies.[68] John E. Miller, a self-described "guerrilla scholar" who has frequently noted the absence of institutional support for midwestern history, has called for more studies of midwestern small towns for decades.[69] Other scholars have also kept the flame of midwestern regionalism alive by bringing attention to the region's writers, artists, and cultural institutions.[70] Future historians of the Midwest will also be able to draw on the important work of geographers,[71] anthropologists,[72] sociologists,[73] economists,[74] journalists,[75] and the authors of more popular works relating to present-day politics.[76] But they will also be facing some strong disciplinary headwinds—the "label Midwest," Andrew Cayton notes, "tends to conjure images that alienate rather than attract contemporary scholars"—and forced to find their way in the ruins of a field of study that is poorly integrated and hobbled by declining resources.[77] The essential ingredients of future success will include a recognition of the wisdom of Guy Stanton Ford's insistence on a regional mission and a commitment to integrating the field around the history of the Midwest as a region, both of which inform the spirit of the University of Iowa Press's new series Iowa and the Midwest Experience.

NOTES

INTRODUCTION

1. A. G. Sulzberger, "Storm upon Storm for South Dakota," *New York Times*, November 20, 2010. For vegetarian Sulzberger's struggles navigating the region's "meat-loving" culture and the "barrage of jokes that followed the announcement of [his] assignment covering the Midwest," see A. G. Sulzberger, "Meatless in the Midwest: A Tale of Survival," *New York Times*, January 10, 2012 ("Are you sure you know what you're getting yourself into?"). In early 2012, Sulzberger moved to the metro desk in New York.

2. Joseph E. Baker, "Four Arguments for Regionalism," *Saturday Review of Literature*, November 28, 1936, 4.

3. Ginette Aley, "Dwelling within the Place Worth Seeking: The Midwest, Regional Identity, and Internal Histories," in *Regionalism and the Humanities*, ed. Wendy J. Katz and Timothy R. Mahoney (Lincoln: University of Nebraska Press, 2008), 99.

4. Christopher Lasch, *The Revolt of the Elites and the Betrayal of Democracy* (New York: W. W. Norton, 1995), 233 ("unremitting onslaught"); James R. Shortridge, *The Middle West: Its Meaning in American Culture* (Lawrence: University Press of Kansas, 1989), 39; Andrew R. L. Cayton and Peter S. Onuf, *The Midwest and the Nation: Rethinking the History of an American Region* (Bloomington: Indiana University Press, 1990), 119–120; Andrew R. L. Cayton and Susan E. Gray, "The Story of the Midwest: An Introduction," in *The Identity of the American Midwest: Essays on Regional History*, ed. Andrew R. L. Cayton and Susan E. Gray (Bloomington: Indiana University Press, 2001), 2, 17–18; Kent Blaser, "Where Is Nebraska Anyway?" *Nebraska History* 80, no. 1 (Spring 1999): 12; Jon K. Lauck, *American Agriculture and the Problem of Monopoly: The Political Economy of Grain Belt Farming, 1953–1980* (Lincoln: University of Nebraska Press, 2000), 168–169; Wallace Stegner, *The American West as Living Space* (Ann Arbor: University of Michigan Press, 1987), 83–84.

5. Arthur Schlesinger Jr., *The Crisis of the Old Order, 1919–1933* (New York: Houghton Mifflin, 1957), 148 ("being suffocated"). See Fred Siegel, "The Anti-American Fallacy," *Commentary* (April 2010).

6. R. Douglas Hurt, "Midwestern Distinctiveness," in Cayton and Gray, *Identity of the American Midwest*, 163.

7. David B. Danbom, "The Professors and the Plowmen in American History Today," *Wisconsin Magazine of History* 69, no. 2 (Winter 1985–1986): 124.

8. James M. Dennis, *Renegade Regionalists: The Modern Independence of Grant Wood, Thomas Hart Benton, and John Steuart Curry* (Madison: University of Wisconsin Press, 1998), 69; John E. Miller, "Midwestern Regionalism during the 1930s: A Democratic Art with Continuing Appeal," *Mid-America* 83, no. 2 (Summer 2001): 76. Thomas Hart Benton was similarly attacked by the Left. Erika Doss, *Benton, Pollock, and the Politics of Modernism: From Regionalism to Abstract Expressionism* (Chicago: University of Chicago Press, 1991), 124–125. The regionalists of the interwar years focused on place, which offended the "internationalism" of the cosmopolitans and Communists, who saw it as "reactionary." Robert L. Dorman, *Revolt of the Provinces: The Regionalist Movement in America, 1920–1945* (Chapel Hill: University of North Carolina Press, 1993), 23. Marxist critics argue that "historical landscape painting only celebrates property and the status quo." Lucy R. Lippard, *The Lure of the Local: Senses of Place in a Multicentered Society* (New York: New Press, 1997), 19.

9. Joyce Carol Oates, "Charles Baxter's Midwest," review of Charles Baxter, *Gryphon: New and Selected Stories* (New York: Pantheon Books, 2010), *New York Times Book Review*, January 14, 2011.

10. David Macleod to author, February 4, 2011.

11. Cayton and Onuf, *Midwest and the Nation*; Cayton and Gray, *Identity of the American Midwest*; Andrew R. L. Cayton, Richard Sisson, and Chris Zacher, eds., *The American Midwest: An Interpretive Encyclopedia* (Bloomington: Indiana University Press, 2006).

12. James H. Madison, ed., *Heartland: Comparative Histories of the Midwestern States* (Bloomington: Indiana University Press, 1988); Kent Blaser, "Making Sense of the Midwest," *Midwest Review* 8 (1991): 76. The Indiana series was conceived by Joan Catapano, who recalled that "I handled the US history list at Indiana and noticed that western, southern, and even northeastern history were well represented in the scholarly publishing world. So I wondered why not the Midwest." The origins of the series "grew out of what I felt was an under representation of Midwestern studies." When launching the series, Catapano worked with Madison, who "shared my belief that the Midwest deserved more attention and study." In 2000, Catapano moved to the University of Illinois Press to become its editor-in-chief. Joan Catapano to author, February 17, 2011.

13. William Cronon, *Nature's Metropolis: Chicago and the Great West* (New York: W. W. Norton, 1991). For this time period, see also Richard White, *The Middle Ground: Indians, Empires, and Republics in the Great Lakes Region, 1650–1815* (New York: Cambridge University Press, 1991); and Nicole Etcheson, *The Emerging Midwest: Upland Southerners and the Political Culture of the Old Northwest, 1787–1861* (Bloomington: Indiana University Press, 1996). On the uptick in published studies of the Midwest in the early 1990s, see Edward Watts, "Hardly Flyover Country: Recent Developments in Midwestern Studies," *MidAmerica* 24 (1997): 36–45.

14. In 2001, due to difficult financial circumstances, the *Filson Club History Quarterly*, which focused on Kentucky, and the journal *Queen City Heritage*, which focused on Cincinnati, combined forces to form the journal *Ohio Valley History*. This new journal is intended to cover the "Ohio valley region, with Cincinnati as its focus." Marianne Kunnen-Jones, "Historians Prevent Journal from Becoming History," *University of Cincinnati Currents*, February 11, 2000; Wayne K. Durrill

and Christopher Phillips, "From the Editors," *Ohio Valley History* 1 (Winter 2001): 3 (source of quotation). During the launch, the journal editors noted that "no journal currently focuses on this region." Durrill and Phillips, "From the Editors," 3. In 2002, two history professors at the University of Akron, Kevin Kern and Gregory Wilson, also launched the *Northeast Ohio Journal of History* to focus on the northeast corner of Ohio. On the journal's focus, see Gregory Wilson, "Thinking about Regions," *Northeast Ohio Journal of History* 2, no. 1 (Fall 2003): 40–42.

15. David S. Brown, *Beyond the Frontier: The Midwestern Voice in American Historical Writing* (Chicago: University of Chicago Press, 2009); Jon K. Lauck, "The 'Interior Tradition' in American History," *Annals of Iowa* 69, no. 1 (Winter 2010): 82–93.

16. John D. Hicks, "My Ten Years on the Wisconsin Faculty," *Wisconsin Magazine of History* 48, no. 4 (Summer 1965): 308.

17. The Newberry fellowships were designed to "assure proper use of the manuscript collections in midwestern civilization." Ray Allen Billington, "Stanley Pargellis: Newberry Librarian, 1942–1962," in *Essays in History and Literature: Presented by Fellows of the Newberry Library to Stanley Pargellis*, ed. Heinz Bluhm (Chicago: Newberry Library, 1965), 8; John Hicks to Stanley Pargellis, March 8, 1948, and John Hicks to Stanley Pargellis, March 3, 1948, both in FF January-March 1948 Correspondence, DB 14, Hicks Papers, Bancroft Library. See NL03/05/03, Box 4, Newberry Library.

18. Howard R. Lamar, "Earl Pomeroy, Historian's Historian," *Pacific Historical Review* 56, no. 4 (November 1987): 549.

19. For research centers focused on the Great Plains, see Frederick C. Luebke, "Regionalism and the Great Plains: Problems of Concept and Method," *Western Historical Quarterly* 15, no. 1 (January 1984): 29, n.31. The journals *Great Plains Quarterly*, *Great Plains Journal*, *Great Plains Research*, and *Heritage of the Great Plains* also focus on the Great Plains. On how the Midwest is "left out" in the "regional division of scholarly turf," see William Cronon, George Miles, and Jay Gitlin, "Becoming West: Toward a New Meaning for Western History," in *Under an Open Sky: Rethinking America's Western Past*, ed. William Cronon, George Miles, and Jay Gitlin (New York: W. W. Norton, 1992), 24.

20. Richard Jensen to author, February 3, 2011. See "The Accomplishments of the Newberry Library Family and Community History Programs: An Interview with Richard Jensen," *Public Historian* 5, no. 4 (Fall 1983): 49–61.

21. To promote regional studies centers, the NEH offered planning grants to Northern Illinois University and the University of Wisconsin–Madison in the "Upper Mississippi Valley" region, to Ohio University and Michigan State University in the "Central" region, and to the University of Nebraska and North Dakota State University in the "Plains" region. Wisconsin, Ohio, and Nebraska advanced to a second stage and earned implementation grants, but then NEH matching funds dried up. Wisconsin, which had not raised the necessary matching funds to create a regional center, instead created the Center for the Study of Midwestern Cultures, which studies midwestern folklore. Despite having raised the necessary matching funds, Nebraska's effort was stymied by NEH's change of direction and lost its donors. The Ohio center "exists mostly as an office for the occasional project." James Leary to author, February 8, 2011; Drew VandeCreek to author, February 8, 2011; John Wunder to author, February 15, 2011; Joseph Slade to author, February 10, 2011 (source of quotation); William Ferris to author, February 7, 2011. The reports relating to these

initiatives are available from the NEH via the Freedom of Information Act process. See also Peter Applebome, "Out from Under the Nation's Shadow; The Hot Subject Today Is the Culture of Regions (Regions? What Regions?)," *New York Times*, February 20, 1999. On the failure of the NEH initiative, see Warren R. Hofstra, "Reconsidering Regional History," *OAH Newsletter* (February 2006): 15.

22. Edward L. Ayers, Patricia Nelson Limerick, Stephen Nissenbaum, and Peter S. Onuf, eds., *All Over the Map: Rethinking American Regions* (Baltimore: Johns Hopkins University Press, 1995).

23. Carl Abbott, "United States Regional History as an Instructional Field: The Practice of College and University History Departments," *Western Historical Quarterly* 21, no. 2 (May 1990): 212.

24. Carl Ubbelohde, "History and the Midwest as a Region," *Wisconsin Magazine of History* 78, no. 1 (Autumn 1994): 44.

25. Susan E. Gray, "Stories Written in the Blood: Race and Midwestern History," in Cayton and Gray, *Identity of the American Midwest*, 123.

26. Wendy J. Katz and Timothy R. Mahoney, "Regionalism and the Humanities: Decline or Revival?" in Katz and Mahoney, *Regionalism and the Humanities*, xxii.

27. James B. M. Schick to author, February 3, 2011; Stephen Meats to author, February 3, 2011.

28. Theodore Karamanski to author, February 3, 2011.

29. Don Hickey to author, January 21, 2011; Jean Karlen to author, May 11, 2011. A *Midwest Review* was published by Wayne State from 1959 to 1963, but when the college started the *Midwest Review* in 1975, it had "no direct relationship to the old *Midwest Review*." Charles M. Hepburn, "Editor's Note," *Midwest Review* 1, no. 1 (Fall 1975): 3.

30. The editors regretted the demise of the journal because it had "become a valued forum in the continuing exploration of Midwestern regional identity." "From the Editors," *Old Northwest* 16, no. 4 (Winter 1992): 223.

31. John E. Hallwas to author, July 22, 2011.

32. Neil Storch, former coeditor of *Upper Midwest History*, interview with author, May 13, 2011.

33. Marv Bergman to author, February 4, 2011.

34. David B. Danbom, "'Cast Down Your Bucket Where You Are': Professional Historians and Local History," *South Dakota History* 33, no. 3 (Fall 2003): 263–273.

35. Robert J. Sloan to author, October 29, 2012.

36. Gretchen Van Houten to author, February 1, 2012.

37. Sandy Crooms to author, February 7, 2013.

38. Joseph A. Amato, interview with author, September 17, 2012.

39. Richard S. Kirkendall, ed., *The Organization of American Historians and the Writing and Teaching of American History* (New York: Oxford University Press, 2011). See author's review in *Annals of Iowa* 71, no. 1 (Winter 2012): 91–93.

40. Stephanie Proffer, "Decision to Close University of Missouri Press Meets with Backlash," *Columbia Missourian*, June 10, 2012; Tim Barker, "UM's Decision to Shutter University Press Draws Criticism," *St. Louis Post-Dispatch*, June 2, 2012.

41. Douglas Reichert Powell explains the "impact of the attenuated cosmopolitanism that is such a powerful force in academic placemaking" at present and intellectuals' "rootlessness" and their treatment of regional sentiments as the reverse of cosmopolitan virtue and how this "constrains the project" of regionalism. See also Powell's

discussion of a *Chronicle of Higher Education* column entitled "What to Do When You've Been Exiled to the Provinces." Douglas Reichert Powell, *Critical Regionalism: Connecting Politics and Culture in the American Landscape* (Chapel Hill: University of North Carolina Press, 2007), 8, 20, 187. The "regional project," John Thomas explains, is "frequently denounced by cosmopolitans." John Thomas, "The Uses of Catastrophe: Lewis Mumford, Vernon L. Parrington, Van Wyck Brooks, and the End of American Regionalism," *American Quarterly* 42, no. 2 (June 1990): 226.

42. Richard Jensen, "On Modernizing Frederick Jackson Turner: The Historiography of Regionalism," *Western Historical Quarterly* 11, no. 3 (July 1980): 316; Joseph A. Amato and Anthony Amato, "Minnesota: A Different America?" *Daedalus* 129, no. 3 (Summer 2000): 66; Richard Shereikis, "Farewell to the Regional Columnist: The Meaning of Bob Greene's Success," *MidAmerica* 8 (1986): 132–133; James H. Madison, "The States of the Midwest: An Introduction," in Madison, *Heartland*, 4; Scott Russell Sanders, *Writing from the Center* (Bloomington: Indiana University Press, 1995), 13; Wayne Franklin and Michael Steiner, "Taking Place: Toward the Regrounding of American Studies," in *Mapping American Culture*, ed. Wayne Franklin and Michael Steiner (Iowa City: University of Iowa Press, 1992), 8–9; Lowry Charles Wimberly, "The New Regionalism," *Prairie Schooner* 6, no. 3 (Summer 1932): 217–221; Kathleen A. Boardman, "Lowry Charles Wimberly and the Retreat of Regionalism," *Great Plains Quarterly* 11 (Summer 1991): 145–146, 152; Pico Iyer, *The Global Soul: Jet Lag, Shopping Malls, and the Search for Home* (New York: Alfred A. Knopf, 2000), 25; Leonard Lutwak, *The Role of Place in Literature* (Syracuse, N.Y.: Syracuse University Press, 1984), 183–184. Paul Shepherd saw the loss of regional attachments as part of a "world-wide blenderizing" of cultures. Paul Shepherd, "Place in American Culture," *North American Review* 262, no. 3 (Fall 1997): 22.

43. David Marion Holman, *A Certain Slant of Light: Regionalism and the Form of Southern and Midwestern Fiction* (Baton Rouge: Louisiana State University Press, 1995), 17; Kent C. Ryden, "Writing the Midwest: History, Literature, and Regional Identity," *Geographical Review* 89, no. 4 (October 1999): 522; Joseph E. Baker, "The Midwestern Origins of America," *American Scholar* 17, no. 1 (Winter 1947–1948): 59.

44. Andrew R. L. Cayton, "The Anti-Region: Place and Identity in the History of the American Midwest," in Cayton and Gray, *Identity of the American* Midwest, 141.

45. Cayton, "Anti-Region," 152.

46. R. Tripp Evans, *Grant Wood: A Life* (New York: Knopf, 2010).

47. Powell, *Critical Regionalism*, 19 (quoting Lucy Lippard).

48. Ubbelohde, "History and the Midwest," 46.

49. Ubbelohde, "History and the Midwest," 37; Martin Ridge, "How the Middle West Became America's Heartland," *Inland* 2 (1976): 13; Milton M. Reigelman, *The Midland: A Venture in Literary Regionalism* (Iowa City: University of Iowa Press, 1975), 42.

50. James R. Shortridge, "The Middle West," in *The Oxford Companion to United States History*, ed. Paul S. Boyer (Oxford: Oxford University Press, 2001); John D. Hicks, "A Political Whirlpool," in *The Heritage of the Middle West*, ed. John J. Murray (Norman: University of Oklahoma Press, 1958), 76. On the "sectional unity" of the Midwest, see John D. Hicks, "The Development of Civilization in the Middle West, 1860–1900," in *Sources of Culture in the Middle West: Backgrounds versus Frontiers*, ed. Dixon Ryan Fox (New York: D. Appleton-Century, 1934), 76–77; and Benjamin F. Shambaugh, ed., *Proceedings of the Mississippi Valley Historical Association for the*

Year 1907–1908 (Cedar Rapids, Iowa: Torch Press, 1909), 1:9. Doug Hurt similarly notes the emergence of the term "Middle West" to apply to Turner's twelve states and also the 1912 recognition by the *Reader's Guide to Periodical Literature*. Hurt, "Midwestern Distinctiveness," 162–163. See also David D. Anderson, "The Origins and Development of the Literature of the Midwest," in *Dictionary of Midwestern Literature*, Philip A. Greasley, gen. ed., Vol. 1, *The Authors* (Bloomington: Indiana University Press, 2001), 11.

51. For exercises in determining which states are midwestern and which are not, see Blaser, "Where Is Nebraska Anyway?" 12; David D. Anderson, "The Dimensions of the Midwest," *MidAmerica* 1 (1974): 7–15; Joseph W. Brownell, "The Cultural Midwest," *Journal of Geography* 59 (1960): 81–85; and Wilbur Zelinsky, *The Cultural Geography of the United States* (Englewood Cliffs, N.J.: Prentice-Hall, 1973), 128–129. When discussing the parameters of regions and the general concept of region, Robert Dorman counsels that "it would be preferable to accept [their] limitations with good humor and scholarly humility as the trade-off for [their] synthetic power, rather than privileging a critique of [them] in the obscurantism of theoretical abstraction, attempting to explain everything by venturing nothing." Robert L. Dorman, "History's Divining Rod," *Reviews in American History* 25, no. 3 (September 1997): 373.

52. For a prairie emphasis on midwestern history, see John D. Hicks, "The Western Middle West, 1900–1914," *Agricultural History* 20, no. 2 (April 1946): 65–77; Ray Allen Billington, *Westward Expansion: A History of the American Frontier*, 4th ed. (New York: Macmillan, 1974), 282–283; and John C. Hudson, *Making the Corn Belt: A Geographical History of Middle-Western Agriculture* (Bloomington: Indiana University Press, 1994). The prairie Midwest contrasts to what Joseph Baker, a University of Iowa English professor, called the "smoke and steel landscape of the Industrial East, which has extended a finger along the Lakes to Chicago." Baker, "Four Arguments for Regionalism," 3. For a work that leans toward a Great Lakes orientation when studying the Midwest, see William Barillas, *The Midwestern Pastoral: Place and Landscape in Literature of the American Heartland* (Athens: Ohio University Press, 2006). C. Elizabeth Raymond defines the "Prairie Midwest" as "Iowa and Illinois; northern Missouri; eastern Kansas, Nebraska, and the Dakotas; southern and western Minnesota; southern Wisconsin and Michigan; and portions of western Indiana." C. Elizabeth Raymond, "The Creation of America's Rural Heartland: An Essay on Prairie Midwestern Regional Identity," 1 (in author's possession). For another view, see Oscar Handlin, "Living in a Valley," *American Scholar* 46 (Summer 1977): 301–312. In *The Great Gatsby*, Nick Carraway distinguishes between the Midwest of "wheat or the prairies or the lost Swede towns" and the Midwest of cities where the "dwellings are still called through decades by a family's name." Ronald Weber, "My Middle West," *Notre Dame Magazine* 14, no. 3 (Autumn 1985): 28. Carey McWilliams discussed how "North Platte [Nebraska] belonged to the Middle West" while Cheyenne, Wyoming, was "spiritually West." Carey McWilliams, "Myths of the West," *North American Review* 232, no. 5 (November 1931): 427. In his description of the region, Frederic Logan Paxson said "from Pittsburgh on the Ohio to Bismarck on the upper Missouri, the extended arms of the Father of Waters gather the Middle West in a vast embrace that still has a meaning." Frederic Logan Paxson, *When the West Is Gone* (New York: Henry Holt, 1930), 89.

53. Paul W. Gates, *The Farmers' Age: Agriculture, 1815–1860* (New York: Harper & Row, 1960), 179. Beverly Bond explained that in northern Indiana, "there were

broad stretches of prairie that broadened out toward the west until they finally covered the landscape, except for a few trees along the watercourses." Beverly W. Bond Jr., *The Civilization of the Old Northwest: A Study of Political, Social, and Economic Development, 1788–1812* (New York: Macmillan, 1934), 1. Carlyle Buley colorfully explained that a "few miles north of Vincennes began the prairies," and described the "open or broken country of the prairies" where, unlike the nearby woods, the "mind became more cheerful." R. Carlyle Buley, *The Old Northwest: Pioneer Period, 1815–1840* (Indianapolis: Indiana Historical Society, 1950), 1:35–36. See also Terry G. Jordan, "Between the Forest and the Prairie," *Agricultural History* 38, no. 4 (October 1964): 205–216; and Michael Martone, "The Flatness," in *A Place of Sense: Essays in Search of the Midwest,* ed. Michael Martone (Iowa City: University of Iowa Press, 1988), 29.

54. Gates, *Farmers' Age,* 179–180. The midwestern prairie is more differentiated than the Great Plains, it should be emphasized. While the plains are flatter and drier, the prairies are more geographically diverse—"rolling grasslands, seemingly limitless level plains, bluffs, forested river bottoms, lakes, and ponds . . . inseparably linked to the grasslands around them"—and they receive more rain. Susanne K. George, "The Prairie State: Root-bound to Nebraska," *Nebraska History* 80, no. 1 (Spring 1999): 19, n.3, quoting David F. Costello, *The Prairie World* (New York: Thomas Y. Crowell, 1969), xi.

55. Shortridge, *Middle West,* 8, 24–25.

56. See John E. Miller, *Memories of Home: Small-Town Boys from the Midwest and the American Dream* (forthcoming from Kansas University Press).

CHAPTER ONE

1. For Turner's focus on "finding the essential," what was "really significant," and the "really influential forces at work," see Frederick Jackson Turner, "The Development of American Society," *Alumni Quarterly* (University of Illinois) 2 (1908): 120–121, RS 26/2/801, University of Illinois Archives.

2. Ann M. Blair, *Too Much to Know: Managing Scholarly Information before the Modern Age* (New Haven, Conn.: Yale University Press, 2011); Neal Gabler, "The Elusive Big Idea," *New York Times,* August 13, 2011. In 1908, Turner was already concerned that "when [the historian] confronts the vast accumulation of material for history, he may well be appalled at the magnitude and the difficulty of his task." Turner, "Development of American Society," 120.

3. Richard Hofstadter, *The Progressive Historians: Turner, Beard, Parrington* (New York: Knopf, 1968), 73.

4. Howard R. Lamar, "Earl Pomeroy, Historian's Historian," *Pacific Historical Review* 56, no. 4 (November 1987): 551 (quoting Paxson); Earl Pomeroy, "Frederic L. Paxson and His Approach to History," *Mississippi Valley Historical Review (MVHR)* 39, no. 4 (March 1953): 683–684.

5. Frederic Logan Paxson, *History of the American Frontier, 1763–1893* (Boston: Houghton Mifflin, 1924), preface.

6. David C. Smith, "Frederick Merk and the Frontier Experience: A Review Essay," *Wisconsin Magazine of History* 63, no. 2 (Winter 1979–1980): 143.

7. Until the middle of the 1700s, British colonials "referred to regions west of their settlements as the 'backcountry,' quite literally, the land behind them as they

faced east toward Europe." Only later did they call them "frontiers." Andrew R. L. Cayton and Frederika J. Teute, "On the Connection of Frontiers," in *Contact Points: American Frontiers from the Mohawk Valley to the Mississippi, 1750–1830*, ed. Andrew R. L. Cayton and Frederika J. Teute (Chapel Hill: University of North Carolina Press, 1998), 1.

8. William M. Fowler Jr., *Empires at War: The Seven Years' War and the Struggle for North America, 1754–1763* (Vancouver: Douglas & McIntyre, 2005), 9, 12.

9. Eric Hinderaker and Peter C. Mancall, *At the Edge of Empire: The Backcountry in British North America* (Baltimore: Johns Hopkins University Press, 2003), 115; Ann Durkin Keating, *Rising Up from Indian Country: The Battle of Fort Dearborn and the Birth of Chicago* (Chicago, University of Chicago Press, 2012): 8, 10. On France's ambitious plans for North America, see David Hackett Fischer, *Champlain's Dream* (New York: Simon & Schuster, 2008). See also Jay Gitlin, *The Bourgeois Frontier: French Towns, French Traders, and American Expansion* (New Haven, Conn.: Yale University Press, 2009).

10. Fred Anderson, *The War That Made America: A Short History of the French and Indian War* (New York: Viking, 2006), vii. Matthew Ward explains that the "escalation to war . . . had little to do with diplomacy and politics in Europe, but was rather the result of developments in the Ohio Valley and on the frontier of Virginia and Pennsylvania." Matthew C. Ward, *Breaking the Backcountry: The Seven Years' War in Virginia and Pennsylvania, 1754–1765* (Pittsburgh: University of Pittsburgh Press, 2003), 35. See also Eliot A. Cohen, *Conquered into Liberty: Two Centuries of Battles along the Great Warpath That Made the American Way of War* (New York: Free Press, 2011), 41–70; and William R. Nester, *The First Global War: Britain, France, and the Fate of North America, 1756–1775* (Westport, Conn.: Praeger, 2000).

11. Hinderaker and Mancall, *At the Edge of Empire*, 105. See also Frederic L. Paxson, "Washington and the Western Fronts, 1753–1795," *Journal of the Illinois State Historical Society* 24, no. 4 (January 1932): 589–605; and John H. Krenkel, "British Conquest of the Old Northwest," *Wisconsin Magazine of History* 35, no. 1 (Autumn 1951): 49–61.

12. Clarence W. Alvord, "Mississippi Valley Problems and the American Revolution," *Minnesota History Bulletin* nos. 5–6 (February–May 1922): 232; Hinderaker and Mancall, *At the Edge of Empire*, 5, 140, 160; Kenneth R. Walker, *A History of the Middle West: From the Beginning to 1970* (Little Rock, Ark.: Pioneer Press, 1972), 49.

13. C. H. Metzger, *The Quebec Act: A Primary Cause of the American Revolution* (New York: United States Catholic Historical Society, 1936).

14. Alvord, "Mississippi Valley Problems," 239; Clarence W. Alvord, "Virginia and the West: An Interpretation," *MVHR* 3, no. 1 (June 1916): 23, 25.

15. Alvord, "Mississippi Valley Problems," 235.

16. Alvord, "Mississippi Valley Problems," 241; Clarence W. Alvord, *The Mississippi Valley in British Politics: A Study of Trade, Land Speculation, and Experiments in Imperialism Culminating in the American Revolution* (Cleveland: Arthur Clark, 1917; repr., New York: Russell & Russell, 1959), 2:250–251; Jack M. Sosin, *Whitehall and the Wilderness: The Middle West in British Colonial Policy, 1760–1775* (Lincoln: University of Nebraska Press, 1961), 4.

17. Kim M. Gruenwald, *River of Enterprise: The Commercial Origins of Regional Identity in the Ohio Valley, 1790–1850* (Bloomington: Indiana University Press, 2002), 11.

18. Paxson, *History of the American Frontier*, 80; Hinderaker and Mancall, *At the Edge of Empire*, 172; Ward, *Breaking the Backcountry*, 10–16; Turner, "Development of American Society," 132–133; Gruenwald, *River of Enterprise*, 155.

19. Francois Furstenberg, "The Significance of the Trans-Appalachian Frontier in Atlantic History," *American Historical Review* 113, no. 3 (June 2008): 663.

20. Some historians give great credit to Clark for securing the West for the new United States. Reuben G. Thwaites, *How George Rogers Clark Won the Northwest, and Other Essays in Western History* (Chicago: A. C. McClurg, 1903); Claude H. Van Tyne, *American Revolution*, vol. 9 (New York: Harper & Brothers, 1907). Alvord also extends great credit to the preferences of British minister Lord Shelburne, who saw in the surrender of the West a "strong foundation laid for eternal amity between England and America." Alvord, "Virginia and the West," 38. See generally, Kenneth W. McKinley, "Ohio, Prize of the Revolution," *Northwest Ohio Quarterly* 13, no. 4 (October 1941): 13–20.

21. Beverly W. Bond Jr., *The Civilization of the Old Northwest: A Study of Political, Social, and Economic Development, 1788–1812* (New York: Macmillan, 1934), 40.

22. James Belich, *Replenishing the Earth: The Settler Revolution and the Rise of the Angloworld, 1783–1939* (New York: Oxford University Press, 2009), 165–169.

23. Clarence E. Carter, "Colonialism in Continental United States," *South Atlantic Quarterly* 47 (January 1948): 18–28; William Cronon, George Miles, and Jay Gitlin, "Becoming West: Toward a New Meaning for Western History," in *Under an Open Sky: Rethinking America's Western Past*, ed. William Cronon, George Miles, and Jay Gitlin (New York: W. W. Norton, 1992), 17.

24. Merrill D. Peterson, "Jefferson, the West, and the Enlightenment," *Wisconsin Magazine of History* 70, no. 4 (Summer 1987): 273, 275–276.

25. Belich, *Replenishing the Earth*, 165.

26. Belich, *Replenishing the Earth*, 165.

27. Paul Finkelman concluded that the "ordinance has been justly praised for insuring religious freedom, civil liberties, and due process; encouraging public education; guaranteeing republican forms of government; and establishing a procedure for converting the region's colonial settlements into states." Paul Finkelman, "The Northwest Ordinance: A Constitution for an Empire of Liberty," in *Pathways to the Old Northwest: An Observance of the Bicentennial of the Northwest Ordinance* (Indianapolis: Indiana Historical Society, 1988), 6. See also Phillip R. Shriver, "Freedom's Proving Ground: The Heritage of the Northwest Ordinance," *Wisconsin Magazine of History* 72, no. 2 (Winter 1988–1989): 126–131; and John Porter Bloom, "The Continental Nation: Our Trinity of Revolutionary Testaments," *Western Historical Quarterly* 6, no. 1 (January 1975): 8–15.

28. Belich, *Replenishing the Earth*, 167. See Peter S. Onuf, *Statehood and Union: A History of the Northwest Ordinance* (Bloomington: Indiana University Press, 1987).

29. Belich, *Replenishing the Earth*, 169.

30. James H. Madison, "Extending Liberty Westward: The Northwest Ordinance of 1787," *OAH Magazine of History* 2, no. 4 (Fall 1987): 15; Lehr Fess, "Charters of Freedom: The Ordinance of 1787," *Northwest Ohio Quarterly* 25, no. 2 (Spring 1953): 121–122.

31. Jon Kukla, *A Wilderness So Immense: The Louisiana Purchase and the Destiny of America* (New York: Knopf, 2003).

32. Gordon S. Wood, *Empire of Liberty: A History of the Early Republic, 1789–1815*

(New York: Oxford University Press, 2009), 357. Frederic Logan Paxson emphasized that the United States "was a new sort of empire, for the ancient empires of the world and contemporary monarchies had done and were doing business on the basis of superiority and force." Frederic Logan Paxson, *When the West Is Gone* (New York: Henry Holt, 1930), 44.

33. Wood, *Empire of Liberty*, 357; August C. Miller Jr., "Jefferson as an Agriculturalist," *Agricultural History* 16, no. 2 (April 1942): 65–78.

34. Joyce Appleby, "The Social Consequences of American Revolutionary Ideals in the Early Republic," in *The Middling Sorts: Explorations in the History of the American Middle Class*, ed. Burton Bledstein and Robert D. Johnston (New York: Routledge, 2001), 34, 313, n.7.

35. Wood, *Empire of Liberty*, 363; William F. Raney, "The Peopling of the Land," in *The Culture of the Middle West* (Appleton, Wis.: Lawrence College Press, 1944), 22.

36. Wood, *Empire of Liberty*, 364–365; Harry N. Scheiber, "On the Concepts of 'Regionalism' and 'Frontier,'" in *The Old Northwest: Studies in Regional History, 1787–1910*, ed. Harry N. Scheiber (Lincoln: University of Nebraska Press, 1969), ix–x.

37. Wood, *Empire of Liberty*, 364 ("more democratic"); Booth Tarkington, "The Middle West," *Harper's Monthly Magazine* (December 1902), 78 ("without snobbishness"); Paxson, *When the West Is Gone*, 32–38; James E. Davis, "'New Aspects of Men and New Forms of Society': The Old Northwest, 1790–1820," *Journal of the Illinois State Historical Society* 69, no. 3 (August 1976): 166; E. Bradford Burns, *Kinship with the Land: Regionalist Thought in Iowa, 1894–1942* (Iowa City: University of Iowa Press, 1996), 130. For a description of Appomattox as an example of regional contrasts, the "final surrender of the southern patrician to the midwestern commoner," see David Marion Holman, *A Certain Slant of Light: Regionalism and the Form of Southern and Midwestern Fiction* (Baton Rouge: Louisiana State University Press, 1995), 8.

38. Henry Hyde Hubbart, *The Older Middle West, 1840–1880: Its Social, Economic and Political Life and Sectional Tendencies before, during and after the Civil War* (New York: D. Appleton-Century, 1936), 9.

39. Wood, *Empire of Liberty*, 373.

40. Reginald Horsman, "The Dimensions of an 'Empire of Liberty': Expansion and Republicanism, 1775–1825," *Journal of the Early Republic* 9, no. 1 (Spring 1989): 1–20.

41. Rush Welter, "The Frontier West as Image of American Society: Conservative Attitudes before the Civil War," *MVHR* 46, no. 4 (March 1960): 593–614.

42. Nicole Etcheson, *The Emerging Midwest: Upland Southerners and the Political Culture of the Old Northwest, 1787–1861* (Bloomington: Indiana University Press, 1996), 15.

43. Etcheson, *Emerging Midwest*, 15–16.

44. Etcheson, *Emerging Midwest*, 19.

45. Etcheson, *Emerging Midwest*, 26. On early Ohio, see R. Douglas Hurt, *The Ohio Frontier: Crucible of the Old Northwest, 1720–1830* (Bloomington: Indiana University Press, 1998); and Andrew R. L. Cayton, *Frontier Republic: Ideology and Politics in the Ohio Country, 1780–1825* (Kent, Ohio: Kent State University Press, 1989).

46. Etcheson, *Emerging Midwest*, 26.

47. Joyce Appleby, "Recovering America's Historic Diversity: Beyond Exceptionalism," *Journal of American History* 79, no. 2 (September 1992): 419, 423–424.

48. Appleby, "Recovering America's Historic Diversity," 426. On the opposition to the United States by the powers of Europe, see William H. Goetzmann, *When the Eagle Screamed: The Romantic Horizon in American Expansionism, 1800–1860* (Norman: University of Oklahoma Press, 2000), xi.

49. Appleby, "Recovering America's Historic Diversity," 425. See also Gordon Wood, *The Idea of America: Reflections on the Birth of the United States* (New York: Penguin Press, 2011), 189–212; and Cronon, Miles, and Gitlin, "Becoming West," 16.

50. David Armitage, *The Declaration of Independence: A Global History* (Cambridge, Mass.: Harvard University Press, 2007), 3; Thomas Bender, *A Nation among Nations: America's Place in World History* (New York: Hill and Wang, 2006), 123; Merle Curti, "The Reputation of America Overseas, 1776–1860," *American Quarterly* 1, no. 1 (Spring 1949): 58–82; Forrest McDonald, "The Relation of the French Peasant Veterans of the American Revolution to the Fall of Feudalism in France, 1789–1792," *Agricultural History* 25, no. 4 (October 1951): 151–161.

51. G. D. Lillibridge, *Beacon of Freedom: The Impact of American Democracy upon Great Britain, 1830–1870* (Philadelphia: University of Pennsylvania Press, 1955), xiii.

52. John D. Barnhart, *Valley of Democracy: The Frontier versus Plantation in the Ohio Valley, 1775–1818* (Bloomington: Indiana University Press, 1953).

53. Paxson, *History of the American Frontier*, 72.

54. Belich, *Replenishing the Earth*, 229.

55. Richard Moe, *The Last Full Measure: The Life and Death of the First Minnesota Volunteers* (New York: Henry Holt, 1993).

56. Belich, *Replenishing the Earth*, 247.

57. Ed Folsom, "Walt Whitman's Prairie Paradise," in *Recovering the Prairie*, ed. Robert F. Sayre (Madison: University of Wisconsin Press, 1999), 54.

58. Belich, *Replenishing the Earth*, 247.

59. Belich, *Replenishing the Earth*, 250.

60. Frederick Merk, *History of the Westward Movement* (New York: Alfred A. Knopf, 1978), 180. See also Bond, *Civilization of the Old Northwest*, 528; Scheiber, "On the Concepts of 'Regionalism' and 'Frontier,'" x–xi; R. Carlyle Buley, *The Old Northwest: Pioneer Period, 1815–1840* (Indianapolis: Indiana Historical Society, 1950), 2:3; Louis Bernard Schmidt, "The Agricultural Revolution in the Prairies and the Great Plains of the United States," *Agricultural History* 8, no. 4 (October 1934): 169; Orin G. Libby, "Some Aspects of Mid-West America," *Minnesota History Bulletin* 4, nos. 5–6 (February–May 1922): 220; Robert Cook, *Baptism of Fire: The Republican Party in Iowa, 1838–1878* (Ames: Iowa State University Press, 1993), 9; Hubbart, *Older Middle West*, 6; Paxson, *When the West Is Gone*, 49.

61. Andrew R. L. Cayton, "'Separate Interests' and the Nation-State: The Washington Administration and the Origins of Regionalism in the Trans-Appalachian West," *Journal of American History* 79, no. 1 (June 1992): 67.

62. R. Carlyle Buley, "The Middle West: Its Heritage and Its Role," *Wabash Bulletin* (December 1943): 20; Jay Hubbell, "The Decay of the Provinces," *Sewanee Review* 35 (1927): 483.

63. Kenneth Winkle, "'The Great Body of the Republic': Abraham Lincoln and the Idea of a Middle West," in *The Identity of the American Midwest: Essays on Regional History*, ed. Andrew R. L. Cayton and Susan E. Gray (Bloomington: Indiana University Press, 2001), 114–115; James H. Madison, "State History in Regional Perspective," in *The State We're In: Reflections on Minnesota History*, ed. Annette Atkins and

Deborah L. Miller (St. Paul: Minnesota Historical Society Press, 2010), 21. On the Northwest Ordinance's "libertarian antislavery heritage," see Harold M. Hyman, *American Singularity: The 1787 Northwest Ordinance, the 1862 Homestead and Morrill Acts, and the 1944 G.I. Bill* (Athens: University of Georgia Press, 1986), 28.

64. Jon K. Lauck, *Prairie Republic: The Political Culture of Dakota Territory, 1879–1889* (Norman: University of Oklahoma Press, 2010).

65. Beverly W. Bond Jr., "American Civilization Comes to the Old Northwest," *MVHR* 19, no. 1 (June 1932): 29.

66. Winkle, "'Great Body of the Republic,'" 113–114.

67. Winkle, "'Great Body of the Republic,'" 111. Nearly 60 percent of all places named for Lincoln in the United States are located in Wisconsin, Iowa, Missouri, Nebraska, and Kansas. Winkle, "'Great Body of the Republic,'" 112.

68. Belich, *Replenishing the Earth*, 435.

69. Richard Lyle Power, *Planting Corn Belt Culture: The Impress of the Upland Southerner and Yankee in the Old Northwest* (Indianapolis: Indiana Historical Society, 1953), 163.

70. Meredith Nicholson, "Valley of Democracy," *Scribner's Magazine* 63, no. 3 (March 1918), 264, 283. See also Meredith Nicholson, *The Valley of Democracy* (New York: C. Scribner's Sons, 1918); and Ralph D. Gray, *Meredith Nicholson: A Writing Life* (Indianapolis: Indiana Historical Society Press, 2007).

71. Belich, *Replenishing the Earth*, 468.

72. Belich, *Replenishing the Earth*, 468; Almon R. Wright, "Food Purchases of the Allies, 1917–1918," *Agricultural History* 16, no. 2 (April 1942): 97–102.

73. Belich, *Replenishing the Earth*, 471.

74. Milo Quaife report attached to Paul M. Angle to Carlyle Buley, December 15, 1948, Buley Papers, Indiana Historical Society.

75. John Dumbrell, *A Special Relationship: Anglo American Relations from the Cold War to Iraq* (New York: Palgrave Macmillan, 2006); Walter Russell Mead, *God and Gold: Britain, America, and the Making of the Modern World* (New York: Vintage, 2008); Duncan Andrew Campbell, *Unlikely Allies: Britain, America, and the Victorian Beginnings of the Special Relationship* (New York: Continuum, 2007).

76. Turner certainly recognized these influences, however, as did Turner's mentor. See William Francis Allen, *Essays and Monographs* (Boston: George H. Ellis, 1890), 105–106.

77. Belich, *Replenishing the Earth*, 165. See generally Gene M. Gressley, "Colonialism: A Western Complaint," *Pacific Northwest Quarterly* 54, no. 1 (January 1963): 1–8.

78. David Donald and Frederick A. Palmer, "Toward a Western Literature, 1820–1860," *MVHR* 35, no. 3 (December 1948): 413–428; Buley, *Old Northwest*, 2:534.

79. Belich, *Replenishing the Earth*, 492; Christopher Lasch, *The New Radicalism in America: The Intellectual as Social Type, 1889–1963* (New York: W. W. Norton, 1965), 319–320.

80. Belich, *Replenishing the Earth*, 493.

81. Ruth Suckow, "Middle Western Literature," *English Journal* 21, no. 3 (March 1932): 182; Joseph E. Baker, "Four Arguments for Regionalism," *Saturday Review of Literature* (November 28, 1936), 3–4; Burns, *Kinship with the Land*.

82. Merle Curti, *The Growth of American Thought* (New York: Harper & Brothers, 1943), 278; Hubbart, *Older Middle West*, 52–72; Wayne A. Wiegand, *Main Street Public Library: Community Places and Reading Spaces in the Rural Heartland, 1876–1956*

(Iowa City: University of Iowa Press, 2011), 8–9; David D. Anderson, "The Queen City and a New Literature," *MidAmerica* 4 (1977): 9–10; David Mead, *Yankee Eloquence in the Middle West: The Ohio Lyceum, 1850–1870* (East Lansing: Michigan State College Press, 1951); John T. Flanagan, "Middlewestern Regional Literature," in *Research Opportunities in American Cultural History*, ed. John Francis McDermott (Lexington: University of Kentucky Press, 1961), 124–139; Robert L. Dorman, *Hell of a Vision: Regionalism and the Modern American West* (Tucson: University of Arizona Press, 2012), 17–22; Wendy J. Katz, "Creating a Western Heart: Art and Reform in Cincinnati's Antebellum Associations," *Ohio Valley History* 1 (Fall 2001): 2–20; David D. Anderson, "The Origins and Development of the Literature of the Midwest," in *Dictionary of Midwestern Literature*, Vol. 1, *The Authors*, ed. Philip A. Greasley (Bloomington: Indiana University Press, 2001), 16; Hubbell, "Decay of the Provinces," 484; John Neufeld, "The Associated Western Literary Societies in the Midwest," *Michigan History* 51 (1967): 154–161; Kenneth H. Wheeler, *Cultivating Regionalism: Higher Education and the Making of the American Midwest* (DeKalb: Northern Illinois University Press, 2011); Richard S. Taylor, "Western Colleges as 'Securities of Intelligence & Virtue': The Towne-Eddy Report of 1846," *Old Northwest* 7 (1981): 41–65. Illinois is known as the "heartland of the service club movement." Jeffery A. Charles, *Service Clubs in American Society: Rotary, Kiwanis, and Lions* (Urbana: University of Illinois Press, 1993), 5.

83. Curti, *Growth of American Thought*, 289.

84. Terry A. Barnhart, "'A Common Feeling': Regional Identity and Historical Consciousness in the Old Northwest, 1820–1860," *Michigan Historical Review* 29, no. 1 (Spring 2003): 51.

85. David S. Brown, *Beyond the Frontier: The Midwestern Voice in American Historical Writing* (Chicago: University of Chicago Press, 2009), 25–50; Jon K. Lauck, "The 'Interior Tradition' in American History," *Annals of Iowa* 69, no. 1 (Winter 2010): 82–93.

86. Edward Watts, *An American Colony: Regionalism and the Roots of Midwestern Culture* (Athens: Ohio University Press, 2002), xxii. On regionalism, see also Kent Blaser, "Where Is Nebraska Anyway?" *Nebraska History* 80, no. 1 (Spring 1999): 3–5.

87. In response to Jack Greene's attempt to merge the American Revolution into the broader story and literature concerning "postcolonialism," Michael Zuckerman notes that Greene inadvertently highlights the uniqueness and "idiosyncrasy of the new nation and the distinctiveness of the regime its Founders devised." Zuckerman explains that in contrast to the grim stories constituting postcolonial studies, "Americans mounted a colonial rebellion like no other and constructed a state like no other," and thus Greene "brings scholars back to American exceptionalism." Michael Zuckerman, "Exceptionalism After All: Or, the Perils of Postcolonialism," *William and Mary Quarterly* 64, no. 2 (April 2007): 260–261.

88. Barnhart, "'Common Feeling,'" 54.

89. Barnhart, "'Common Feeling,'" 53. David Anderson concluded that the "Midwest has virtually no colonial tradition." David D. Anderson, "Notes toward a Definition of the Mind of the Midwest," *MidAmerica* 3 (1976): 9.

90. Andrew R. L. Cayton, "The Anti-Region: Place and Identity in the History of the American Midwest," in Cayton and Gray, *Identity of the American Midwest*, 150.

91. Cayton, "Anti-Region," 150.

92. Cayton, "Anti-Region," 159.

93. Cayton, "Anti-Region," 157. David Anderson concluded that the Midwest "inherited from the beginning a national consciousness that rivals when it does not overwhelm its regional awareness." Anderson, "Notes," 10.

94. Cayton, "Anti-Region," 158; Madison, "State History in Regional Perspective," 21; Ronald Weber, *The Midwestern Ascendency in American Writing* (Bloomington: Indiana University Press, 1992), 7.

95. Jennifer Marie Holly Wells, "The Construction of Midwestern Literary Regionalism in Sinclair Lewis's and Louise Erdrich's Novels: Regional Influences on Carol Kennicott and Fleur Pillager" (Ph.D. diss., Drew University, 2009), 8–10.

96. Jon Gjerde, *The Minds of the West: Ethnocultural Evolution in the Rural Middle West, 1830–1917* (Chapel Hill: University of North Carolina Press, 1997); Mark Wyman, *Immigrants in the Valley: Irish, Germans, and Americans in the Upper Mississippi Country, 1830-1860* (Chicago: Nelson-Hall, 1984): 11–12.

97. Madison, "State History in Regional Perspective," 21. See Elizabeth A. Perkins, "Distinctions and Partitions Among Us: Identity and Interaction in the Ohio Valley," in Cayton and Teute, *Contact Points*, 206–211; Louis B. Wright, *Culture on the Moving Frontier* (Bloomington: Indiana University Press, 1955), 81–82; Martin Ridge, "How the Middle West Became America's Heartland," *Inland* 2 (1976): 11–12; William Carter, *Middle West Country* (Boston: Houghton Mifflin, 1975), 26–27; William N. Parker, "From Northwest to Midwest: Social Bases of a Regional History," in *Essays in Nineteenth Century Economic History: The Old Northwest,* ed. David C. Klingaman and Richard K. Vedder (Athens: Ohio University Press, 1975), 6–12; Wilbur Zelinsky, *The Cultural Geography of the United States* (Englewood Cliffs, N.J.: Prentice-Hall, 1973), 26; John C. Hudson, "North American Origins of Middlewestern Frontier Populations," *Annals of the Association of American Geographers* 78, no. 3 (September 1988): 395–413; James B. Bergquist, "Tracing the Origins of a Midwestern Culture: The Case of Central Indiana," *Indiana Magazine of History* 77, no. 1 (March 1981): 1–3.

98. Buley, "Middle West," 14; Etcheson, *Emerging Midwest*, xii; Power, *Planting Corn Belt Culture*, 162–174; Paxson, *History of the American Frontier*, 7; Bond, "American Civilization," 28; Colin Woodward, *American Nations: A History of the Eleven Rival Regional Cultures of North America* (New York: Viking, 2011), 173–188; Paxson, *When the West Is Gone*, 30–32. Tocqueville also noted the "mingling" of customs and classes on the American frontier. See Lasch, *New Radicalism in America*, xi.

99. Etcheson, *Emerging Midwest*, 137–138.

100. Etcheson, *Emerging Midwest*, 139.

101. Etcheson, *Emerging Midwest*, 139.

102. Etcheson, *Emerging Midwest*, 141; Joseph E. Baker, "The Midwestern Origins of America," *American Scholar* 17, no. 1 (Winter 1947–1948): 58–68.

103. See James Shortridge, *The Middle West: Its Meaning in American Culture* (Lawrence: University Press of Kansas, 1989).

104. Bruce Cumings, *Dominion from Sea to Sea: Pacific Ascendency and American Power* (New Haven, Conn.: Yale University Press, 2009), 4.

105. Emerson quoted in Frederick Sontag, *American Life* (Lanham, Md.: University Press of America, 2006), 87.

106. Cumings, *Dominion from Sea to Sea*, 14. Around the turn of the twentieth century, the Mississippi Valley produced 75 percent of the nation's farm products. Ernest M. Pollard, "The Conservation of the Natural Resources of the Mississippi Valley," in

Proceedings of the Mississippi Valley Historical Association for the Year 1907–1908, ed. Benjamin F. Shambaugh (Cedar Rapids, Iowa: Torch Press, 1909), 1:99.

107. Cumings, *Dominion from Sea to Sea*, 38.

108. Cumings, *Dominion from Sea to Sea*, 38 (emphasis added).

109. Belich, *Replenishing the Earth*, 163.

110. Belich, *Replenishing the Earth*, 164.

111. See Claiborne A. Skinner, *The Upper Country: French Enterprise in the Colonial Great Lakes* (Baltimore: Johns Hopkins University Press, 2008); and Susan Sleeper-Smith, *Rethinking the Fur Trade: Cultures of Exchange in an Atlantic World* (Lincoln: University of Nebraska Press, 2009).

112. Belich, *Replenishing the Earth*, 185. See also Andrew R. L. Cayton, "Artery and Border: The Ambiguous Development of the Ohio Valley in the Early Republic," *Ohio Valley History* 1 (Winter 2001): 19–22.

113. John C. Weaver, *The Great Land Rush and the Making of the Modern World, 1650–1900* (Montreal and Kingston: McGill-Queen's University Press, 2003). See also Michael Martone, "Correctionville, Iowa," *North American Review* 276, no. 4 (December 1991): 4–9.

114. Weaver, *Great Land Rush*, 349. On the smallholder tradition in the Midwest, see Gilbert C. Fite, "The American West of Farmers and Stockmen," in *Historians and the American West*, ed. Michael P. Malone (Lincoln: University of Nebraska Press, 1983), 212.

115. Weaver, *Great Land Rush*, 349.

116. Cayton, "Anti-Region," 154; Ginette Aley, "Dwelling within the Place Worth Seeking: The Midwest, Regional Identity, and Internal Histories," in *Regionalism and the Humanities*, ed. Wendy J. Katz and Timothy R. Mahoney (Lincoln: University of Nebraska Press, 2008), 103.

117. Madison, "State History in Regional Perspective," 23; Parker, "From Northwest to Midwest," 16.

118. Jon C. Teaford, *Cities of the Heartland: The Rise and Fall of the Industrial Midwest* (Bloomington: Indiana University Press, 1993), xi.

119. Cumings, *Dominion from Sea to Sea*, 19. Belich also examines the importance of Chicago at length in *Replenishing the Earth*. See also William Cronon, *Nature's Metropolis: Chicago and the Great West* (New York: W. W. Norton, 1991).

120. Cumings, *Dominion from Sea to Sea*, 37.

121. Frank L. Klement, "Middle Western Copperheadism and the Genesis of the Granger Movement," *MVHR* 38, no. 4 (March 1952): 679–694; Russel B. Nye, *Midwestern Progressive Politics: A Historical Study of Its Origins and Development, 1870–1950* (East Lansing: Michigan State College Press, 1951).

122. Katharine Q. Seelye, "Detroit Census Confirms a Desertion Like No Other," *New York Times*, March 22, 2011.

123. Robert Bothwell, *The Penguin History of Canada* (Toronto: Penguin, 2006), 35, 38, 58.

124. Richard White, *The Middle Ground: Indians, Empires, and Republics in the Great Lakes Region, 1650–1815* (New York: Cambridge University Press, 1991), 240–256.

125. David R. Wrone, "Indian Treaties and the Democratic Idea," *Wisconsin Magazine of History* 70, no. 2 (Winter 1986–1987): 82–106.

126. Andrew R. L. Cayton and Peter S. Onuf, *The Midwest and the Nation: Re-*

thinking the History of an American Region (Bloomington: Indiana University Press, 1990), 9.

127. Richard Sewell, *Ballots for Freedom: Antislavery Politics in the United States, 1837–1860* (New York: W. W. Norton, 1980), 326–342; Michael J. McManus, "Wisconsin Republicans and Negro Slavery: Attitudes and Behavior, 1857," *Civil War History* 25, no. 1 (March 1979): 36–54.

128. Cayton and Onuf, *Midwest and the Nation*, 16–17; Earle D. Ross, "A Generation of Prairie Historiography," *MVHR* 33, no. 3 (December 1946): 406; Paul Finkelman, "Prelude to the Fourteenth Amendment: Black Rights in the Antebellum North," *Rutgers Law Journal* 17 (1986): 415–482; Paul Finkelman, "Fugitive Slaves, Midwestern Racial Tolerance, and the Value of 'Justice Delayed,'" *Iowa Law Review* 78 (October 1992): 89–141; Michael J. McManus, *Political Abolitionism in Wisconsin, 1840–1861* (Kent, Ohio: Kent State University Press, 1998); Eric Foner, *Free Soil, Free Labor, Free Men: The Ideology of the Republican Party before the Civil War* (New York: Oxford University Press, 1970); Arthur Zilversmit, *The First Emancipation: The Abolition of Slavery in the North* (Chicago: University of Chicago Press, 1967); Donald G. Mathews, "The Methodist Schism of 1844 and the Popularization of Antislavery Sentiment," *MidAmerica* 51, no. 1 (January 1968): 3–23; Thomas D. Hamm, April Beckman, Marissa Florio, Kirsti Giles, and Marie Hopper, "'A Great and Good People': Midwestern Quakers and the Struggle against Slavery," *Indiana Magazine of History* 100, no. 1 (March 2004): 3–25. In her recent book about Wisconsin, Iowa, and Minnesota, Leslie Schwalm downplays the distinctiveness of the American North, but also notes the French origins of slaves in the Midwest, midwestern courts' favorable treatment of African Americans, the abolition of all forms of bondage in Illinois, the defeat of attempts to exclude African Americans from the Midwest, the spread of midwestern abolitionism, whites who were sympathetic to African Americans, and the enfranchisement of African Americans in Wisconsin, Minnesota, and Iowa. Leslie A. Schwalm, *Emancipation's Diaspora: Race and Reconstruction in the Upper Midwest* (Chapel Hill: University of North Carolina Press, 2009), 16–17, 22, 29, 31, 181. See also Leon Litwak, *North from Slavery: The Negro in the Free States, 1790–1860* (Chicago: University of Chicago Press, 1965).

129. Aferdteen Harrison, *Black Exodus: The Great Migration from the American South* (Jackson: University Press of Mississippi, 1992). Although critical of racism in the North, Thomas Sagrue's recent book begins with the story of a "small-town Midwesterner" whose experience in Iowa and Minnesota demonstrates the distinction between North and South. Thomas Sagrue, *Sweet Land of Liberty: The Forgotten Struggle for Civil Rights in the North* (New York: Random House, 2008), 13.

CHAPTER TWO

1. Hugh Honour, *Romanticism* (Boulder, Colo.: Westview Press, 1979); Paul V. Murphy, *The Rebuke of History: The Southern Agrarians and American Conservative Thought* (Chapel Hill: University of North Carolina Press, 2001); Neil Jumonville, *Critical Crossings: The New York Intellectuals in Postwar America* (Berkeley: University of California Press, 1991); Harvey J. Kaye, *The British Marxist Historians: An Introductory Analysis* (New York: Basil Blackwell, 1984).

2. James Gleick, *The Information: A History. A Theory. A Flood.* (New York: Pantheon Books, 2011). The philosopher and mathematician Gottfried Leibiz was

already complaining in the seventeenth century about "that horrible mass of books that keeps on growing." Nicholas Jolley, ed., *The Cambridge Companion to Leibniz* (Cambridge: Cambridge University Press, 1995), 61, n.28. T. S. Eliot complained that "in our time, we read too many books, or are oppressed by the thought of the new books which we are neglecting to read." Eliot quoted in Michael Kammen, *In the Past Lane: Historical Perspectives on American Culture* (New York: Oxford University Press, 1997), 11. Thirty years ago, Bernard Bailyn said, "Only a besotted Faust would attempt to keep up with even a large part of this proliferating literature in any detail." Bernard Bailyn, "The Challenge of Modern Historiography," *American Historical Review* 87, no. 1 (February 1982): 2. See also John E. Miller, "Epistemology in Flux: Embattled Truth in an Information Age," *South Dakota Review* 24, no. 3 (Autumn 1986): 7–20; and W. Stull Holt, "An Evaluation of the Report on Theory and Practice in Historical Study," *Pacific Historical Review* 18, no. 2 (May 1949): 239–242.

3. David S. Brown, *Beyond the Frontier: The Midwestern Voice in American Historical Writing* (Chicago: University of Chicago Press, 2009). See also Jon K. Lauck, "The 'Interior Tradition' in American History," *Annals of Iowa* 69, no. 1 (Winter 2010): 82–93.

4. David S. Brown, *Richard Hofstadter: An Intellectual Biography* (Chicago: University of Chicago Press, 2007).

5. Brown, *Beyond the Frontier*, 190.

6. Brown, *Beyond the Frontier*, xv.

7. Brown, *Beyond the Frontier*, 9.

8. On Turner's focus on the Midwest, see Robert F. Berkohofer Jr., "Space, Time, Culture and the New Frontier," *Agricultural History* 38, no. 1 (January 1964): 23.

9. Curtis P. Nettels, "History Out of Wisconsin," *Wisconsin Magazine of History* 39, no. 2 (Winter 1955–1956): 116. See also Curtis Nettels, "Frederick Jackson Turner and the New Deal," *Wisconsin Magazine of History* 17, no. 3 (March 1934): 258.

10. Michael C. Steiner, "The Significance of Turner's Sectional Thesis," *Western Historical Quarterly* 10, no. 4 (October 1979): 443 (quoting Turner letter from 1922); Frederick Jackson Turner to Theodore Blegen, March 16, 1923, Blegen Papers, University of Minnesota Archives; John W. Caughey, "The Insignificance of the Frontier in American History or 'Once Upon a Time There Was an American West,'" *Western Historical Quarterly* 5, no. 1 (January 1974): 6; Ray Allen Billington, "Why Some Historians Rarely Write History: A Case Study of Frederick Jackson Turner," *Mississippi Valley Historical Review (MVHR)* 50, no. 1 (June 1963): 15; Ellen Fitzpatrick, *History's Memory: Writing America's Past, 1880–1980* (Cambridge, Mass.: Harvard University Press, 2002), 81; John D. Hicks, "The Development of Civilization in the Middle West, 1860–1900," in *Sources of Culture in the Middle West: Backgrounds versus Frontiers*, ed. Dixon Ryan Fox (New York: D. Appleton-Century, 1934), 74; Ray Allen Billington, *The Genesis of the Frontier Thesis: A Study in Historical Creativity* (Pasadena, Calif.: Huntington Library Press, 1971), 6, 29, 93–94; Harry R. Stevens, "Cross Section and Frontier," *South Atlantic Quarterly* 52, no. 3 (July 1953): 445–448.

11. Clarence Paine was from Eden Valley Township, Minnesota; had worked on a farm and in a lumber camp; had founded a business college in Iowa; and had become interested in promoting the efforts of the Iowa Historical Department when Morton tapped him to work on a large-scale history of Nebraska. James L. Sellers, "Before We Were Members: The MVHA," *MVHR* 40, no. 1 (June 1953): 6; Benjamin F. Shambaugh, "The Sixteenth Annual Meeting of the Mississippi Valley Historical

Association," *MVHR* 10, no. 2 (September 1923): 112; "Clarence S. Paine, Historian, Dies," *Lincoln Daily Star*, June 14, 1916. Because he gave Paine his platform, Morton is considered the "genuine spiritual godfather" of the MVHA. Sellers, "Before We Were Members," 6. On Morton, see James C. Olson, *J. Sterling Morton* (Lincoln: University of Nebraska Press, 1942).

12. Benjamin F. Shambaugh, ed., *Proceedings of the Mississippi Valley Historical Association for the Year 1907–1908* (Cedar Rapids, Iowa: Torch Press, 1909), 1:9. Although Turner never served as president of the MVHA, it was "quintessentially the organization of Frederick Jackson Turner, who dominated its proceedings and consciousness for many years." Stanley N. Katz, "The Rise of a Modern and Democratic Learned Society," in *The Organization of American Historians and the Writing and Teaching of American History*, ed. Richard S. Kirkendall (New York: Oxford University Press, 2011), 14. On the MVHA, Michael Kammen notes, "Turner's influence was ubiquitous and persistent." After reviewing the published work of the MVHA, Kammen concluded that "no other figure dominates, personally and intellectually, as much as Turner." Michael Kammen, "The Mississippi Valley Historical Association, 1907–1952," in Kirkendall, *Organization of American Historians*, 22.

13. Midwesterners had "long resented what they saw as control of the profession by a northeastern (and especially New England) elite." Peter Novick, *That Noble Dream: The "Objectivity Question" and the American Historical Profession* (New York: Cambridge University Press, 1988), 181. Historians complained of the "difficulty of getting articles on Western history accepted by journals edited in the East." Nettels, "History Out of Wisconsin," 115. On the hostility to western history at Yale, see Jon K. Lauck, "The Old Roots of the New History: Howard Lamar and the Intellectual Origins of *Dakota Territory*," *Western Historical Quarterly* 39, no. 3 (Autumn 2008): 262. On the hostility to western history at Harvard, see Frederick Merk to Milo Quaife, October 15, 1916, General Administrative Correspondence of Wisconsin Historical Society, 1900–2000, Wisconsin Historical Society (WHS). On the friction between midwestern historians and the easterners, see Kammen, "Mississippi Valley Historical Association," 18–20.

14. Sellers, "Before We Were Members," 8; Nettels, "History Out of Wisconsin," 115; Vernon Carstensen to Merle Curti, July 1, 1951, FF 18, DB 8, Curti Papers, WHS.

15. John R. Wunder, "The Founding Years of the OAH," *OAH Newsletter* 34 (November 2006); Novick, *That Noble Dream*, 182; Ian Tyrell, "Public at the Creation: Place, Memory, and Historical Practice in the Mississippi Valley Historical Association, 1907–1950," *Journal of American History* 94, no. 1 (June 2007): 27.

16. Novick, *That Noble Dream*, 183.

17. Some leaders of the MVHA objected to the president, Dunbar Rowland, sending his statement on MVHA letterhead without having the MVHA's approval, and Professor Claude H. Van Tyne of the University of Michigan resigned from the board of editors in protest. See numerous letters in Vol. 2, MVHA Correspondence, Alvord Papers, State Historical Society of Missouri (SHSM). Alvord generally tried to keep the MVHA out of the AHA "fiasco." Clarence Alvord to Van Tyne, October 18, 1915, Vol. 2, MVHA Correspondence, Alvord Papers, SHSM. Early MVHA leaders Benjamin Shambaugh and Frederic Logan Paxson opposed being drawn into the AHA imbroglio. Paxson to Alvord, November 12, 1915, and Shambaugh to Alvord, November 13, 1915, both in Vol. 2, MVHA Correspondence, Alvord Papers, SHSM. The AHA reform movement was led by Frederic Bancroft. Alvord to MVHR Board of Editors,

October 1, 1915, Vol. 2, MVHA Correspondence, Alvord Papers, SHSM; Paxson to Turner, January 23, 1915, Turner Papers, Huntington Library. The MVHA's neutrality in the AHA battle stemmed in part from the fact that Turner, then at Harvard, was being attacked as part of the AHA "oligarchy." R. R. Palmer, "The American Historical Association in 1970," *American Historical Review* 76, no. 1 (February 1971): 5. Turner sought moderate reforms within the AHA. Ray Allen Billington, "Tempest in Clio's Teapot: The American Historical Association Rebellion of 1915," *American Historical Review* 78, no. 2 (April 1973): 354. See also Allan G. Bogue, *Frederick Jackson Turner: Strange Roads Going Down* (Norman: University of Oklahoma Press, 1998), 305–319.

18. Shambaugh, "Sixteenth Annual Meeting of the Mississippi Valley Historical Association," 113; Kammen, "Mississippi Valley Historical Association," 18–20.

19. Wunder, "Founding Years of the OAH."

20. Alvord believed that the AHA had "been run by a ring." Alvord to Dunbar Rowland, October 19, 1915, Vol. 2, MVHA Correspondence, Alvord Papers, SHSM; Solon J. Buck, "Clarence Walworth Alvord, Historian," *MVHR* 15, no. 3 (December 1928): 314; Wunder, "Founding Years of the OAH"; Theodore C. Blegen, "Our Widening Province," *MVHR* 31, no. 1 (June 1944): 5; James L. Sellers, "The Semicentennial of the Mississippi Valley Historical Association," *MVHR* 44, no. 3 (December 1957): 498 ("good deal"). For more on the formative growth of the MVHA, see Tyrell, "Public at the Creation," 19–46.

21. Clarence W. Alvord, "The Study and Writing of History in the Mississippi Valley," in Shambaugh, *Proceedings of the Mississippi Valley Historical Association*, 1:101, 104.

22. Buck, "Clarence Walworth Alvord," 309–314. On the work at Illinois, see Dixon Ryan Fox, "State History II," *Political Science Quarterly* 37, no. 1 (March 1922): 99–118.

23. Frederic Logan Paxson, *History of the American Frontier, 1763–1893* (Boston: Houghton Mifflin, 1924), preface, 111, n.1.

24. By 1934, Shambaugh had already published 720 works. Julian P. Boyd, "State and Local Historical Societies in the United States," *American Historical Review* 40, no. 1 (October 1934): 31.

25. Shambaugh received his B.A. and M.A. from the University of Iowa and his Ph.D. from the Wharton School. He transformed the *Iowa Historical Record* into the more scholarly *Iowa Journal of History and Politics* in 1903. Wunder, "Founding Years of the OAH," n.13; William D. Aeschbacher, "The Mississippi Valley Historical Association, 1907–1965," *Journal of American History* 54, no. 2 (September 1967): 348; Alan M. Schroder, "Benjamin F. Shambaugh," in *Historians of the American Frontier*, ed. John R. Wunder (Westport, Conn.: Greenwood Press, 1988), 611–612.

26. See letters discussing creation of the *MVHR*, 1913–1914, Vol. 1, MVHA Correspondence, Alvord Papers, SHSM; Buck, "Clarence Walworth Alvord," 315.

27. Board of Editors Minutes, December 29, 1913, Vol. 1, MVHA Correspondence, Alvord Papers, SHSM.

28. Alvord to Albert Friedenberg, March 17, 1914, Vol. 1, MVHA Correspondence, Alvord Papers, SHSM.

29. Wunder, "Founding Years of the OAH"; David Thelen, "Of Audiences, Borderlands, and Comparisons: Toward the Internationalization of American History," *Journal of American History* 79, no. 2 (September 1992): 436; Rebecca Conard,

Benjamin Shambaugh and the Intellectual Foundations of Public History (Iowa City: University of Iowa Press, 2002), 11. Shambaugh analyzed Iowa's constitutional development in *The Constitutions of Iowa* (Iowa City: State Historical Society of Iowa, 1934). See also "Benjamin F. Shambaugh," *Palimpsest* 21, no. 5 (May 1940): 133–139. On the importance afforded by historians to training secondary teachers in the early twentieth century, see Robert B. Townsend, *History's Babel: Scholarship, Professionalization, and the Historical Enterprise in the United States, 1880-1940* (Chicago: University of Chicago Press, 2013).

30. Shambaugh, "Sixteenth Annual Meeting of the Mississippi Valley Historical Association," 112.

31. Alvord to MVHR Board of Editors, March 31, 1914, Vol. 1, MVHA Correspondence, Alvord Papers, SHSM.

32. Shambaugh to Alvord, April 3, 1914, Vol. 1, MVHA Correspondence, Alvord Papers, SHSM.

33. Paxson, *History of the American Frontier*, preface.

34. Pease was a professor of history at Illinois from 1914 to 1948. W. N. Davis Jr., Fred Dietz, and Robert S. Fletcher, "Historical News and Comments," *MVHR* 35, no. 4 (March 1949): 719–720. Illinois also produced Clarence E. Carter, born in Jacksonville, Illinois, who earned his B.A. from Illinois, his M.A. from Wisconsin, and his Ph.D. from Illinois in 1908. He taught at Miami University in Ohio, and then edited the massive *Territorial Papers* series for the Department of State and then the National Archives, a series that included many midwestern states. Solon J. Buck, "Clarence E. Carter, 1881–1961," *American Archivist* 25, no. 1 (January 1962): 59–60. The Territorial Papers Act of 1925 required the secretary of state to collect and publish these papers. *Territorial Papers of the United States Senate, 1789–1873* (Washington, D.C.: National Archives and Records Service, General Services Administration, 1973), 1. See Carter's 1955 MVHA presentation, reprinted as Clarence E. Carter, "The Territorial Papers of the United States: A Review and a Commentary," *MVHR* 42, no. 3 (December 1955): 510–524; and Carter's 1938 presidential address to the MVHA, "The United States and Documentary Historical Publication," *MVHR* 25 (June 1938): 3–24.

35. Pelzer was born to a German farm family in Cass County, Iowa. See Pelzer file, Special Collections Department, University of Iowa Libraries.

36. Martin Ridge, "Turner the Historian: A Long Shadow," *Journal of the Early Republic* 13, no. 2 (Summer 1993): 137; W. L. Williamson, "A Sidelight on the Frontier Thesis: A New Turner Letter," *Newberry Library Bulletin* 3 (April 1953): 46–49; Robert P. Wilkins, "Orin G. Libby, 1864–1952," *Arizona and the West* 16, no. 2 (Summer 1974): 107; Gordon L. Iseminger, "Dr. Orin G. Libby: A Centennial Commemoration of the Father of North Dakota History," *North Dakota History* 68, no. 4 (2001): 2–3.

37. Boyd, "State and Local Historical Societies," 32.

38. Barnhart to Hicks, n.d., FF 1925, Carton 13, Hicks Papers, Bancroft Library; "Memorial Tribute to John D. Barnhart," *Indiana Magazine of History* 64, no. 2 (June 1968): 109–112. Barnhart taught at Nebraska, Nebraska Wesleyan, and Minnesota Teachers College–Morehead.

39. Paxson to Turner, May 1, 1906, and Paxson to Turner, March 30, 1910, both in Turner Papers, Huntington Library; Ira G. Clark, "Frederic Logan Paxson, 1877–1948," *Journal of the Southwest* 3, no. 2 (Summer 1961): 107.

40. Paul Hass, "Reflections on 150 Years of Publishing," *Wisconsin Magazine of*

History 88, no. 2 (Winter 2004–2005): 4–5; John D. Hicks, "My Ten Years on the Wisconsin Faculty," *Wisconsin Magazine of History* 48, no. 4 (Summer 1965): 308; William B. Hesseltine, *Pioneer's Mission: The Story of Lyman Copeland Draper* (Madison: State Historical Society of Wisconsin, 1954).

41. Turner started teaching at Wisconsin in 1889 and "for the next dozen years was a staunch friend and colleague of Thwaites and an eloquent booster of the Society, which inspired his research and teaching for forty years." Thwaites edited the *Collections*, edited and published 168 books, and also wrote 15 books himself. Hass, "Reflections," 5. See Frederick Jackson Turner, *Reuben Gold Thwaites: A Memorial Address* (Madison: State Historical Society of Wisconsin, 1914). When Turner returned to Wisconsin in 1889, he started "a formal seminary" in the Society library and started to study the "social foundations of American history." Wisconsin granted its first doctorate in history in 1893. Nettels, "History Out of Wisconsin," 114.

42. Paxson, who served on the search committee for a new leader of the Society, said Quaife's history of Chicago was the "kind of historical work that we should like to see associated with the Society." Paxson to Turner, December 11, 1913, Turner Papers, Huntington Library.

43. Quaife later moved to the Detroit Public Library to oversee the Burton Historical Collection, becoming known as the "unofficial voice of Midwestern history." David A. Walker, "Milo Milton Quaife," in Wunder, *Historians of the American Frontier*, 497–499; John D. Hicks, "State and Local History," *Wisconsin Magazine of History* 39, no. 2 (Winter 1955–1956): 136.

44. Hass, "Reflections," 8.

45. These included Libby, Thwaites, Paxson, Quaife, Buck, Schafer, Louise Kellogg, John D. Hicks, Carter, Frederick Merk, and Merle Curti. Nettels, "History Out of Wisconsin," 115. Underscoring the leadership role taken by the State Historical Society of Wisconsin, Paxson said that the Society wanted to "keep ahead of our neighbors" in other states. Paxson to Turner, November 10, 1913, Turner Papers, Huntington Library.

46. Margaret Landis, "Connelley Kept Record Straight," *Kansan*, November 17, 1985; Edgar Langsdorf, "The First Hundred Years of the Kansas State Historical Society," *Kansas Historical Quarterly* 41 (1975): 265–425; Anne Polk Diffendal, "A Centennial History of the Nebraska State Historical Society, 1878–1978," *Nebraska History* 59, no. 3 (Fall 1978): 333–334, 345–349, 357–364 (also noting friction between Paine and Sheldon); Mary Wheelhouse Berthel and Harold Dean Carter, "The Minnesota Historical Society: Highlights of a Century," *Minnesota History* 30, no. 4 (December 1949): 313–315; Russell W. Fridley, "Critical Choices for the 'Minnesota Historical Society,'" *Minnesota History* 46, no. 4 (Winter 1978): 134, 136; James Sellers, "A. E. Sheldon's History Gives Complete Story of State Development," *Nebraska History* 13 (June 1932): 110–112; Robert L. Dorman, *Hell of a Vision: Regionalism and the Modern American West* (Tucson: University of Arizona Press, 2012), 34–35. On Iowa, see Benjamin F. Shambaugh, "A Brief History of the State Historical Society of Iowa," *Iowa Journal of History and Politics* 1 (1903): 139–152.

47. On Merk's admiration for Turner, see Rodman W. Paul, "Frederick Merk, Teacher and Scholar: A Tribute," *Western Historical Quarterly* 9, no. 2 (April 1978): 142; and Wilbur R. Jacobs, *On Turner's Trail: 100 Years of Writing Western History* (Lawrence: University Press of Kansas, 1994), 179–186.

48. Frederick B. Merk to author, May 24, 2012. Merk's family "had been part of the

great nineteenth century German migration to Wisconsin." Ruth Karp, "Frederick Merk: Fifty–Third President of the Mississippi Valley Historical Association" (graduate thesis, Northwestern University, 1967), 1. I want to extend particular thanks to Frederick B. Merk III, the son of Prairie Historian Frederick Merk, for his generous help with this project and for sharing materials about his father, including the Karp thesis.

49. Hicks to Barnhart, May 21, 1932, Barnhart Papers, Lilly Library, Indiana University. Paxson said he would "leave Madison the happier knowing that you are going to carry on." Paxson to Hicks, May 14, 1932, FF 1932, Carton 13, Hicks Papers, Bancroft Library. Paxson said Hicks "is a wise man and makes a good platform appearance." Paxson to Mr. Williams, August 20, 1932, FF 1932, Carton 13, Hicks Papers, Bancroft Library. Before leaving Nebraska, Hicks arranged for the MVHA to meet in Lincoln. Dwight Bedell to Hicks, June 18, 1931, FF MVHA Correspondence 1931–57, DB 5, James Sellers Papers, University of Nebraska Archives. On Hicks's background, see John D. Hicks, "The Significance of the Small Town in American History," in *Reflections of Western Historians*, ed. John Alexander Carroll (Tucson: University of Arizona Press, 1967), 155–166.

50. Paxson told Hicks that "your Nebraska group stands high at Wisconsin" and that the "Nebraska reputation is excellent" and singled out Dick as one "of your boys" whom he was "glad to have." Dick said that Paxson took Hicks's "word as law in regard to Nebraska graduates." Paxson to Hicks, October 8, 1928, Dick to Hicks, December 17, 1928, Paxson to Hicks, January 25, 1929, and Paxson to Hicks, January 22, 1930, all in Carton 13, Hicks Papers, Bancroft Library; Christine Nasso, ed., "Everett Dick," *Contemporary Authors* (Detroit: Gale Research, 1977), 25:188–189. Hicks claimed Dick as "one of my discoveries" at Nebraska. Hicks to Stanley Pargellis, March 8, 1948, FF January–March 1948 Correspondence, DB 14, Hicks Papers, Bancroft Library. James Sellers, who was born in North Platte, Nebraska, also earned his Ph.D. from Wisconsin in 1922, taught at Nebraska from 1930 to 1959, edited *Nebraska History*, and served as president of the MVHA. James C. Olson, "James Lee Sellers," *Nebraska History* 47, no. 2 (June 1966): 123–126.

51. Buley to Stanley Pargellis, August 15, 1944, Buley Papers, Indiana Historical Society; R. Carlyle Buley, *The Old Northwest: Pioneer Period, 1815–1840*, 2 vols. (Indianapolis: Indiana Historical Society, 1950). At Indiana, Buley followed in the tradition of Logan Esarey, who was from rural Indiana, earned an Indiana Ph.D., and launched the professional study of the state's history. R. Carlyle Buley, "Logan Esarey, Hoosier," *Indiana Magazine of History* 38, no. 4 (December 1942): 348.

52. Pelzer also edited the *MVHR* from 1941 to 1946. Ellis earned his M.A. at the University of North Dakota under Libby, and at Missouri Ellis trained historians Lewis Atherton, from Missouri, and Gilbert Fite, from South Dakota. During these years, Fred Shannon also earned his Ph.D. at Iowa working under Arthur Schlesinger Sr. His dissertation became the Pulitzer Prize–winning two-volume book *The Organization and Administration of the Union Army, 1861–1865* (Cleveland: Arthur H. Clark, 1928). Robert H. Jones, "Fred Albert Shannon," *Great Plains Journal* 19 (1979): 55.

53. Malin said that Hodder "meant more to the cause of history in Kansas that any other man." James C. Malin, "Frank Heywood Hodder, 1860–1935," *Kansas Historical Quarterly* 5, no. 2 (May 1936): 115; Thomas B. Colbert, "James C. Malin," *Great Plains Journal* 19 (1979): 48. At first, Hodder was not enthused about the MVHA, but became its president in 1925. Alvord, Shambaugh, and James E. James Memo to

MVHA Executive Committee, circa 1913, Vol. 1, MVHA Correspondence, Alvord Papers, SHSM; Buck to Alvord, April 6, 1916, Vol. 2, MVHA Correspondence, Alvord Papers, SHSM. In the 1890s, Hodder was the only history professor at Kansas. John V. Mering, "Frank Heywood Hodder, 1860–1935," *Arizona and the West* 14, no. 2 (Summer 1972): 111.

54. Boyd, "State and Local Historical Societies," 28, 33; Andrew R. L. Cayton and Susan E. Gray, "The Story of the Midwest: An Introduction," in *The Identity of the American Midwest: Essays on Regional History*, ed. Andrew R. L. Cayton and Susan E. Gray (Bloomington: Indiana University Press, 2001), 22; Buley, *Old Northwest*, 1:551–556; Eric Hinderaker, "Liberating Contrivances: Narrative and Identity in Midwestern Histories," in Cayton and Gray, *Identity of the American Midwest*, 53–65, 215, n.34.

55. Buck to Alvord, May 3, 1916, Vol. 2, MVHA Correspondence, Alvord Papers, SHSM.

56. Clara Paine to Alvord, October 18, 1916, Vol. 2, MVHA Correspondence, Alvord Papers, SHSM.

57. Buck, "Clarence Walworth Alvord," 311.

58. Buck, "Clarence Walworth Alvord," 311–312. The series included Buck's *Illinois in 1818* (1917), Pease's *The Frontier State, 1818–1848* (1918), and Alvord's *The Illinois Country, 1673–1818* (1920).

59. J. G. Randall, "Theodore Calvin Pease," *Journal of the Illinois State Historical Society* 41, no. 4 (December 1948): 354, 357–359; Davis, Dietz, and Fletcher, "Historical News and Comments," 720.

60. Randall, "Theodore Calvin Pease," 361–362; Davis, Dietz, and Fletcher, "Historical News and Comments," 720. Pease was also chairman of the AHA's Manuscripts Commission. The Society of American Archivists held its second annual meeting in Springfield, Illinois, in 1938.

61. Randall, "Theodore Calvin Pease," 362.

62. Blegen to Barnhart, November 12, 1931, Barnhart Papers, Lilly Library, Indiana University; Theodore C. Blegen, "Solon Justus Buck: Scholar–Administrator," *American Archivist* 23, no. 3 (July 1960): 259–261; Robert L. Dorman, *Revolt of the Provinces: The Regionalist Movement in America, 1920–1945* (Chapel Hill: University of North Carolina Press, 1993), 117. Buck tried to hire Hicks to work at the Minnesota Historical Society when Hicks was at Hamline University. John D. Hicks, "My Six Years at Hamline," *Minnesota History* 39, no. 6 (Summer 1965): 220.

63. Wilkins, "Orin G. Libby," 108; Iseminger, "Dr. Orin G. Libby," 6–7; Waldemar Westergaard, "Orin Grant Libby," *North Dakota Historical Quarterly* 42, no. 1 (Summer 1956): 70.

64. Unknown to Paxson, December 12, 1913, Libby Papers, University of North Dakota; Wilkins, "Orin G. Libby," 110.

65. Barnhart to Hicks, June 19, 1928, FF 1928, Carton 13, Hicks Papers, Bancroft Library. On such journals, see James H. Rodabaugh, "Historical Societies: Their Magazines and Their Editors," *Wisconsin Magazine of History* 45, no. 2 (Winter 1961–1962): 115–123.

66. Solon J. Buck, "The Progress and Possibilities of Mississippi Valley History," *MVHR* 10, no. 1 (June 1923): 5–6. See also Solon J. Buck, "The Upper Missouri Historical Expedition," *MVHR* 12, no. 3 (December 1925): 385–391.

67. Hicks, "State and Local History," 137; Shambaugh, *Constitutions of Iowa*, 11;

Schroder, "Benjamin F. Shambaugh," 614; Walker, "Milo Milton Quaife," 98–110; Robert Galen Bell, "James C. Malin and the Grasslands of North America," *Agricultural History* 46, no. 3 (July 1972): 415.

68. Theodore C. Blegen, *Grassroots History* (Minneapolis: University of Minnesota Press, 1947), 5. Theodore Blegen said that Solon Buck's "instruction turned me away from the Stuart period of English history into American western and American social history," and Blegen became a strong champion of local history. Blegen, "Solon Justus Buck," 260. See also Turner to Blegen, March 16, 1923, Blegen Papers, University of Minnesota Archives.

69. Buck to Blegen, February 4, 1937, Box 6, Buck Papers, National Archives; Merk to Malin, March 15, 1952, Mss. Coll. 183, Malin Papers, Kansas State Historical Society (KSHS). See also Gilbert C. Fite, "The American West of Farmers and Stockmen," in *Historians and the American West*, ed. Michael P. Malone (Lincoln: University of Nebraska Press, 1983), 217.

70. Allan G. Bogue, "Tilling Agricultural History with Paul Wallace Gates and James C. Malin," *Agricultural History* 80, no. 4 (Autumn 2006): 437, 448, 453.

71. Hicks, "State and Local History," 137.

72. Buck to Barnhart, January 18, 1938, Barnhart Papers, Lilly Library, Indiana University; James C. Malin, "On the Nature of Local History," *Wisconsin Magazine of History* 40, no. 4 (Summer 1957): 227; Frederic L. Paxson, "A Generation of the Frontier Hypothesis: 1893–1932," *Pacific Historical Review* 2, no. 1 (March 1933): 39; Iseminger, "Dr. Orin G. Libby," 3.

73. Buck, "Clarence Walworth Alvord," 320.

74. Malin, "On the Nature of Local History," 228.

75. Malin, "On the Nature of Local History," 228.

76. Board of Editors Minutes, December 29, 1913, Vol. 1, MVHA Correspondence, Alvord Papers, SHSM; Shambaugh to Alvord, January 16, 1914, Vol. 1, MVHA Correspondence, Alvord Papers, SHSM.

77. Alvord circular letter, March 7, 1914, Vol. 1, MVHA Correspondence, Alvord Papers, SHSM; Alvord to the Authors of "Historical Activities," February 10, 1914, Vol. 1, MVHA Correspondence, Alvord Papers, SHSM; Sellers to Buck, August 2, 1929, Sellers Papers, University of Nebraska Archives. When searching for an editor of the *MVHR*, Sellers said that the MVHA "can hardly afford to go east of the Alleghenies to secure an editor; Princeton of all the eastern schools has had the least contact with the school of frontier history and, it seems to me, is completely disqualified to take over the editorship." Sellers to Hicks, July 17, 1940, Sellers Papers, University of Nebraska Archives.

78. Alvord authored circular, January 30, 1914, Vol. 1, MVHA Correspondence, Alvord Papers, SHSM; Clarence Paine to Alvord, March 4, 1914, Vol. 1, MVHA Correspondence, Alvord Papers, SHSM.

79. Alvord to Clarence Paine, June 17, 1914, Vol. 1, MVHA Correspondence, Alvord Papers, SHSM; Vernon Carstensen to Merle Curti, February 14, 1951, FF 18, DB 8, Curti Papers, WHS; Gates to Ray Billington, November 15, 1951, Gates Papers, Cornell University.

80. Alvord to Clarence Paine, June 24, 1914, Vol. 1, MVHA Correspondence, Alvord Papers, SHSM.

81. Sellers, "Semicentennial of the Mississippi Valley Historical Association," 516–517. For a negative assessment of the MVHA's regionalism, see Ray Allen Billington,

"From Association to Organization: The OAH in the Bad Old Days," *Journal of American History* 65, no. 1 (June 1978): 75–84.

82. Richard Jensen, "On Modernizing Frederick Jackson Turner: The Historiography of Regionalism," *Western Historical Quarterly* 11, no. 3 (July 1980): 307; Jacobs, *On Turner's Trail*, 158; Kerwin Lee Klein, *Frontiers of Historical Imagination: Narrating the European Conquest of Native America, 1890–1990* (Berkeley: University of California Press, 1999), 92–96; Martin Ridge, "Frederick Jackson Turner and His Ghost: The Writing of Western History," in *Writing the History of the American West* (Worcester, Mass.: American Antiquarian Society, 1991), 68.

83. Earle D. Ross, "A Generation of Prairie Historiography," *MVHR* 33, no. 3 (December 1946): 392–393.

84. Steiner, "Significance of Turner's Sectional Thesis," 442 (quoting Turner); Billington, "Why Some Historians Rarely Write History," 12–13.

85. Frederick Jackson Turner, "Is Sectionalism in America Dying Away?" *American Journal of Sociology* 13, no. 5 (March 1908): 661–662; Turner to Barnhart, April 1, 1931, Barnhart Papers, Lilly Library, Indiana University.

86. Steiner, "Significance of Turner's Sectional Thesis," 439. Turner was posthumously awarded the Pulitzer Prize for his book *The Significance of Sections in American History* (New York: Henry Holt, 1932). Turner used the term "sectionalism" because the term "regionalism" was "not widely used in the United States until the last decade of his life." Michael C. Steiner, "Frontier to Region: Frederick Jackson Turner and the New Western History," *Pacific Historical Review* 64, no. 4 (November 1995): 486.

87. Fulmer Mood, "The Theory of the History of an American Section in the Practice of R. Carlyle Buley," *Indiana Magazine of History* 48, no. 1 (March 1952): 14.

88. Turner quoted in Allan G. Bogue, "The Significance of the History of the American West: Postscripts and Prospects," *Western Historical Quarterly* 24, no. 1 (February 1993): 48. See also Martin Ridge, "The Life of an Idea: The Significance of Frederick Jackson Turner's Frontier Thesis," *Montana: The Magazine of Western History* 41, no. 1 (Winter 1991): 11.

89. Clarence Paine to Alvord, October 9, 1915, Vol. 2, MVHA Correspondence, Alvord Papers, SHSM; Katz, "Rise of a Modern and Democratic Learned Society," 14.

90. Paxson, *History of the American Frontier*, 7, n.3.

91. Paxson to Turner, November 2, 1910, Turner Papers, Huntington Library; Hicks, "My Ten Years on the Wisconsin Faculty," 306; John D. Hicks, "Historical News and Comments," *MVHR* 36, no. 2 (September 1949): 372.

92. Frederick Merk to Merle Curti, March 21, 1959, FF 1, DB 26, Curti Papers, WHS; David C. Smith, "Frederick Merk and the Frontier Experience: A Review Essay," *Wisconsin Magazine of History* 63, no. 2 (Winter 1979–1980): 143.

93. Schroder, "Benjamin F. Shambaugh," 613; "Memorial Tribute to John D. Barnhart," 110.

94. Morton Rothstein interview, University of Wisconsin Collection #92, 1976.

95. John Morton Blum, "A Celebration of Frederick Merk, 1887–1977," *Virginia Quarterly Review* 54, no. 3 (Summer 1978).

96. Paxson, "Generation of the Frontier Hypothesis," 43–46; Gerald D. Nash, *Creating the West: Historical Interpretations, 1890–1990* (Albuquerque: University of New Mexico Press, 1991), 30, 35; Louis Pelzer, Merle Curti, Edward Everett Dale, Everett Dick, and Paul W. Gates, "Projects in American History and Culture," *MVHR* 31, no. 4 (March 1945): 510.

97. Blegen to Curti, May 25, 1944, FF 4, DB 6, Curti Papers, WHS; Buck letter, September 27, 1935, Box 6, Buck Papers, National Archives. See Theodore C. Blegen, *Norwegian Migration to America*, 2 vols. (Northfield, Minn.: Norwegian-American Historical Association, 1931–1940). The Prairie Historians also frequently corresponded with Turner's student Marcus Hansen, who was from Iowa, and Carl Wittke, who was from Ohio. Hansen and Wittke both emphasized immigration. See Marcus L. Hansen, *The Atlantic Migration, 1607–1860* (Cambridge, Mass.: Harvard University Press, 1940), which won the Pulitzer Prize in 1941, and Carl F. Wittke, *We Who Built America: The Saga of the Immigrant* (New York: Prentice–Hall, 1939). See also Joseph Schafer, *The Yankee and the Teuton in Wisconsin* (Menasha, Wis.: n.p., 1922).

98. Nash, *Creating the West*, 31.

99. Paxson to Malin, November 16, 1936, Mss. Coll. 183, Malin Papers, KSHS ("good row"); Paxson to Joseph Schafer, FF 5, DB 3, Schafer Papers, WHS; Gates to Merk, May 1, 1935, Gates Papers, Cornell University; Fred Shannon to Ray Billington, August 9, 1945, FF Ray A. Billington, DB 1, Shannon Papers, University of Illinois Archives; Buley, *Old Northwest*, 1:10, n.17; Fred A. Shannon, "A Post Mortem on the Labor-Safety Valve Theory," *Agricultural History* 19, no. 1 (January 1945): 31–37; Joseph Schafer, "Was the West a Safety Valve for Labor?" *MVHR* 24 (1937): 299–314; Henry M. Littlefield, "Has the Safety Valve Come Back to Life?" *Agricultural History* 28 (January 1964): 47–49.

100. Paxson to Malin, February 7, 1947, Mss. Coll. 183, Malin Papers, KSHS; Paxson to Joseph Schafer, FF 5, DB 3, Schafer Papers, WHS.

101. Frederick Merk to Merle Curti, December 15, 1949, FF 1, DB 26, Curti Papers, WHS.

102. Nash, *Creating the West*, 64–65; Steiner, "Significance of Turner's Sectional Thesis," 444; Steiner, "Frontier to Region," 491–492; Bogue, *Frederick Jackson Turner*, 55, 185, 195, 205. On Turner as the "key figure in [the] reorientation of American historiography" toward immigration, see Allan H. Spear, "Marcus Lee Hansen and the Historiography of Immigration," *Wisconsin Magazine of History* 44, no. 4 (Summer 1961): 258–259.

103. Frederick Jackson Turner, "The Development of American Society," *Alumni Quarterly* (University of Illinois) 2 (1908): 121, RS 26/2/801, University of Illinois Archives; Merle Curti, "The Democratic Theme in American Historical Literature," *MVHR* 39, no. 1 (June 1952): 13; Nash, *Creating the West*, 47. See the excellent discussion of this point in Donald G. Holtgrieve, "Frederick Jackson Turner as a Regionalist," *Professional Geographer* 17 (May 1974): 159–165.

104. Richard Hofstadter, *The Progressive Historians: Turner, Beard, Parrington* (New York: Knopf, 1968), 95.

105. Alvord, "Study and Writing of History," 101; Clarence Walworth Alvord, "The Relation of the State to Historical Work," *Minnesota History Bulletin* 1, no. 1 (February 1915): 16.

106. Paxson, *History of the American Frontier*, 7; Frederic Logan Paxson, *When the West Is Gone* (New York: Henry Holt, 1930), 33.

107. Buley, *Old Northwest*, 2:1.

108. John D. Barnhart, *Valley of Democracy: The Frontier versus Plantation in the Ohio Valley, 1775–1818* (Bloomington: Indiana University Press, 1953), 7; "Memorial Tribute to John D. Barnhart," 110; John D. Barnhart, "Sources of Southern Migration into the Old Northwest," *MVHR* 22 (1936): 49–62; John D. Barnhart, "The Southern

Influence in the Formation of Indiana," *Indiana Magazine of History* 33 (1937): 261–276; John D. Barnhart, "The Southern Influence in the Formation of Illinois," *Journal of the Illinois State Historical Society* 32 (1939): 358–378.

109. Orin G. Libby, "Some Aspects of Mid-West America," *Minnesota History Bulletin* 4, nos. 5–6 (February–May 1922): 214.

110. Pelzer et al., "Projects in American History and Culture," 510.

111. Shambaugh, *Constitutions of Iowa*, 25.

112. John D. Barnhart, "The Democratization of Indiana Territory," *Indiana Magazine of History* 43, no. 1 (March 1947): 9–10.

113. Buley, *Old Northwest*, 1:31. See also R. Carlyle Buley, "The Middle West: Its Heritage and Its Role," *Wabash Bulletin* (December 1943): 12–13.

114. Buley, *Old Northwest*, 2:2.

115. Buley, *Old Northwest*, 2:489.

116. "Atlantic History" started in the 1970s, but the 1990s "saw the greatest explosion of Atlantic scholarship." Alison Games, "Atlantic History: Definitions, Challenges, and Opportunities," *American Historical Review* 111, no. 3 (June 2006): 744. If one reads the Prairie Historians, this perspective is not a "surprisingly recent phenomenon," as Games writes. Games, "Atlantic History," 745. Martin Ridge has explained Turner's emphasis on writing about the broader world. Ridge, "Turner the Historian," 137.

117. Francois Furstenberg, "The Significance of the Trans-Appalachian Frontier in Atlantic History," *American Historical Review* 113, no. 3 (June 2008): 676; Bogue, *Frederick Jackson Turner*, 189.

118. Furstenberg, "Significance of the Trans–Appalachian Frontier," 676.

119. Furstenberg, "Significance of the Trans-Appalachian Frontier," 676–677.

120. Jack P. Greene, "Colonial History and National History: Reflections on a Continuing Problem," *William and Mary Quarterly* 64, no. 2 (April 2007): 235.

121. Frederick Jackson Turner, "The Significance of History," *Wisconsin Journal of Education* 21 (October–November 1891): 230–234, 253, reprinted in Ray Allen Billington, ed., *Frontier and Section: Selected Essays of Frederick Jackson Turner* (Englewood Cliffs, N.J.: Prentice-Hall, 1961), 26.

122. Clarence Walworth Alvord, "When Minnesota Was a Pawn of International Politics," *Minnesota History Bulletin* 4, nos. 7–8 (August—November 1922): 309–330.

123. Clarence Walworth Alvord, *The Mississippi Valley in British Politics: A Study of Trade, Land Speculation, and Experiments in Imperialism Culminating in the American Revolution*, 2 vols. (Cleveland: Arthur Clark, 1917). Alvord cowrote (with Lee Bidgood) *The First Explorations of the Trans-Allegheny Region by the Virginians, 1650–1674* (Cleveland: Arthur Clark, 1912). Buck, "Clarence Walworth Alvord, Historian," 313. See Alvord, "When Minnesota Was a Pawn," 309–330.

124. H. E. Egerton, review of Clarence Walworth Alvord, *The Mississippi Valley in British Politics*, in *English Historical Review* 32, no. 126 (April 1917): 299. Another reviewer called the book a "classic." Philip C. Sturges, *Western Political Quarterly* 14, no. 1, part 1 (March 1961): 242.

125. Buck, "Clarence Walworth Alvord," 318–319. See also Clarence Walworth Alvord and Clarence Carter, *The Critical Period, 1763–65* (Springfield: Illinois State Historical Library, 1915); Clarence Walworth Alvord and Clarence Carter, *The New Regime, 1765–1767* (Springfield: Illinois State Historical Library, 1916); Clarence Carter, *Great Britain and the Illinois Country, 1763–1774* (Washington, D.C.:

American Historical Association, 1910); Reuben Gold Thwaites, *How George Rogers Clark Won the Northwest* (Chicago: A. C. McClurg, 1903); Theodore C. Pease, with Ernestine Jackson, *Illinois on the Eve of the Seven Years' War, 1747–1755* (Springfield: Illinois State Historical Library, 1940); John D. Barnhart, *Henry Hamilton and George Rogers Clark in the American Revolution with the Unpublished Journal of Lieut. Gov. Henry Hamilton* (Crawfordsville, Ind.: R. E. Banta, 1951); Theodore C. Pease, "The Ordinance of 1787," *MVHR* 25, no. 2 (September 1938): 167–180; and Theodore C. Pease, "1780: The Revolution at Crisis in the West," *Journal of the Illinois State Historical Society* 23, no. 4 (January 1931): 664–681.

126. Paxson, *History of the American Frontier*, 1; Frederic Logan Paxson, *The Independence of the South American Republics: A Study in Recognition and Foreign Policy* (Philadelphia: Ferris and Leach, 1903).

127. Thomas C. McClintock, "Frederick Merk," in Wunder, *Historians of the American Frontier*, 429. See Frederick Merk, *The Oregon Question: Essays in Anglo-American Diplomacy and Politics* (Cambridge, Mass.: Harvard University Press, 1967); Frederick Merk, *Albert Gallatin and the Oregon Problem: A Study in Anglo-American Diplomacy* (Cambridge, Mass.: Harvard University Press, 1950). See also Frederic Logan Paxson, "Washington and the Western Fronts, 1753–1795," *Journal of the Illinois State Historical Society* 24, no. 4 (January 1932): 589–605.

128. Blum, "Celebration of Frederick Merk."

129. Nash, *Creating the West*, 17–18, 108–110; Steiner, "Significance of Turner's Sectional Thesis," 458. The diplomatic historian Samuel Flagg Bemis earned his Ph.D. at Harvard in 1916 "with Turner's advice" and studied early American diplomacy and wrote books such as *Jay's Treaty: A Study in Commerce and Diplomacy* (New York: Macmillan, 1923), and *Pinckney's Treaty* (Baltimore: Johns Hopkins University Press, 1926). Nash, *Creating the West*, 19.

130. Bogue, *Frederick Jackson Turner*, 434.

131. Barnhart, *Valley of Democracy*, 19; Paxson, *History of the American Frontier*, 7.

132. Paxson, *History of the American Frontier*, 8.

133. Paxson, *History of the American Frontier*, 97.

134. Alvord, "When Minnesota Was a Pawn," 312.

135. Barnhart, *Valley of Democracy*, 20.

136. Paxson, *History of the American Frontier*, 11.

137. Barnhart, *Valley of Democracy*, 9; Paxson, *History of the American Frontier*, 80.

138. Paxson, *History of the American Frontier*, 104.

139. Paxson, *History of the American Frontier*, 94.

140. Paxson, *History of the American Frontier*, 95.

141. Nettels, "History Out of Wisconsin," 116; Furstenberg, "Significance of the Trans-Appalachian Frontier," 676; Ridge, "Turner the Historian," 137; Kammen, "Mississippi Valley Historical Association," 22, 28–29.

142. O. G. Libby, "The New Northwest," *MVHR* 7, no. 4 (March 1921): 346.

143. Libby, "New Northwest," 346.

144. Barnhart, *Valley of Democracy*, 216.

145. Theodore Calvin Pease, *The Frontier State, 1818–1848* (Springfield: Illinois Centennial Commission, 1918), 20.

146. Frederick Merk to Merle Curti, June 28, 1926, FF 1, DB 26, Curti Papers, WHS.

147. Frederick Merk to Merle Curti, March 14, 1949, Merk to Curti, November 14, 1950, both in FF 1, DB 26, Curti Papers, WHS. A Curti student, G. D. Lillibridge from

South Dakota, also emphasized this theme. G. D. Lillibridge, *Beacon of Freedom: The Impact of American Democracy upon Britain, 1830–1870* (Philadelphia: University of Pennsylvania Press, 1955).

148. Merle Curti, "The Reputation of America Overseas, 1776–1860," *American Quarterly* 1, no. 1 (Spring 1949): 59.

149. Curti, "Reputation of America Overseas," 61–62.

150. Nettels, "History Out of Wisconsin," 115–116.

151. Frederick Jackson Turner, "The Significance of the Frontier in American History," in *Rereading Frederick Jackson Turner: "The Significance of the Frontier in American History" and Other Essays* (New Haven, Conn.: Yale University Press, 1998), 53.

152. Curti, "Democratic Theme," 10, 12–13.

153. John D. Hicks to Merle Curti, May 6, 1952, FF 17, DB 19, Curti Papers, WHS.

154. John D. Hicks, *A Short History of American Democracy* (Boston: Houghton Mifflin, 1943).

155. Merle Curti, *The Growth of American Thought* (New York: Harper & Brothers, 1943).

156. Barnhart, *Valley of Democracy*, ix.

157. Barnhart, *Valley of Democracy*, viii.

158. Barnhart, *Valley of Democracy*, 3.

159. Barnhart, *Valley of Democracy*, 3, 4.

160. Donald K. Pickens, "The Turner Thesis and Republicanism: A Historiographical Commentary," *Pacific Historical Review* 61, no. 3 (May 1992): 319–340.

161. Buley, *Old Northwest*, 1:1; Robert W. Johannsen, "Introduction," in Theodore Calvin Pease, *The Frontier State, 1818–1848* (Urbana: University of Illinois Press, 1987 [first published as Vol. 2 of the *Centennial History of Illinois* by the Illinois Centennial Commission, 1918]), xxvi.

162. Allan G. Bogue, "Social Theory and the Pioneer," *Agricultural History* 34, no. 1 (January 1960): 34, n.3.

163. Malcolm J. Rohrbough, "Louis Pelzer," in Wunder, *Historians of the American Frontier*, 487.

164. Nash, *Creating the West*, 31.

165. Merk quoted in Smith, "Frederick Merk," 145.

166. Curti treated constitutionalism as an "essential element of democracy." Curti, "Democratic Theme," 8.

167. Libby's dissertation under Turner about the ratification votes on the federal Constitution is described as "Libby's magnum opus" and the "foundation for a new sophisticated study of the Constitution," which "brought him immediate acclaim in the American historical profession." Wilkins, "Orin G. Libby," 107–108. See also Iseminger, "Dr. Orin G. Libby," 3.

168. Pease, "Ordinance of 1787," 167.

169. McLaughlin's *A Constitutional History of the United States* (New York: Appleton-Century, 1936) won the Pulitzer Prize in 1936. Curti said McLaughlin was a "pioneer" in bringing the theme of democracy into American history. Curti, "Democratic Theme," 18. See McLaughlin's presidential address to the AHA entitled "American History and American Democracy," *American Historical Review* 20, no. 2 (January 1915): 255–276, along with his *Steps in the Development of American Democracy* (New York: Abingdon Press, 1920) and "The Uses of an Historical Society," *North Dakota Historical Society Collections* 1 (1906): 53–67. Alvord also persuaded McLaughlin to

make the University of Chicago a guarantor of the *MVHR*. McLaughlin to Alvord, March 3, 1914, Vol. 1, MVHA Correspondence, Alvord Papers, SHSM.

170. Theodore Calvin Pease, *The Leveller Movement: A Study in the History and Political Theory of the English Great Civil War* (Washington, D.C.: American Historical Association, 1916). The book won the Herbert Baxter Adams prize in 1915. Johannsen, "Introduction," xv; R. Douglas Hurt, "Theodore Calvin Pease," in Wunder, *Historians of the American Frontier*, 472. The book began as an assignment in McLaughlin's seminar at Chicago. Randall, "Theodore Calvin Pease," 355, 360; Theodore Calvin Pease, *The Laws of the Northwest Territory, 1788–1800* (Springfield: Illinois State Historical Library, 1925).

171. Clark, "Frederic Logan Paxson," 108; Frederic Logan Paxson, "The Constitution of Texas, 1845," *Southwestern Historical Quarterly* 18 (April 1915): 386–398; Frederic Logan Paxson, "A Constitution of Democracy: Wisconsin, 1847," *MVHR* 2 (June 1915): 3–24; Frederic Logan Paxson, "The Admission of the 'Omnibus' States, 1889–1890," *Proceedings of the State Historical Society of Wisconsin* 49 (1911): 76–93; Frederic Logan Paxson, "Influence of Frontier Life on the Development of American Law," *Proceedings of the State Historical Society of Wisconsin* 13 (1919–1921): 477–489.

172. John D. Hicks, "My Years as a Graduate Student," *Wisconsin Magazine of History* 47, no. 4 (Summer 1964): 283. See John D. Hicks, *The Constitutions of the Northwest States* (Lincoln: University of Nebraska Studies, 1924). After moving to Berkeley, Paxson also advised Earl Pomeroy, who studied the development of western territories and drew heavily upon Clarence Carter's collections of documents about the territories. Earl Pomeroy, *The Territories and the United States, 1861–1890: Studies in Colonial Administration* (Philadelphia: University of Pennsylvania Press, 1947).

173. Hicks to Barnhart, June 4, 1935, Barnhart Papers, Lilly Library, Indiana University; John D. Barnhart, "Sources of Indiana's First Constitution," *Indiana Magazine of History* 39 (1943): 55–94; John D. Barnhart, "The Tennessee Constitution of 1796: A Product of the Old West," *Journal of Southern History* 9 (1943): 532–549; Barnhart, "Democratization of Indiana," 1–22.

174. Buck to Hicks, May 26, 1936, Box 8, Buck Papers, National Archives.

175. Hurt, "Theodore Calvin Pease," 474.

176. Steiner, "Significance of Turner's Sectional Thesis," 443.

177. Solon Buck, *The Granger Movement: A Study of Agricultural Organization and Its Political, Economic, and Social Manifestations, 1870–1880* (Cambridge, Mass.: Harvard University Press, 1913); Blegen, "Solon Justus Buck," 260. See also Solon Buck, "Agricultural Organization in Illinois, 1870–1880," *Journal of the Illinois State Historical Society* 3, no. 1 (April 1910): 10–23. Turner praises Buck's work on the Grangers in Turner to Buck, November 4, 1906, and Turner to Buck, June 24, 1910, both in Collection P1494, Box 1, Buck Papers, Minnesota Historical Society. On Turner's efforts to convince Harvard to publish Buck's Granger book, see Turner to Buck, May 1, 1912, and Turner to Buck, November 1, 1912, both in Collection P1494, Box 1, Buck Papers, Minnesota Historical Society.

178. Frederic Logan Paxson, review of Solon Buck, *The Granger Movement*, in *MVHR* 1, no. 1 (June 1914): 139.

179. Paxson, *History of the American Frontier*, 573.

180. Solon Buck, *The Agrarian Crusade* (New Haven, Conn.: Yale University Press, 1920).

181. Ridge, "Turner the Historian," 143, n.36 (on Barnhart and Turner). Merk,

Arthur Schlesinger Sr., and Barnhart agreed that Schlesinger would be the first reader of Barnhart's dissertation on Nebraska Populism. Merk to Barnhart, February 19, 1926, Barnhart Papers, Lilly Library, Indiana University; "Memorial Tribute to John D. Barnhart," 111; John D. Barnhart, "Rainfall and the Populist Party in Nebraska," *American Political Science Review* 19 (1925): 527–540; John D. Barnhart and John D. Hicks, "The Farmers' Alliance," *North Carolina Historical Review* 6 (1929): 254–280.

182. Barnhart, "Rainfall and the Populist Party," 527.

183. Paxson to Hicks, December 1, 1928, FF 1928, Carton 13, Hicks Papers, Bancroft Library; Paxson to Hicks, October 11, 1930, FF 1930, Carton 13, Hicks Papers, Bancroft Library.

184. Buck to Hicks, January 2, 1929, FF 1929, Carton 13, Hicks Papers, Bancroft Library.

185. Barnhart to Hicks, January 21, 1925, FF 1925, Carton 13, Hicks Papers, Bancroft Library; Barnhart to Hicks, December 8, 1925, FF 1916, Carton 13, Hicks Papers, Bancroft Library; Barnhart to Hicks, July 16, 1928, FF 1928, Carton 13, Hicks Papers, Bancroft Library; Barnhart to Hicks, August 13, 1930, FF 1930, Carton 13, Hicks Papers, Bancroft Library; Hicks to Barnhart, May 7, 1932, Barnhart Papers, Lilly Library, Indiana University.

186. John D. Hicks, *The Populist Revolt: A History of the Farmers' Alliance and the People's Party* (Minneapolis: University of Minnesota Press, 1931); Martin Ridge, "Populism Redux: John D. Hicks and *The Populist Revolt*," *Reviews in American History* 13, no. 1 (March 1985): 142. Hicks said that the rise of the Populist Party was "coincident with the annihilation of the frontier." Hicks, *Populist Revolt*, vii. The *Populist Revolt* also earned Hicks his post at Wisconsin. Hicks recalled that Carl Russell Fish began his search for a replacement for Paxson "by removing my book, *The Populist Revolt*, from the office shelf, and taking it home with him. In a matter of days he wrote me what he chose to call 'a love letter,' inviting me to join the Wisconsin staff." Hicks, "My Ten Years on the Wisconsin Faculty," 305.

187. Merk to Hicks, February 10, 1932, FF 1932, Carton 13, Hicks Papers, Bancroft Library.

188. Smith, "Frederick Merk," 144. Merk's later presidential address to the AHS focused on the developments in the East that contributed to agrarian unrest in the West. Frederick Merk, "Eastern Antecedents of the Grangers," *Agricultural History* 23, no. 1 (January 1949): 1–8.

189. Hicks, "My Ten Years on the Wisconsin Faculty," 309.

190. Hicks, "My Ten Years on the Wisconsin Faculty," 309; Hicks to A. Whitney Griswold, April 13, 1942, FF Correspondence January–June 1942, Carton C10, Hicks Papers, Bancroft Library. For extensive discussions between Hicks and Saloutos about the book, see Box 14, Hicks Papers, Bancroft Library. See Theodore Saloutos and John D. Hicks, *Agricultural Discontent in the Middle West, 1900–1939* (Madison: University of Wisconsin Press, 1951).

191. Barnhart, *Valley of Democracy*, 8; Nettels, "History Out of Wisconsin," 118; Ridge, "Frederick Jackson Turner and His Ghost," 69. John Hicks said that Turner "wrote and thought mainly in nineteenth century terms, and with the country more in mind than the city." Hicks to G. W. Pierson, November 25, 1941, FF Correspondence July–December 1941, DB 10, Hicks Papers, Bancroft Library.

192. James C. Malin, "Mobility and History: Reflections on the Agricultural Policies

of the United States in Relation to a Mechanized World," *Agricultural History* 17, no. 4 (October 1943): 177.

193. Harold D. Woodman, "The State of Agricultural History," in *The State of American History*, ed. Herbert J. Bass (Chicago: Quadrangle Books, 1970), 220–221; Novick, *That Noble Dream*, 182; Jess Gilbert, "Eastern Urban Liberals and Midwestern Agrarian Intellectuals: Two Group Portraits of Progressives in the New Deal Department of Agriculture," *Agricultural History* 74, no. 2 (Spring 2000): 169. The "dean of rural sociology," a discipline that emerged during these same decades, was a Kansan named John Gillette. Sidney Baldwin, *Poverty and Politics: The Rise and Decline of the Farm Security Administration* (Chapel Hill: University of North Carolina Press, 1968), 40, n.36. Rural sociology emerged out of Theodore Roosevelt's Country Life Commission. Baldwin, *Poverty and Politics*, 39; Clayton S. Ellsworth, "Theodore Roosevelt's Country Life Commission," *Agricultural History* 34, no. 4 (October 1960): 172. On the emergence of the field of agricultural economics at Wisconsin, see Jess Gilbert and Ellen Baker, "Wisconsin Economists and New Deal Agricultural Policy: The Legacy of Progressive Professors," *Wisconsin Magazine of History* 80, no. 4 (Summer 1997): 294–302; and Donald L. Winters, "The Persistence of Progressivism: Henry Cantwell Wallace and the Movement for Agricultural Economics," *Agricultural History* 41, no. 2 (April 1967): 117. See also Richard S. Kirkendall, *Social Scientists and Farm Politics in the Age of Roosevelt* (Columbia: University of Missouri Press, 1966), 11–29. A related organization, the Society for the Study of Midwestern Literature, was formed when the Modern Language Association rejected David D. Anderson's proposal for a panel discussion about midwestern writers. David D. Anderson, interview with author, November 11, 2011. On the biographical similarities of early twentieth-century regionalists, see Dorman, *Revolt of the Provinces*, 33. On the common "rural roots" of Iowa regionalists, see E. Bradford Burns, *Kinship with the Land: Regionalist Thought in Iowa, 1894–1942* (Iowa City: University of Iowa Press, 1996), 18.

194. Pelzer et al., "Projects in American History and Culture," 507.

195. Schmidt was head of the Department of History and Government at Iowa State from 1919 to 1945 and "pioneered courses in agricultural history and farmers' movements." W. Turrentine Jackson, "A Dedication to the Memory of Louis Bernard Schmidt, 1879–1963," *Arizona and the West* 15, no. 2 (Summer 1973): 103–104. See Louis Bernard Schmidt, "The Economic History of American Agriculture as a Field for Study," *MVHR* 3, no. 1 (June 1916): 39–50; and Louis Bernard Schmidt, "The Role and Techniques of Agrarian Pressure Groups," *Agricultural History* 30, no. 2 (April 1956): 49–58.

196. Louis Bernard Schmidt, "The Agricultural Revolution in the Prairies and the Great Plains of the United States," *Agricultural History* 8, no. 4 (October 1934): 173. Turner's "writings about the frontier had emphasized the importance of agricultural history," and Turner "made agricultural history—or a part of it at least—the central theme in American history." Woodman, "State of Agricultural History," 221, 225. See Ridge, "Life of an Idea," 6.

197. From 1889, when the post was given cabinet rank, until the 1930s, the secretary of agriculture was from the prairie states or Great Plains. Schmidt, "Agricultural Revolution," 181, 184.

198. Turner noted in a letter how he had "started a lot of these men [who led the AHS] off in historical study of agriculture." Ridge, "Frederick Jackson Turner and His Ghost," 69.

199. Merle Curti and Vernon Carstensen, *The University of Wisconsin: A History, 1848–1925*, 2 vols. (Madison: University of Wisconsin Press, 1949); Vernon Carstensen, "The Origin and Early Development of the Wisconsin Idea," *Wisconsin Magazine of History* 39, no. 3 (Spring 1956): 181–188; Earle D. Ross, *Democracy's College: The Land-Grant Movement in the Formative Stage* (Ames: Iowa State College Press, 1942); Schmidt, "Agricultural Revolution," 181–182. David Smith said that Merk "embodied" the ideal that Justin Morrill envisioned for land-grant colleges such as Wisconsin. Smith, "Frederick Merk," 142.

200. Clark, "Frederic Logan Paxson," 108; Hicks, "Historical News and Comments," 373.

201. Earl Pomeroy, "Frederic L. Paxson and His Approach to History," *MVHR* 39, no. 4 (March 1953): 690.

202. Allan G. Bogue, *From Prairie to Corn Belt: Farming on the Illinois and Iowa Prairies in the Nineteenth Century* (Chicago: University of Chicago Press, 1963).

203. Bogue recently said, "I was born a Midwesterner because southwestern Ontario is essentially Midwestern in its natural environment—farther west than Ohio, farther south than much of Minnesota and Wisconsin." Allan Bogue, interview with author, May 7, 2007; Bogue, "Tilling Agricultural History," 438.

204. Margaret Beattie Bogue also met her future husband in Gates's seminar. About the time Allan Bogue published *From Prairie to Corn Belt*, Margaret Beattie Bogue published *Patterns from the Sod: Land Use and Tenure in the Grand Prairie, 1850–1900* (Springfield: Illinois State Historical Library, 1959). Bogue spent much of his early career "trying to understand the agricultural history of the Midwestern prairie states and the grasslands immediately beyond." Allan G. Bogue, *The Farm on North Talbot Road* (Lincoln: University of Nebraska Press, 2001), xii.

205. Bogue, *From Prairie to Corn Belt*, preface. Bogue discusses the release of the book with Malin in Bogue to Malin, July 22, 1961, Bogue to Malin, December 24, 1962, and Bogue to Malin, July 13, 1964, all in Mss. Coll. 183, Malin Papers, KSHS. Gates was the reader for the publisher of the book. Bogue to Malin, January 9, 1963, Mss. Coll. 183, Malin Papers, KSHS. Bogue thanked Malin for his comments on the book and expressed "shock" at the negative review of the book in the *MVHR* by Mary Hargreaves, who had been a student of Gates (when he taught at Bucknell) and Merk (when she was in graduate school at Harvard). Bogue to Malin, July 13, 1964, Mss. Coll. 183, Malin Papers, KSHS. See Hargreaves's review, *MVHR* 51, no. 1 (June 1964), 115–116.

206. Bogue, *From Prairie to Corn Belt*, 1. Bogue said, "Iowa is virgin territory almost for quantitative analysis on the pioneer process." Bogue to Malin, January 10, 1954, Mss. Coll. 183, Malin Papers, KSHS. Bogue was also less glowing about the Iowa claims clubs than Benjamin Shambaugh had been. Allan G. Bogue, "The Iowa Claims Clubs: Symbol and Substance," *MVHR* 45, no. 2 (September 1958): 231–253; Schroder, "Benjamin F. Shambaugh," 615–616.

207. Bogue, *From Prairie to Corn Belt*, 287.

208. Bogue, *From Prairie to Corn Belt*, 193.

209. Allan G. Bogue, *Money at Interest: The Farm Mortgage on the Middle Border* (Lincoln: University of Nebraska Press, 1955). Bogue said he wanted to evaluate the "claims of the agrarians." Bogue to Malin, September 9, 1949, Mss. Coll. 183, Malin Papers, KSHS. Bogue said Ray Allen Billington's treatment of western mortgages made his survey textbook a "damn waste of paper and money." Bogue to Malin, March 19, 1950, Mss. Coll. 183, Malin Papers, KSHS.

210. Jensen, "On Modernizing Frederick Jackson Turner," 317; Gerald D. Nash, "John D. Hicks," in Wunder, *Historians of the American Frontier*, 308. Merk wrote *Economic History of Wisconsin during the Civil War Decade* (Madison: State Historical Society of Wisconsin, 1916) while at the State Historical Society of Wisconsin, which Harvard accepted as his dissertation. Paul, "Frederick Merk," 140. The famous business historian Alfred Chandler was a student of Merk. Blum, "Celebration of Frederick Merk." Turner's focus on economic history, and the work of his "historical followers, helped to lay the groundwork for the more aggressive use of the economic interpretation of history that came with Beard's generation." Hofstadter, *Progressive Historians*, 72.

211. Bogue to Malin, March 19, 1959, and Bogue to Malin, February 11, 1971, both in Mss. Coll. 183, Malin Papers, KSHS; E. David Cronon, "Merle Curti: An Appraisal and Bibliography of His Writings," *Wisconsin Magazine of History* 54, no. 2 (Winter 1970–1971): 121; Wilkins, "Orin G. Libby," 110; Smith, "Frederick Merk," 143.

212. Bogue to Malin, August 14, 1968, Mss. Coll. 183, Malin Papers, KSHS; Allan G. Bogue, "The Quest for Numeracy: Data and Methods in American Political History," *Journal of Interdisciplinary History* 21, no. 1 (Summer 1990): 89–116. See also the work of Bogue's student Robert Swierenga, "Computers and American History: The Impact of the 'New' Generation," *Journal of American History* 60, no. 4 (March 1974): 1045–1070.

213. Bogue, "Social Theory and the Pioneer," 34; Nash, *Creating the West*, 69.

214. McClintock, "Frederick Merk," 435; Margaret Beattie Bogue and Allan G. Bogue, "Paul W. Gates," *Great Plains Journal* 19 (1979): 22; Paul W. Gates, *The Farmers' Age: Agriculture, 1815–1860* (New York: Harper & Row, 1960), 51; Paul W. Gates, "The Homestead Law in an Incongruous Land System," *American Historical Review* 41 (July 1936): 652–681; Paul W. Gates, "The Role of the Land Speculator in Western Development," *Pennsylvania Magazine of History and Biography* 46 (July 1942): 314–333; Paul W. Gates, *Frontier Landlords and Pioneer Tenants* (Ithaca, N.Y.: Cornell University Press, 1945). For a survey of work on this topic, see Paul W. Gates, "Research in the History of the Public Lands," *Agricultural History* 48, no. 1 (January 1974): 31–50. For a survey of Gates's work, see Harry N. Scheiber, "The Economic Historian as Realist and as Keeper of Democratic Ideals: Paul Wallace Gates's Studies of American Land Policy," *Journal of Economic History* 40, no. 3 (September 1980): 585–593; and Frederick Merk, "Foreword," in *The Frontier in American Development: Essays in Honor of Paul Wallace Gates*, ed., David M. Ellis (Ithaca, N.Y.: Cornell University Press, 1969), ix–xxx.

215. Frederick Merk to Merle Curti, December 15, 1949, FF 1, DB 26, Curti Papers, WHS; Merk to Gates, September 11, 1935, Gates Papers, Cornell University.

216. Buck, "Progress and Possibilities of Mississippi Valley History," 8; Pelzer et al., "Projects in American History and Culture," 504–506; Frederick Merk, *History of the Westward Movement* (New York: Alfred A. Knopf, 1978), 605; Smith, "Frederick Merk," 143; Paxson, *History of the American Frontier*, 43–70; Vernon Carstensen, ed., *The Public Lands: Studies in the History of the Public Domain* (Madison: University of Wisconsin Press, 1963). Carstensen's students include Malcolm Rohrbough, whose first book was *The Land Office Business: The Settlement and Administration of American Public Lands, 1789–1837* (New York: Oxford University Press, 1968), and Richard White, whose first book was *Land Use, Environment, and Social Change: The Shaping of Island County, Washington* (Seattle: University of Washington Press, 1979). See

also Fite, "American West of Farmers and Stockmen," 211–212. On similar studies by social scientists, see Jess Gilbert, "Agrarian Intellectuals in a Democratizing State: A Collective Biography of USDA Leaders in the Intended New Deal," in *The Country-side in the Age of the Modern State: Political Histories of Rural America*, ed. Catherine McNicol Stock and Robert D. Johnston (Ithaca, N.Y.: Cornell University Press, 2001), 224.

217. Bogue, *Frederick Jackson Turner*, 239–242, 430; Everett E. Edwards, "Middle Western Agricultural History as a Field of Research," *MVHR* 24, no. 3 (December 1937): 317–318; Steiner, "Significance of Turner's Sectional Thesis," 451, 454; Jensen, "On Modernizing Frederick Jackson Turner," 308; Libby, "Some Aspects of Mid-West America," 213; Smith, "Frederick Merk," 143; Elmer Ellis, "Louis Pelzer: Scholar, Teacher, Editor," *MVHR* 33, no. 2 (September 1946): 209.

218. James Malin, "Ecology and History," *Scientific Monthly* 70, no. 5 (May 1950): 297; Michael P. Malone, "Beyond the Last Frontier: Toward a New Approach to Western History," *Western Historical Quarterly* 20, no. 4 (November 1989): 412. Dan Flores deemed Malin's work the "first real ecological history written by an American." Dan Flores, review of James C. Malin, *History and Ecology: Studies of the Grassland*, ed. Robert P. Swierenga (Lincoln: University of Nebraska Press, 1984), in *Western Historical Quarterly* 16, no. 4 (October 1985): 456. Prairie Historian Theodore Blegen also helped to found the Forest History Society. Tyrell, "Public at the Creation," 40.

219. Malin, "Ecology and History," 297; James C. Malin, "Space and History: Reflections on the Closed-Space Doctrines of Turner and Mackinder and the Challenge of Those Ideas by the Air Age," Part 2, *Agricultural History* 18, no. 3 (April 1944): 120; Merk to Malin, January 27, 1947, Merk to Malin, May 6, 1947, Bogue to Malin, February 11, 1956, and Bogue to Malin, March 11, 1956, all in Malin Papers, KSHS.

220. Gilman M. Ostrander, "Turner and the Germ Theory," *Agricultural History* 32, no. 4 (October 1958): 258–261; Nettels, "History Out of Wisconsin," 117; James C. Malin, "Space and History: Reflections on the Closed-Space Doctrines of Turner and Mackinder and the Challenge of Those Ideas by the Air Age," Part 1, *Agricultural History* 18, no. 2 (April 1944): 66.

221. Allan G. Bogue, "Frederick Jackson Turner," *History Teacher* 27, no. 2 (February 1994): 199.

222. Barnhart, *Valley of Democracy*, viii.

223. Paxson, *History of the American Frontier*, 1–2. On the influence of English institutions in the settlement of the West ("American democracy was born in West-minster Hall"), see the 1947 AHA presidential address by Thomas J. Wertenbaker, "The Molding of the Middle West," *American Historical Review* 53, no. 2 (January 1948): 223–234 (quote on 228).

224. Steiner, "Significance of Turner's Sectional Thesis," 451, 454; Jensen, "On Modernizing Frederick Jackson Turner," 308.

225. Merk to Malin, January 27, 1947, Merk to Malin, November 18, 1947, and Hicks to Malin, February 7, 1942, all in Malin Papers, KSHS; Gates, *Farmers' Age*, 180; Pelzer et al., "Projects in American History and Culture," 506–507; Edwards, "Middle Western Agricultural History," 317–318.

226. Merk to Malin, May 6, 1947, and Merk to Malin, March 15, 1952, both in Malin Papers, KSHS.

227. Merk to Malin, November 18, 1947, Malin Papers, KSHS. Bogue said *Grassland* "is one of the relatively few *tours de force* in the historiography of western America."

Allan G. Bogue, "Farming in the Northern American Grasslands: A Survey of Publications, 1947–80," *Agricultural History Review* 30, no. 1 (1982): 51.

228. Hicks to Malin, May 15, 1944, Malin Papers, KSHS.

229. Bogue to Malin, November 2, 1947, Bogue to Malin, June 7, 1963, and Bogue to Malin, November 26, 1950, all in Malin Papers, KSHS.

230. Malin, "Ecology and History," 295; Malin, "Space and History," Part 1, 65; Malin, "Space and History," Part 2, 107.

231. Everett Dick, "Going Beyond the Ninety-Fifth Meridian," *Agricultural History* 17, no. 2 (April 1943): 105.

232. The novelist Ivan Doig also noted how Carstensen "prodded" his students to "think about our patterns on this land." Richard White, "Obituary," *Western Historical Quarterly* 24, no. 1 (February 1993): 138. On the origins of environmental history within the MVHA, see Karl Brooks, "The Wild One: Environmental History as Redheaded Stepchild," in Kirkendall, *Organization of American Historians*, 212.

233. Malin, "On the Nature of Local History," 228. In a 1923 letter to Theodore Blegen, Turner discussed "history from the bottom up." Ridge, "Life of an Idea," 6, n.6. Martin Ridge noted the "irony in the fact that the phrase ['history from the bottom up'] was popular in the 1960s among radical social historians who rejected Turnerian thinking. Jesse Lemisch was probably unaware of its origin." Ridge, "Life of an Idea," 6, n.6. On Curti and the early social history, see James A. Henretta, "The Making of an American Community: A Thirty-Year Retrospective," *Reviews in American History* 16, no. 3 (September 1988): 506–512. Turner's mentor at Wisconsin, William Allen, was, Turner said, "ahead of his time" for focusing on "social and economic forces." Billington, *Genesis of the Frontier Thesis*, 5. On the numerous topics that earlier historians had already studied prior to the later work of the supposed "new" historians, see Fitzpatrick, *History's Memory*.

234. Howard R. Lamar, "Earl Pomeroy, Historian's Historian," *Pacific Historical Review* 56, no. 4 (November 1987): 551; Pease, *Frontier State*.

235. Hicks, "My Ten Years on the Wisconsin Faculty," 306.

236. Hicks, "My Ten Years on the Wisconsin Faculty," 306. Fulmer Mood similarly concluded that "social history can be so divorced from political history that the social data as such end up wearying or confusing the reader, who sees no path or pattern through the jungle of particulars spread out before him." Mood, "Theory of the History of an American Section," 5–6.

237. Hicks, "My Ten Years on the Wisconsin Faculty," 306.

238. Hicks, "My Ten Years on the Wisconsin Faculty," 306.

239. Fulmer Mood noted that before Turner, most historians focused on "political and institutional history" but that Turner promoted economic and "social history." Mood, "Theory of the History of an American Section," 4.

240. Steiner, "Frontier to Region," 490; Hofstadter, *Progressive Historians*, 72.

241. Louis Pelzer, "History Made By Plain Men," *Iowa Journal of History and Politics* 11, no. 3 (July 1913): 307–322; Pelzer et al., "Projects in American History and Culture," 517; Pease, *Frontier State*, 20–23; Buck, "Progress and Possibilities of Mississippi Valley History," 6–10; Smith, "Frederick Merk," 143; R. Carlyle Buley, "Glimpses of Pioneer Mid-west Social and Cultural History," *MVHR* 23, no. 4 (March 1937): 481–510; Buley, *Old Northwest*, 1:138–239; Buley to Stanley Pargellis, August 15, 1944, Buley Papers, Indiana Historical Society; Herbert A. Kellar, "Louis Pelzer: Scholar, Teacher, Editor," *MVHR* 33, no. 2 (September 1946): 204; Alvord, "Relation of the

State to Historical Work," 8, 15; Paxson, *History of the American Frontier*, 113; Fred A. Shannon, "The Life of the Common Soldier in the Union Army, 1861–1865," *MVHR* 13, no. 4 (March 1927): 465–482; Joseph Schafer, "The Wisconsin Domesday Book," *Wisconsin Magazine of History* 4, no. 1 (September 1920): 61–74; Stephanie J. Shaw, "The Long and Influential Life of Social History in the MVHR and the JAH," in Kirkendall, *Organization of American Historians*, 127–132.

242. Alvord, "Relation of the State to Historical Work," 8, 15.

243. Kellar, "Louis Pelzer," 204 ("interested in people"); Philip D. Jordan, "Louis Pelzer: Scholar, Teacher, Editor," *MVHR* 33, no. 2 (September 1946): 215 ("social customs and manners").

244. Blegen, *Grassroots History*, 6, 15.

245. Everett Dick, *The Sod-House Frontier: A Social History of the Northern Plains from the Creation of Kansas and Nebraska to the Admission of the Dakotas* (Lincoln, Neb.: Johnson, 1954); Everett Dick, *Vanguards of the Frontier: A Social History of the Northern Plains and Rocky Mountains from the Earliest White Contacts to the Coming of the Homemaker* (New York: D. Appleton-Century, 1941); Everett Dick, *The Lure of the Land: A Social History of the Public Lands from the Articles of Confederation to the New Deal* (Lincoln: University of Nebraska Press, 1970). Malin joked that Dick's *The Sod-House Frontier* should have been named *The Sawed House Frontier* because of the fast transition from soddies to lumber homes. Bogue, "Tilling Agricultural History," 450. At Union College in Lincoln, Nebraska, Dick lived with his family in a dormitory and wrote *The Sod-House Frontier* in the basement, which had a dirt floor. In 1952, a survey of historians indicated that *The Sod-House Frontier* was among the top fifteen books published between 1936 and 1950. Gilbert C. Fite, "Everett Dick," *Great Plains Journal* 19 (1979): 17, 21.

246. Barbara Howard, "Pulitzer Prize Awarded to Dr. Buley: Two Volumes on Northwest Win Citation for History," *Indiana Daily Student*, May 8, 1951.

247. Buley to Charles D. Anderson, August 20, 1947, Rosemary B. York to Buley, May 6, 1948, Arthur W. Wang to Buley, July 7, 1948, and Edward C. Aswell to Buley, August 16, 1948, all in Buley Papers, Indiana Historical Society.

248. Buley to Stanley Pargellis, August 15, 1944, Buley Papers, Indiana Historical Society.

249. "Hoosiers Honor Prof. Buley: 135 Pay Tribute to Prize Winner," *Indiana Daily Student*, June 2, 1951.

250. Buley to Philip D. Jordan, May 24, 1951, Buley Papers, Indiana Historical Society.

251. Libby, "New Northwest," 345–346.

252. Alvord to Clarence Paine, June 24, 1914, Vol. 1, MVHA Correspondence, Alvord Papers, SHSM; Unknown to Clarence Paine, September 28, 1914, Vol. 1, MVHA Correspondence, Alvord Papers, SHSM.

253. Buck to Hicks, March 5, 1941, Hicks to Buck, April 23, 1941, and Buck to Hicks, April 21, 1941, all in Box 8, Buck Papers, National Archives.

254. Blegen, *Grassroots History*, 11.

255. Bogue to Malin, August 10, 1971, Malin Papers, KSHS; Hicks, "My Ten Years on the Wisconsin Faculty," 315. When Merk left the State Historical Society of Wisconsin to continue his studies at Harvard, Quaife worried he might become "an effete Easterner." Quaife to Merk, October 5, 1916, General Administrative Correspondence of WHS, 1900–2000, WHS.

256. Hofstadter, *Progressive Historians*, 79–80.

257. Novick, *That Noble Dream*, 180–181, 185.

258. On the decline of regionalism by the 1950s, see Douglas Reichert Powell, *Critical Regionalism: Connecting Politics and Culture in the American Landscape* (Chapel Hill: University of North Carolina Press, 2007), 19; and Michael C. Steiner and David M. Wrobel, "Many Wests: Discovering a Dynamic Western Regionalism," in *Many Wests: Place, Culture, and Identity*, ed. Michael C. Steiner and David M. Wrobel (Lawrence: University Press of Kansas, 1997), 6. E. Bradford Burns also argues that World War II ended the regionalist movement in Iowa. Burns, *Kinship with the Land*, 11, 167, 176. Burns saw World War II as the "coup de grace" for Iowa regionalism. Burns, *Kinship with the Land*, 163.

259. Warren I. Susman, "History and the American Intellectual: Uses of a Usable Past," *American Quarterly* 16, part 2, Supplement (Summer 1964): 254–255; Warren I. Susman, "The Useless Past: American Intellectuals and the Frontier Thesis, 1910–1930," *Bucknell Review* 11 (March 1963): 17.

260. Novick, *That Noble Dream*, 368; Tyrell, "Public at the Creation," 28.

261. Novick, *That Noble Dream*, 183, 367. Gates criticized Barnhart for continuing to adhere to the idea of the MVHA as "a provincial organization with its principal interest in the Mississippi Valley." Gates to Richard Lyle Power, November 24, 1951, Gates Papers, Cornell University. Ray Billington sought to end the "Nebraska matriarchy" of Clara Paine. Ray Billington to Gates, February 5, 1952, Gates Papers, Cornell University. Billington noted that the "Nebraska matriarchy is strong among the ex-presidents on the board" of the MVHA. Billington to Fred Shannon, January 10, 1952, FF Ray A. Billington, DB 1, Shannon Papers, University of Illinois Archives. Billington thought the "small group of obstructionists about Lincoln must be overruled." Billington to Gates, January 14, 1964, Gates Papers, Cornell University. On the growth of a national outlook for the MVHA, see Tyrell, "Public at the Creation," 43–46. Regionalism in sociology also began to disappear during this period. Carl Abbott, "United States Regional History as an Instructional Field: The Practice of College and University History Departments," *Western Historical Quarterly* 21, no. 2 (May 1990): 200.

262. During an earlier debate, John Hicks argued that "we must retain the Mississippi Valley name and connotation" of the MVHA. Hicks to Sellers, June 18, 1945, Sellers Papers, University of Nebraska Archives. Curti thought the "arguments for keeping the old name [of the MVHA were] stronger," but supported changing the name of the *MVHR*. Curti to Sellers, September 27, 1951, and October 2, 1951, Sellers Papers, University of Nebraska Archives. One opponent of the name change noted the "obligation to our guarantors who carried us through the early days and the hard years," including Paine, Alvord, Turner, Libby, Thwaites, and Paxson. Unsigned opposition document entitled "Changing the Name of the Mississippi Valley Historical Association," Sellers Papers, University of Nebraska Archives. John Barnhart also opposed the name change. Clara Paine to James Sellers, June 28, 1951, Sellers Papers, University of Nebraska Archives. Elmer Ellis and Paul Gates favored the name change. Ellis to Paul Gates, n.d. [likely 1951], and Clara Paine to James Sellers, June 28, 1951, both in Sellers Papers, University of Nebraska Archives. For the Barnhart versus Gates debate over the name change, see *MVHR* 38, no. 2 (September 1951): 350–352.

263. Michael Steiner review of E. Bradford Burns, *Kinship with the Land,* in *Indiana*

Magazine of History 94, no. 4 (December 1998): 365 (source of quotation). Carl Coke Rister, a historian at the University of Oklahoma, favored changing the name of the MVHA because such a name "implied regionalism." Rister to James Sellers, September 25, 1951, Sellers Papers, University of Nebraska Archives. Paul Gates criticized the name of the MVHA as being too "provincial" and "regional." Paul Gates, "Historical News and Comments," *MVHR* 38, no. 2 (September 1951): 351. See also Frederick C. Luebke, "Regionalism and the Great Plains: Problems of Concept and Method," *Western Historical Quarterly* 15, no. 1 (January 1984): 22.

264. Curti replaced Hicks at Wisconsin after Elmer Ellis declined the position, and after moving to California, Hicks confessed to missing the "generous hospitality of the Middle West." John D. Hicks, *My Life with History: An Autobiography* (Lincoln: University of Nebraska Press, 1968), 211, 215. On Hicks's departure from Wisconsin for Berkeley, see Hicks to Guy Stanton Ford, January 20, 1942, Ford Papers, University of Minnesota Archives. See also Hicks to Louis Pelzer, April 13, 1942, FF Correspondence January–June 1942, Carton C10, Hicks Papers, Bancroft Library, in which Hicks vowed to maintain his "deep-seated interest in the Mississippi Valley Historical Association." In 1944, Hicks agreed to accept an offer to return to Wisconsin and went so far as to resign from Berkeley, but changed his mind, concluding that "California needs a lot of Wisconsin in its system" and resolving to do the "job of pioneering" at Berkeley while drawing on the "eleven generations of American pioneers" in his family. Hicks to Paul Knaplund, April 7, 1944, FF January–June Correspondence, DB 10, Hicks Papers, Bancroft Library. In 1964, Carstensen also moved west, leaving Wisconsin for the University of Washington.

265. Thomas T. McAvoy, "What Is the Midwestern Mind?" in *The Midwest: Myth or Reality?* (Notre Dame, Ind.: University of Notre Dame Press, 1961), 62.

266. Buley to Stanley Pargellis, August 15, 1944, Buley Papers, Indiana Historical Society.

CHAPTER THREE

1. Michael C. Steiner, "Frontier to Region: Frederick Jackson Turner and the New Western History," *Pacific Historical Review* 64, no. 4 (November 1995): 491, 497, n.53.

2. J. L. Sellers, "Louise Phelps Kellogg," *Wisconsin Magazine of History* 37, no. 4 (Summer 1954): 210; Glenda Riley, "Frederick Jackson Turner Overlooked the Ladies," *Journal of the Early Republic* 13, no. 2 (Summer 1993): 218–219; Allan G. Bogue, *Frederick Jackson Turner: Strange Roads Going Down* (Norman: University of Oklahoma Press, 1998), 236; Buck to Hicks, November 7, 1935, Box 8, Buck Papers, National Archives; Frederick Merk to Merle Curti, March 21, 1959, FF 1, DB 26, Curti Papers, Wisconsin Historical Society (WHS); Buck to Hicks, April 23, 1937, FF 1937, Carton 13, Hicks Papers, Bancroft Library; Benjamin F. Shambaugh, "The Sixteenth Annual Meeting of the Mississippi Valley Historical Association," *Mississippi Valley Historical Review (MVHR)* 10, no. 2 (September 1923): 115, 121; Bogue to Malin, October 24, 1954, Mss. Coll. 183, Malin Papers, Kansas State Historical Society (KSHS); Allan G. Bogue, "Tilling Agricultural History with Paul Wallace Gates and James C. Malin," *Agricultural History* 80, no. 4 (Autumn 2006): 456; Paul Gates to Merle Curti, April 28, 1953, FF 16, DB 17, Curti Papers, WHS; Howard R. Lamar, "Commentary," in *Writing the History of the American West* (Worcester, Mass.: American Antiquarian Society,

1991), 107. Louise Phelps Kellogg, from Milwaukee, was a "pillar" of the State Historical Society of Wisconsin for four decades and its chief of research, a Minnesota Ph.D.,
the president of the MVHA, a "bulldog researcher," and an active editor. In 1948, the
State Historical Society of Wisconsin also hired Livia Appel away from the University
of Minnesota Press, and she was a "crackerjack editor" who guided sixteen books
into print. Paul Hass, "Reflections on 150 Years of Publishing," *Wisconsin Magazine
of History* 88, no. 2 (Winter 2004–2005): 6–7, 9; John D. Hicks, "My Ten Years on the
Wisconsin Faculty," *Wisconsin Magazine of History* 48, no. 4 (Summer 1965): 308; Ian
Tyrell, "Public at the Creation: Place, Memory, and Historical Practice in the Missis-
sippi Valley Historical Association, 1907–1950," *Journal of American History* 94, no. 1
(June 2007): 31. The Minnesotan Agnes Larson also earned a Harvard Ph.D. under
Merk, taught at St. Olaf College and Mankato Normal, and wrote *The White Pine
Industry of Minnesota* (Minneapolis: University of Minnesota Press, 1949). Her sis-
ter, Henrietta, earned her degree from Columbia and taught business history in the
College of Business at Harvard. Grace Lee Nute worked at the Minnesota Historical
Society, earned a Ph.D. from Harvard, and taught in Minnesota at Hamline University
and Macalester College. Iowa's Ruth Gallaher had her political science dissertation,
Legal and Political Status of Women in Iowa, published by the State Historical Society of Iowa in 1918, and she was a key member of the SHSI staff for many years, with
duties including the editing of the *Iowa Journal of History and Politics* and the *Palimpsest* before she left the state in the 1940s to teach in Kentucky. I thank Lori Lahlum
for introducing me to the Larsons and Nute, and Robert Burchfield for introducing
me to Ruth Gallaher. See also Barbara Stuhler and Gretchen Kreuter, eds., *Women of
Minnesota: Selected Biographical Essays* (St. Paul: Minnesota Historical Society, 1977);
"Grace Nute, 94, Dies; Historian and Teacher," *New York Times*, May 16, 1990.

3. John D. Hicks to Merle Curti, October 1, 1942, FF 17, DB 19, Curti Papers, WHS.

4. John D. Hicks to Merle Curti, May 6, 1952, FF 17, DB 19, Curti Papers, WHS.

5. Paxson to Hicks, October 11, 1930, FF 1930, Carton 13, Hicks Papers, Bancroft Library. Hicks's course at Nebraska and his book on Populism also inspired
Mari Sandoz. Robert L. Dorman, *Revolt of the Provinces: The Regionalist Movement
in America, 1920–1945* (Chapel Hill: University of North Carolina Press, 1993), 238.

6. Bogue thought that farm women had been a "relatively neglected" topic of
study. Bogue to Malin, July 15, 1975, Mss. Coll. 183, Malin Papers, KSHS. On the
growth of the study of midwestern women, see Ginette Aley, "'Knotted Together Like
Roots in the Darkness': Rural Midwestern Women and Region—A Bibliographic
Guide," *Agricultural History* 77, no. 3 (Summer 2003): 453–481.

7. Allan G. Bogue, Margaret Beattie Bogue, Walter LaFeber, and Joel Silbey, "In
Memoriam: Paul Wallace Gates," *Perspectives* (May 1999). In 1962, the University
of Iowa historian and native Nebraskan Christopher Lasch would present a paper
entitled "How New Was the New Woman?" at the MVHA annual meeting and was
interested in the history of women throughout his career. Christopher Lasch, "Sup-
plementary Statements A and B," William Leuchtenburg Papers, University of North
Carolina–Chapel Hill. On Lasch's midwestern background, see Jon K. Lauck, "The
Prairie Populism of Christopher Lasch," *Great Plains Quarterly* 32, no. 3 (Summer
2012): 183–205.

8. Louis Pelzer, "The Negro and Slavery in Iowa," *Iowa Journal of History and
Politics* 2 (October 1904): 471–484; Theodore Calvin Pease, *The Frontier State, 1818–
1848* (Springfield: Illinois Centennial Commission, 1918), 47; Fred Shannon, "The

Federal Government and the Negro Soldier, 1861–1865," *Journal of Negro History* 11, no. 4 (October 1926): 563–583. Louis Pelzer accepted with enthusiasm Fred Shannon's article in the *Journal of Negro History* as partial fulfillment of Shannon's publication requirement to earn his Ph.D. Pelzer to Shannon, November 18, 1926, FF Louis Pelzer, DB 2, Shannon Papers, University of Illinois Archives.

9. Robert R. Dykstra, *Bright Radical Star: Black Freedom and White Supremacy on the Hawkeye Frontier* (Cambridge, Mass.: Harvard University Press, 1993).

10. Louis Pelzer, Merle Curti, Everett E. Dale, Everett Dick, and Paul W. Gates, "Projects in American History and Culture," *MVHR* 31, no. 4 (March 1945): 510.

11. Peter Novick, *That Noble Dream: The "Objectivity Question" and the American Historical Profession* (New York: Cambridge University Press, 1988), 225.

12. Gordon L. Iseminger, "Dr. Orin G. Libby: A Centennial Commemoration of the Father of North Dakota History," *North Dakota History* 68, no. 4 (2001): 18; Quaife to Buley, June 11, 1950, Buley Papers, Indiana Historical Society.

13. John D. Hicks, *The Populist Revolt: A History of the Farmers' Alliance and People's Party* (Minneapolis: University of Minnesota Press, 1931), 47.

14. R. Carlyle Buley, *The Old Northwest: Pioneer Period, 1815–1840* (Indianapolis: Indiana Historical Society, 1950), 1:31.

15. Buley said that "keeping an organization out of social reform, religious doctrine, and seventeen other things does not prevent individual members thereof from being interested in same." Buley to Philip D. Jordan, May 24, 1951, and Buley to Curti, May 17, 1951, both in Buley Papers, Indiana Historical Society. Gates argued against meetings in segregated cities and praised his department's "colored secretary" and "colored stenographer." Paul Gates to Merle Curti, April 25, 1950, FF 16, DB 17, Curti Papers, WHS. In the 1950s, the MVHA ceased holding meetings in cities where accommodations were still segregated and also passed resolutions against Cold War loyalty oaths. Novick, *That Noble Dream*, 349, 329; Tyrell, "Public at the Creation," 20.

16. Curtis P. Nettels, "History Out of Wisconsin," *Wisconsin Magazine of History* 39, no. 2 (Winter 1955–1956): 117; John Schacht, "American Labor and Working Class History at Iowa: Part I," *Books at Iowa* 53 (November 1990); Jess Gilbert and Ellen Baker, "Wisconsin Economists and New Deal Agricultural Policy: The Legacy of Progressive Professors," *Wisconsin Magazine of History* 80, no. 4 (Summer 1997): 289–291; George D. Blackwood, "Frederick Jackson Turner and John Rogers Commons: Complementary Thinkers," *MVHR* 41, no. 3 (December 1954): 471–488.

17. Frederick Merk, *The Labor Movement in Wisconsin during the Civil War* (Madison: State Historical Society of Wisconsin, 1916).

18. Schacht, "American Labor and Working Class History"; Tyrell, "Public at the Creation," 37.

19. Illinois also hosted a Labor and Industrial Relations Institute. Paul W. Gates to Fred Shannon, September 30, 1953, FF Paul Gates, DB 2, Shannon Papers, University of Illinois Archives.

20. Paul W. Gates, *The Farmers' Age: Agriculture, 1815–1860* (New York: Harper & Row, 1960), 196.

21. James A. Hijiya, "Why the West Is Lost," *William and Mary Quarterly* 51, no. 2 (April 1994): 277.

22. Alvord to MVHR Board of Editors, January 6, 1915, Vol. 2, MVHA Correspondence, Alvord Papers, State Historical Society of Missouri (SHSM); Orin G. Libby review of Warren K. Moorehead, *The American Indian in the United States, 1850–1914*

(Andover, Mass.: Andover Press, 1914), in *MVHR* 2, no. 2 (September 1915): 293; Orin G. Libby, "The New Northwest," *MVHR* 7, no. 4 (March 1921): 347; Orin G. Libby, "Some Aspects of Mid–West America," *Minnesota History Bulletin* 4, nos. 5–6 (February–May 1922): 215.

23. Robert P. Wilkins, "Orin G. Libby, 1864–1952," *Arizona and the West* 16, no. 2 (Summer 1974): 109.

24. Wilkins, "Orin G. Libby," 109.

25. Alvord to Clarence Paine, March 27, 1916, Vol. 2, MVHA Correspondence, Alvord Papers, SHSM; Benjamin F. Shambaugh, ed., *Proceedings of the Mississippi Valley Historical Association for the Year 1907–1908* (Cedar Rapids, Iowa: Torch Press, 1909), 1:31; David Thelen, "Of Audiences, Borderlands, and Comparisons: Toward the Internationalization of American History," *Journal of American History* 79, no. 2 (September 1992): 436.

26. Frederick Merk, *History of the Westward Movement* (New York: Alfred A. Knopf, 1978); Frederic Logan Paxson, *History of the American Frontier, 1763–1893* (Boston: Houghton Mifflin, 1924), 1.

27. Bogue, "Tilling Agricultural History," 442; Thomas LeDuc, "The Work of the Indian Claims Commission under the Act of 1946," *Pacific Historical Review* 26, no. 1 (February 1957): 1–16; Paul Wallace Gates, ed., *The Rape of Indian Lands* (New York: Arno Press, 1979). Edward Dale, who earned his Ph.D. from Harvard under Turner, also served on the Department of the Interior survey that produced the Meriam Report of 1928 calling for reforms in federal Indian policies. Tyrell, "Public at the Creation," 37.

28. Bogue, "Tilling Agricultural History," 449; James C. Malin, "Ecology and History," *Scientific Monthly* 70, no. 5 (May 1950): 296.

29. Paxson to Malin, January 24, 1922, and Buck to Malin, January 27, 1922, both in Mss. Coll. 183, Malin Papers, KSHS.

30. Pelzer et al., "Projects in American History," 510.

31. Theodore C. Blegen, "Our Widening Province," *MVHR* 31, no. 1 (June 1944): 6; Tyrell, "Public at the Creation," 42.

32. Eric Hinderaker, "Liberating Contrivances: Narrative and Identity in Midwestern Histories," in *The Identity of the American Midwest: Essays on Regional History*, ed. Andrew R. L. Cayton and Susan E. Gray (Bloomington: Indiana University Press, 2001), 48–68. See also Frederick E. Hoxie, "The Presence of Native American History," in *The Organization of American Historians and the Writing and Teaching of American History*, ed. Richard S. Kirkendall (New York: Oxford University Press, 2011), 198–199; and Ellen Fitzpatrick, *History's Memory: Writing America's Past, 1880–1980* (Cambridge, Mass.: Harvard University Press, 2002), 98–140. American Indian history was also strong in the Western History Association, formed in 1961. John Porter Bloom, "Ten Years of Western History Conferences: An Appraisal," *Western Historical Quarterly* 2, no. 1 (January 1971): 115.

33. See generally Novick, *That Noble Dream*; David S. Brown, *Beyond the Frontier: The Midwestern Voice in American Historical Writing* (Chicago: University of Chicago Press, 2009); William Palmer, *From Gentlemen's Club to Professional Body: The Evolution of the History Department in the United States, 1940–1980* (Charleston, S.C.: BookSurge Publishing, 2008); and William Palmer, "All Coherence Gone? A Cultural History of Leading History Departments in the United States, 1970–2010," *Journal of the Historical Society* 12, no. 2 (June 2012): 113, 115.

34. Brown, *Beyond the Frontier*, 48. In an 1888 letter and a 1901 newspaper column, Turner trafficked in Jewish stereotypes and expressed skepticism about the new immigrant groups to the United States, but he also thought that Jews in the United States would be very successful immigrants. Bogue, *Frederick Jackson Turner*, 55, 185–186.

35. Philip Taft, "Reflections on Selig Perlman as a Teacher and Writer," *Industrial and Labor Relations Review* 29, no. 2 (January 1976): 251. On Perlman and labor history at Wisconsin, see Selig Perlman, "John Rogers Commons, 1862–1945," *Wisconsin Magazine of History* 29, no. 1 (September 1945): 25–31.

36. Novick, *That Noble Dream*, 330.

37. Palmer, *From Gentlemen's Club to Professional Body*, 132, 154, n.14 (citing oral history of Robert Brentano and Stanley Kutler).

38. Gerald Nash, "John D. Hicks," in *Historians of the American Frontier*, ed. John R. Wunder (Westport, Conn.: Greenwood Press, 1988), 306–310; Hicks, "My Ten Years on the Wisconsin Faculty," 309.

39. Novick, *That Noble Dream*, 172.

40. Merk to Gates, June 26, 1936, Gates Papers, Cornell University.

41. Bogue to Malin, September 24, 1957, Mss. Coll. 183, Malin Papers, KSHS.

42. In 1956, Wisconsin hired the European historian George Mosse away from Iowa. Palmer, *From Gentlemen's Club to Professional Body*, 166. See generally George Mosse, *Confronting History: A Memoir* (Madison: University of Wisconsin Press, 2000). In 1958, Wisconsin hired a second Jewish professor of history, Theodore Hamerow, who had been teaching at Illinois. In 1963, Wisconsin also hired Harvey Goldberg away from Ohio State. Palmer, *From Gentlemen's Club to Professional Body*, 167.

43. Brown, *Beyond the Frontier*, 113.

44. Brown, *Beyond the Frontier*, 113–114.

45. Richard Hofstadter, *The Age of Reform: From Bryan to F.D.R.* (New York: Knopf, 1955).

46. Novick, *That Noble Dream*, 337–339. See Walter T. K. Nugent, *The Tolerant Populists: Kansas Populism and Nativism* (Chicago: University of Chicago Press, 1963). The University of Chicago Press published Nugent's book after a "rave report" from Hicks. Walter Nugent, "Where Have All the Flowers Gone . . . When Will They Ever Learn?" *Reviews in American History* 37 (2009): 206.

47. Novick, *That Noble Dream*, 340.

48. Novick, *That Noble Dream*, 339. See Norman Pollack, "The Myth of Populist Anti-Semitism," *American Historical Review* 68, no. 1 (October 1962): 76–80.

49. Bogue to Malin, December 19, 1961, Mss. Coll. 183, Malin Papers, KSHS.

50. Bogue to Malin, December 19, 1961, Mss. Coll. 183, Malin Papers, KSHS.

51. Pollack to author, March 24, 2011. For a critique of Pollack's Marxist interpretation of populism, see Irwin Under, "Critique of Norman Pollack's 'Fear of Man,'" *Agricultural History* 39, no. 2 (April 1965): 75–80. On the rise of New Left, see Jonathan M. Wiener, "Radical Historians and the Crisis in American History, 1959–1980," *Journal of American History* 76, no. 2 (September 1989): 399–434. Jesse Lemisch argues that Pollack's *The Populist Response to Industrial America* (Cambridge, Mass.: Harvard University Press, 1962) "deserves to be thought of as the first work of New Left history." Jesse Lemisch, "History at Yale in the Dark Ages, 1953–76," *History News Network* (2006).

52. Novick, *That Noble Dream*, 338; David Brown, *Richard Hofstadter: An Intellectual Biography* (Chicago: University of Chicago Press, 2006), 117–119.

53. Novick, *That Noble Dream*, 341. Lawrence Goodwyn similarly argued that the "blithely condescending tints that colored Hofstadter's portrait of the agrarian movement suggest that he may have subconsciously seen American farmers as surrogate East European peasants with a corresponding penchant for pogroms." Lawrence Goodwyn, "Rethinking 'Populism': Paradoxes of Historiography and Democracy," *Telos* 87 (1991): n.4, 41.

54. Novick, *That Noble Dream*, 341, n.32.

55. Brown, *Richard Hofstadter*, 112. The phrase "the new conservatism" refers to Hofstadter's reaction against McCarthyism.

56. On the tradition of faculty dinner parties and general sociability, see Palmer, "All Coherence Gone?" 131–133.

57. Iseminger, "Dr. Orin G. Libby," 17–18; Wilkins, "Orin G. Libby," 108.

58. William J. Peterson, "Louis Pelzer: Scholar, Teacher, Editor," *MVHR* 33, no. 2 (September 1946): 206.

59. David A. Walker, "Milo Milton Quaife," in Wunder, *Historians of the American Frontier*, 498.

60. "Memorial Tribute to John D. Barnhart," *Indiana Magazine of History* 64, no. 2 (June 1968): 111.

61. Paul Gates to Merle Curti, January 3, 1955, FF 16, DB 17, Curti Papers, WHS; Tyrell, "Public at the Creation," 30.

62. Blegen to Buck, November 12, 1940, Box 6, Buck Papers, National Archives.

63. Hicks, "My Ten Years on the Wisconsin Faculty," 316.

64. Hicks to Sellers, December 6, 1932, Sellers Papers, University of Nebraska Archives.

65. Hicks, "My Ten Years on the Wisconsin Faculty," 304.

66. Claude H. Van Tyne to Clarence Alvord, September 28, 1915, Vol. 2, MVHA Correspondence, Alvord Papers, SHSM.

67. Novick, *That Noble Dream*, 363. Shannon complains to Hicks about the power of the department head in Shannon to Hicks, May 4, 1938, FF 1938, Carton 13, Hicks Papers, Bancroft Library.

68. Novick, *That Noble Dream*, 419.

69. Wilkins, "Orin G. Libby," 108.

70. Tully Hunter, "Frederic Logan Paxson," in Wunder, *Historians of the American Frontier*, 459; John D. Hicks, "My Years as a Graduate Student," *Wisconsin Magazine of History* 47, no. 4 (Summer 1964): 289. On the Quaker influence on the development of the American "Midlands," see Colin Woodward, *American Nations: A History of the Eleven Rival Regional Cultures of North America* (New York: Viking, 2011), 183.

71. Hicks, "My Years as a Graduate Student," 279–280.

72. Hicks to Sellers, December 6, 1932, Sellers Papers, University of Nebraska Archives.

73. Bogue, "Tilling Agricultural History," 441.

74. Dick to Hicks, December 17, 1928, FF 1928, Carton 13, Hicks Papers, Bancroft Library. On the religious inclinations of prominent midwestern New Dealers of this era, see Jess Gilbert, "Agrarian Intellectuals in a Democratizing State: A Collective Biography of USDA Leaders in the Intended New Deal," in *The Countryside in the*

Age of the Modern State: Political Histories of Rural America, ed. Catherine McNicol Stock and Robert D. Johnston (Ithaca, N.Y.: Cornell University Press, 2001), 217–222.

75. Wilkins, "Orin G. Libby," 108; Iseminger, "Dr. Orin G. Libby," 17–18.

76. J. G. Randall, "Theodore Calvin Pease," *Journal of the Illinois State Historical Society* 41, no. 4 (December 1948): 365.

77. Paxson to Hicks, May 23, 1934, and Paxson to Hicks, April 13, 1937, both in FF 1934, Carton 13, Hicks Papers, Bancroft Library.

78. "Memorial Tribute to R. Carlyle Buley," *Indiana Magazine of History* 64, no. 4 (December 1968): 325.

79. John D. Hicks, "My Six Years at Hamline," *Minnesota History* 39, no. 6 (Summer 1965): 223.

80. Bogue, "Tilling Agricultural History," 456.

81. Paxson to Hicks, August 20, 1932, FF 1932, Carton 13, Hicks Papers, Bancroft Library. When Hicks arrived in Berkeley in 1942, Paxson ensured that his office was "clean and newly painted" and accessorized with a "new swivel chair" and included a balcony with "a fine Bay view." Paxson to Hicks, August 5, 1942, and Paxson to Hicks, July 29, 1942, both in FF June–August 1942 Correspondence, DB 10, Hicks Papers, Bancroft Library.

82. See letters, Vols. 1–2, MVHA Correspondence, Alvord Papers, SHSM; Alvord to MVHR Board of Editors, January 29, 1914, Vol. 1, MVHA Correspondence, Alvord Papers, SHSM ("asthetic"); Shambaugh to Alvord, February 13, 1914, Vol. 1, MVHA Correspondence, Alvord Papers, SHSM ("undignified").

83. Paxson to Alvord, January 23, 1914, Vol. 1, MVHA Correspondence, Alvord Papers, SHSM.

84. Alvord to Clarence Paine, February 17, 1914, Vol. 1, MVHA Correspondence, Alvord Papers, SHSM.

85. Bogue to Malin, October 2, 1950, Mss. Coll. 183, Malin Papers, KSHS.

86. Bogue to Malin, January 6, 1961, Mss. Coll. 183, Malin Papers, KSHS.

87. Vernon Carstensen to Merle Curti letters in FF 18, DB 8, Curti Papers, WHS; Bogue to Malin, June 10, 1953, Mss. Coll. 183, Malin Papers, KSHS.

88. Pelzer to Hicks, February 16, 1929, and Pelzer to Hicks, February 26, 1929, both in FF 1929, Carton 13, Hicks Papers, Bancroft Library; Buck to Blegen, September 17, 1936, Box 6, Buck Papers, National Archives.

89. Paxson to Turner, March 30, 1910, Paxson to Turner, November 2, 1910, and Paxson to Turner, November 2, 1910, all in Turner Papers, Huntington Library.

90. John D. Hicks to Merle Curti, June 16, 1942, FF 17, DB 19, Curti Papers, WHS; Hicks to Curti, June 21, 1942, FF Correspondence January–June 1942, Carton 10, Hicks Papers, Bancroft Library.

91. Paxson to Hicks, November 21, 1932, FF 1932, Carton 13, Hicks Papers, Bancroft Library.

92. Wilkins, "Orin G. Libby," 108.

93. Wilkins, "Orin G. Libby," 110.

94. Paul Gates to Merle Curti, March 17, 1948, FF 16, DB 17, Curti Papers, WHS.

95. Morton Rothstein interview, University of Wisconsin Collection #92, 1976; Paul Gates to Merle Curti, July 11, 1949, FF 16, DB 17, Curti Papers, WHS.

96. Hicks, "My Ten Years on the Wisconsin Faculty," 305, 310. Hicks complained that one author's [Louis Hacker] "eternal harping on the class struggle wearies, but his book is probably fuller and better than others except when he goes Marxist."

Hicks to Merle Curti, August 7, 1942, FF Correspondence June–August 1942, Carton 10, Hicks Papers, Bancroft Library.

97. Novick, *That Noble Dream*, 246.

98. Carstensen to Curti, July 8, 1948, Carstensen to Curti, December 4, 1950, Carstensen to Curti, November 25, 1956, and Carstensen to Curti, March 19, 1967, all in FF 18, DB 8, Curti Papers, WHS. When he moved to Seattle, Carstensen was concerned about all the Goldwater signs he saw, thought the rise of Reagan in California would "give aid and courage to the troglodytes around the country," and worried that the "leather jacket motorcycle set" was attacking "the peace makers." Carstensen to Curti, September 19, 1964, Carstensen to Curti, February 14, 1967, and Carstensen to Curti, April 10, 1966, all in FF 18, DB 8, Curti Papers, WHS.

99. Novick, *That Noble Dream*, 225, 245.

100. Novick, *That Noble Dream*, 240, 243.

101. Carl Ubberlohde, "R. Carlyle Buley," in Wunder, *Historians of the American Frontier*, 162; Buley to Philip D. Jordan, May 24, 1951, Buley Papers, Indiana Historical Society.

102. Hicks to Buck, December 30, 1944, Box 8, Buck Papers, National Archives; Hicks, "My Ten Years on the Wisconsin Faculty," 315; Novick, *That Noble Dream*, 247.

103. Malin, "Ecology and History," 296; James C. Malin, "Space and History: Reflections on the Closed-Space Doctrines of Turner and Mackinder and the Challenge of Those Ideas by the Air Age," Part 1, *Agricultural History* 18, no. 2 (April 1944): 66, 73.

104. Gerald D. Nash, *Creating the West: Historical Interpretations, 1890–1990* (Albuquerque: University of New Mexico Press, 1991), 32, 222; Gene M. Gressley, "The Turner Thesis: A Problem of Historiography," *Agricultural History* 32, no. 4 (October 1958): 233.

105. Burton J. Bledstein, "Frederick Jackson Turner: A Note on the Intellectual and the Professional," *Wisconsin Magazine of History* 54 (Autumn 1970): 51.

106. Warren I. Susman, "The Useless Past: American Intellectuals and the Frontier Thesis, 1910–1930," *Bucknell Review* 11 (March 1963): 17.

107. Brown, *Beyond the Frontier*, 82.

108. Clarence Paine to Alvord, January 26, 1914, Vol. 1, MVHA Correspondence, Alvord Papers, SHSM.

109. Bogue, *Frederick Jackson Turner*, 249–254; Allan G. Bogue, "'Not by Bread Alone': The Emergence of the Wisconsin Idea and the Departure of Frederick Jackson Turner," *Wisconsin Magazine of History* 86, no. 1 (Autumn 2002): 10–23.

110. Iseminger, "Dr. Orin G. Libby," 3–5; Wilkins, "Orin G. Libby," 108. On the friction between Turner and Libby, see Bogue, *Frederick Jackson Turner*, 168–176.

111. Robert W. Johannsen, "Introduction," in Theodore Calvin Pease, *The Frontier State, 1818–1848* (Urbana: University of Illinois Press, 1987 [first published as Vol. 2 of the Centennial History of Illinois by the Illinois Centennial Commission, 1918]), xvii, xix.

112. Solon J. Buck, "Clarence Walworth Alvord, Historian," *MVHR* 15, no. 3 (December 1928): 317.

113. Paxson to Turner, November 11, 1919, and Paxson to Turner, November 20, 1919, both in Turner Papers, Huntington Library; Walker, "Milo Milton Quaife," 498; Quaife to Buley, December 28, 1950, Buley Papers, Indiana Historical Society.

114. Quaife to Buley, October 24, 1945, and Quaife to Buley, December 28, 1950, both in Buley Papers, Indiana Historical Society.

115. Paxson to Hicks, January 1, 1924, FF 1925, Carton 13, Hicks Papers, Bancroft Library.

116. Hicks to Barnhart, May 7, 1932, and Hicks to Barnhart, May 21, 1932, both in Barnhart Papers, Lilly Library, Indiana University.

117. Paul Gates to Merle Curti, October 27, 1950, and Paul Gates to Merle Curti, January 30, 1953, both in FF 16, DB 17, Curti Papers, WHS.

118. Barnhart to Hicks, June 19, 1928, and Barnhart to Hicks, November 23, 1928, both in FF 1928, Carton 13, Hicks Papers, Bancroft Library.

119. Vernon Carstensen to Merle Curti, [August 1950?], Carstensen to Curti, April 24, 1956, Carstensen to Curti, April 8, 1965, Carstensen to Curti, January 4, 1957, Carstensen to Curti, February 18, 1957, and Carstensen to Curti, January 26, 1957, all in FF 18, DB 8, Curti Papers, WHS.

120. Robert Galen Bell, "James C. Malin and the Grasslands of North America," *Agricultural History* 46, no. 3 (July 1972): 424. Fred Shannon, never one to pull punches, criticized Malin for his "constant nursing of a persecution complex" and concluded that Malin should "wake up and begin to realize that the whole world is not leagued against you" or Shannon would "be compelled to feel that [Malin's] condition is verging on the psychopathic." Fred Shannon to James Malin, April 7, 1947, FF James C. Malin, DB 1, Shannon Papers, University of Illinois Archives.

121. Rodman W. Paul, "Frederick Merk, Teacher and Scholar: A Tribute," *Western Historical Quarterly* 9, no. 2 (April 1978): 144.

122. John Morton Blum, "A Celebration of Frederick Merk, 1887–1977," *Virginia Quarterly Review* 54, no. 3 (Summer 1978).

123. Herbert A. Kellar, "Louis Pelzer: Scholar, Teacher, Editor," *MVHR* 33, no. 2 (September 1946): 205.

124. Elmer Ellis, "Louis Pelzer: Scholar, Teacher, Editor," *MVHR* 33, no. 2 (September 1946): 211 ("rugged"); Philip D. Jordan, "Louis Pelzer: Scholar, Teacher, Editor," *MVHR* 33, no. 2 (September 1946): 215 ("marrow").

125. Louis Bernard Schmidt, "A Dedication to the Memory of Louis Pelzer, 1879–1946," *Arizona and the West* 2, no. 4 (Winter 1960): 303.

126. Michael C. Steiner, "The Significance of Turner's Sectional Thesis," *Western Historical Quarterly* 10, no. 4 (October 1979): 440; Avery Craven, "Frederick Jackson Turner, Historian," *Wisconsin Magazine of History* 25, no. 4 (June 1942): 424.

127. Kellar, "Louis Pelzer," 204.

128. Jordan, "Louis Pelzer," 214; Malcolm J. Rohrbough, "Louis Pelzer," in Wunder, *Historians of the American Frontier*, 483.

129. Nash, "John D. Hicks," 306.

130. John D. Hicks to Merle Curti, October 1, 1942, FF 17, DB 19, Curti Papers, WHS.

131. Gilbert C. Fite, "Everett Dick," *Great Plains Journal* 19 (1979): 15–17.

132. E. David Cronon, "Merle Curti: An Appraisal and Bibliography of his Writings," *Wisconsin Magazine of History* 54, no. 2 (Winter 1970–1971): 119.

133. Vernon Carstensen to Merle Curti, April 6, 1957, FF 18, DB 8, Curti Papers, WHS.

134. Bogue, "Tilling Agricultural History," 437.

135. Bogue, "Tilling Agricultural History," 440.

136. Bogue to Malin, September 11, 1947, Mss. Coll. 183, Malin Papers, KSHS.

137. Clarence Walworth Alvord, "The Relation of the State to Historical Work," *Minnesota History Bulletin* 1, no. 1 (February 1915): 4.

138. Alvord, "Relation of the State to Historical Work," 8.

139. Solon J. Buck, "The Living Past," *Pennsylvania History* 8, no. 1 (January 1941): 53. On the need to preserve historical materials, see Buck's luncheon address at the 1926 MVHA annual meeting in Springfield, Illinois. Solon Buck, "The Promotion of American History and History in America," *Minnesota History* 7, no. 2 (June 1926): 122–126.

140. Buck to Blegen, December 4, 1935, and assorted correspondence, Box 6, Buck Papers, National Archives.

141. W. N. Davis Jr., Fred Dietz, and Robert S. Fletcher, "Historical News and Comments," *MVHR* 35, no. 4 (March 1949): 720. Pease was also chairman of the AHA's Manuscripts Commission. The Society of American Archivists held its second annual meeting in Springfield, Illinois, in 1938. Randall, "Theodore Calvin Pease," 361–362.

142. Hicks to Buck, June 29, 1938, FF 1938, Carton 13, Hicks Papers, Bancroft Library; Hicks to Malin, February 27, 1941, and Hicks to Malin, March 7, 1941, both in Mss. Coll. 183, Malin Papers, KSHS; Buck to Blegen, September 28, 1935, and Buck to Blegen, March 28, 1940, both in Box 6, Buck Papers, National Archives.

143. Novick, *That Noble Dream*, 175.

144. Buck, "Clarence Walworth Alvord," 316.

145. Johannsen, "Introduction," xxviii.

146. Hicks to Shannon, May 12, 1938, FF 1938, Carton 13, Hicks Papers, Bancroft Library; Hicks to Malin, January 8, 1942, Mss. Coll. 183, Malin Papers, KSHS (advocating Theodore Saloutos).

147. Hicks to Buck, October 31, 1935, and Buck to Hicks, November 7, 1935, both in Box 8, Buck Papers, National Archives.

148. Gates to Malin, December 10, 1943, Mss. Coll. 183, Malin Papers, KSHS; Paul Gates to Merle Curti, October 27, 1950, FF 16, DB 17, Curti Papers, WHS.

149. Bogue to Malin, December 24, 1962, Mss. Coll. 183, Malin Papers, KSHS. On Bogue's hiring at Iowa, see Stow Persons, "History at Iowa: The Modern Era," 6–7, University of Iowa Libraries. Turner was similarly diverted by other duties. See Ray Allen Billington, "Why Some Historians Rarely Write History: A Case Study of Frederick Jackson Turner," *MVHR* 50, no. 1 (June 1963): 14.

150. Thelen, "Of Audiences, Borderlands, and Comparisons," 433.

151. Solon Buck, "The Progress and Possibilities of Mississippi Valley History," *MVHR* 10, no. 1 (June 1923): 16.

152. Pelzer et al., "Projects in American History," 502.

153. Pelzer et al., "Projects in American History," 501–502.

154. Shambaugh to Alvord, October 4, 1915, Vol. 2, MVHA Correspondence, Alvord Papers, SHSM; Benjamin J. Shambaugh, ed., *Applied History* (Iowa City: State Historical Society of Iowa, 1914); Merle Curti, "The Democratic Theme in American Historical Literature," *MVHR* 39, no. 1 (June 1952): 13; Hicks, "My Ten Years on the Wisconsin Faculty," 306; "Historical News," *American Historical Review* 54, no. 2 (January 1949): 479.

155. Bogue to Malin, March 6, 1967, Mss. Coll. 183, Malin Papers, KSHS.

156. The Prairie Historians' work ethic comports with their midwestern heritage. Liahna Babener, "The Romance of Suffering: Midwesterners Remember the Homestead," *MidAmerica* 22 (1995): 25–34.

157. Clarence Paine to Alvord, September 14, 1914, Vol. 1, MVHA Correspondence, Alvord Papers, SHSM.

158. Alvord to Dunbar Rowland, November 22, 1915, Vol. 2, MVHA Correspondence, Alvord Papers, SHSM.

159. Buck, "Clarence Walworth Alvord," 317.

160. Jordan, "Louis Pelzer," 211–213; Schmidt, "Dedication to the Memory of Louis Pelzer," 305; Rohrbough, "Louis Pelzer," 485.

161. Schmidt, "Dedication to the Memory of Louis Pelzer," 213.

162. Iseminger, "Dr. Orin G. Libby," 21.

163. Ira G. Clark, "Frederic Logan Paxson, 1877–1948," *Journal of the Southwest* 3, no. 2 (Summer 1961): 110.

164. Hicks, "My Years as a Graduate Student," 288.

165. Hicks, "My Six Years at Hamline," 218.

166. Fite, "Everett Dick," 17.

167. Bogue to Malin, November 5, 1955, Mss. Coll. 183, Malin Papers, KSHS (quoting unnamed historian).

168. Bogue to Malin, June 11, 1950, and Bogue to Malin, July 1, 1957, both in Mss. Coll. 183, Malin Papers, KSHS.

169. Bogue to Malin, April 28, 1952, and Bogue to Malin, October 24, 1954, both in Mss. Coll. 183, Malin Papers, KSHS.

170. Bogue to Malin, November 27, 1954, Mss. Coll. 183, Malin Papers, KSHS.

171. Buley to Curti, May 17, 1951, Buley Papers, Indiana Historical Society.

172. Blegen to Curti, January 8, 1960, FF 4, DB 6, Curti Papers, WHS.

173. Bogue, *Frederick Jackson Turner*, 189.

174. Alvord to Editor, *Literary Digest*, February 16, 1914, Vol. 1, MVHA Correspondence, Alvord Papers, SHSM; Alvord to George Sioussat, May 29, 1917, Vol. 2, MVHA Correspondence, Alvord Papers, SHSM. The members of the MVHA, Ian Tyrell explains, "saw it as their duty to discipline memory, to subject it to critical analysis, and to broaden its context beyond the personal and the local." Tyrell, "Public at the Creation," 23.

175. Clarence Walworth Alvord, "The Daniel Boone Myth," *Journal of the Illinois State Historical Society* 19, nos. 1–2 (April–July 1926): 16–30.

176. Buck, "Clarence Walworth Alvord," 319–320.

177. Milo M. Quaife, "Critical Evaluation of the Sources for Western History," *MVHR* 1, no. 2 (September 1914): 169.

178. Buley, *Old Northwest*, vii.

179. Ubberlohde, "R. Carlyle Buley," 163.

180. Iseminger, "Dr. Orin G. Libby," 3 (Iseminger's description).

181. Kellar, "Louis Pelzer," 205–206; Ellis, "Louis Pelzer," 209 ("restricted").

182. Clark, "Frederic Logan Paxson," 109; "Interview with Gilbert Fite," *Historian* 56, no. 1 (Autumn 1993): 15. See also James C. Malin, *Essays on Historiography* (Lawrence, Kans.: James C. Malin, 1946); and James C. Malin, *On the Nature of History: Essays about History and Dissidence* (Lawrence, Kans.: James C. Malin, 1954).

183. Earl Pomeroy, "Frederic L. Paxson and His Approach to History," *MVHR* 39, no. 4 (March 1953): 682–684.

184. Shambaugh to Alvord, April 1, 1916, Vol. 2, MVHA Correspondence, Alvord Papers, SHSM; Clarence Paine to Alvord, April 10, 1916, Vol. 2, MVHA Correspondence, Alvord Papers, SHSM.

185. Richard Hofstadter, *The Progressive Historians: Turner, Beard, Parrington* (New York: Knopf, 1968), 72.

186. H. Roger Grant, "Lewis Atherton," *Great Plains Journal* 19 (1979): 11. Becker was from Iowa, earned a Ph.D. from Wisconsin, and taught at Kansas from 1902 to 1916. For his treatment of Kansas, see Carl Becker, "Kansas," in *Essays in American History Dedicated to Frederick Jackson Turner* (New York: Henry Holt, 1910), 85–111.

187. Shambaugh to Alvord, October 4, 1915, Vol. 2, MVHA Correspondence, Alvord Papers, SHSM. See Shambaugh, *Applied History*; Alvord to Shambaugh, October 5, 1915, Vol. 2, MVHA Correspondence, Alvord Papers, SHSM.

188. Curti, "Democratic Theme," 22.

189. Alvord to George Sioussat, May 29, 1917, Vol. 2, MVHA Correspondence, Alvord Papers, SHSM.

190. Quaife to Alvord, June 5, 1917, Vol. 2, MVHA Correspondence, Alvord Papers, SHSM.

191. Libby to Alvord, June 5, 1917, Vol. 2, MVHA Correspondence, Alvord Papers, SHSM.

192. Frederic Logan Paxson review of Charles A. Beard and Mary R. Beard, *The Rise of American Civilization*, 2 vols. (New York: Macmillan, 1927), in *MVHR* 14 (September 1927): 233.

193. Malin, "Ecology and History," 297; James C. Malin, "Space and History: Reflections on the Closed–Space Doctrines of Turner and Mackinder and the Challenge of Those Ideas by the Air Age," Part 2, *Agricultural History* 18, no. 3 (April 1944): 120; Jon K. Lauck, "Dorothea Lange and the Limits of the Liberal Narrative," *Heritage of the Great Plains* 45, no. 1 (Summer 2012): 4–37.

194. Curti, "Democratic Theme," 26.

195. Pelzer et al., "Projects in American History," 501.

196. Bogue to Malin, April 5, 1968, Mss. Coll. 183, Malin Papers, KSHS; Curti, "Democratic Theme," 19. Bogue also criticized an article written for *Harpers* by Walter Prescott Webb entitled "The American West: Perpetual Mirage" and commented on "how remunerative it can be for a historian to disregard all the canons of historical scholarship." Bogue to Malin, September 24, 1957, Mss. Coll. 183, Malin Papers, KSHS. Bogue said he would not "knuckle under and be a conformist" and said he would "rather be a James Malin than a Ray Billington who runs for the presidency of the MVHA in every book review he writes." Bogue to Malin, March 11, 1956, Mss. Coll. 183, Malin Papers, KSHS.

197. Christopher Lasch, *The Revolt of the Elites and the Betrayal of Democracy* (New York: W. W. Norton, 1995), 14; James T. Kloppenberg, "Objectivity and Historicism: A Century of American Historical Writing," *American Historical Review* 94, no. 4 (October 1989): 1029.

198. Kloppenberg, "Objectivity and Historicism," 1029, 1015.

199. Kloppenberg, "Objectivity and Historicism," 1030. See also John E. Miller, "Epistemology in Flux: Embattled Truth in an Information Age," *South Dakota Review* 24, no. 3 (Autumn 1986): 7–20.

200. John Hicks to Merle Curti, October 5, 1944, FF Correspondence August–December 1942, DB 10, Hicks Papers, Bancroft Library.

201. Hicks to Curti, October 5, 1944, FF Correspondence August–December 1942, DB 10, Hicks Papers, Bancroft Library. As Alvin Kernan has noted when discussing the recent hand-wringing about the difficulty of scholarly interpretation, "there was

nothing new in this." Alvin Kernan, *In Plato's Cave* (New Haven, Conn.: Yale University Press 1999), 193.

202. Hofstadter, *Progressive Historians*, xvi ("Brahmins"); Charles Grier Sellers Jr., "Andrew Jackson versus the Historians," *MVHR* 44, no. 4 (March 1958): 619.

203. Craven, "Frederick Jackson Turner," 424; Avery Craven, "A History Still Unwritten," *Western Historical Quarterly* 2, no. 4 (October 1971): 377.

CHAPTER FOUR

1. Tony Judt, "A Clown in Regal Purple: Social History and the Historians," *History Workshop* no. 7 (Spring 1979): 89, n.1.

2. On regional assertiveness, see Wallace Stegner and Richard Etulain, *Stegner: Conversations on History and Literature*, rev. ed. (Reno: University of Nevada Press, 1996), 190.

3. Ruth Suckow, "Middle Western Literature," *English Journal* 21, no. 3 (March 1932): 176.

4. Robert L. Dorman, *Revolt of the Provinces: The Regionalist Movement in America, 1920–1945* (Chapel Hill: University of North Carolina Press, 1993), 10.

5. The "fiercest disputes" in history departments are no longer over which candidate is most qualified for a position, William Palmer notes, but "about what field a position would cover." William Palmer, "All Coherence Gone? A Cultural History of Leading History Departments in the United States, 1970–2010," *Journal of the Historical Society* 12, no. 2 (June 2012): 131. Those who support a revival of midwestern history will need to argue in favor of the field of midwestern history.

6. Joseph Schafer, "The Social Value of Historical Memorials," *Wisconsin Magazine of History* 9, no. 2 (December 1925): 213.

7. Dixon Ryan Fox, "State History I," *Political Science Quarterly* 36, no. 4 (December 1921): 573.

8. Fox, "State History," 573.

9. Fox, "State History," 573. See also Wilfred M. McClay, "The Particularities of Place," *New Atlantis* no. 31 (Spring 2011): 33–40. On the psychological costs of placelessness, see David Glassberg, *Sense of History: The Place of the Past in American Life* (Amherst: University of Massachusetts Press, 2001), 111–127. On the social and personal costs of disconnection from place, see Susan J. Matt, *Homesickness: An American History* (New York: Oxford University Press, 2011); and "The New Globalist Is Homesick," *New York Times*, March 21, 2012. See also Scott Russell Sanders, *Writing from the Center* (Bloomington: Indiana University Press, 1995), 9–21; Wallace Stegner, *Where the Bluebird Sings to the Lemonade Springs: Living and Writing in the West* (New York: Wings Books, 1992), 199–206; Wayne Franklin and Michael Steiner, "Taking Place: Toward the Regrounding of American Studies," in *Mapping American Culture*, ed. Wayne Franklin and Michael C. Steiner (Iowa City: University of Iowa Press, 1992), 5–6; and Harold P. Simonson, *Beyond the Frontier: Writers, Western Regionalism, and a Sense of Place* (Fort Worth: Texas Christian University Press, 1989), 3–4.

10. Avery Craven, "The Advance of Civilization into the Middle West in the Period of Settlement," in *Sources of Culture in the Middle West: Backgrounds versus Frontier*, ed. Dixon Ryan Fox (1934; repr., New York: Russell & Russell, 1964),

40; Avery Craven, "A History Still Unwritten," *Western Historical Quarterly* 2, no. 4 (October 1971): 378, 382.

11. Jon K. Lauck, "The Prairie Populism of Christopher Lasch," *Great Plains Quarterly* 32, no. 3 (Summer 2012): 183–205; Christopher Lasch, *The Minimal Self: Psychic Survival in Troubled Times* (New York: W. W. Norton, 1984), 17.

12. Richard Lingeman, *Sinclair Lewis: Rebel from Main Street* (New York: Random House, 2002); Mark Schorer, *Sinclair Lewis: An American Life* (New York: McGraw-Hill, 1961); Fred Hobson, *Mencken: A Life* (Baltimore: Johns Hopkins University Press, 1995); Anthony Channell Hilfer, *The Revolt from the Village, 1915–1930* (Chapel Hill: University of North Carolina Press, 1969), 4; C. Elizabeth Raymond, "The Creation of America's Rural Heartland: An Essay on Prairie Midwestern Regional Identity," 3–6 (in author's possession); James C. Malin, *Essays on Historiography* (Lawrence, Kans.: James C. Malin, 1946), 109–110; Richard O. Davies, *Main Street Blues: The Decline of Small-Town America* (Columbus: Ohio State University Press, 1998), 6; Stephen H. Webb, "What Is the Midwest? Notes on a Geographical Identity," *Reviews in Religion and Theology* 16, no. 2 (2009): 171; Timothy B. Spears, *Chicago Dreaming: Midwesterners and the City, 1871–1919* (Chicago: University of Chicago Press, 2005), 111–146; Guy Reynolds, "Willa Cather's Case: Region and Reputation," in *Regionalism and the Humanities*, ed. Wendy J. Katz and Timothy R. Mahoney (Lincoln: University of Nebraska Press, 2008), 81–84. On the "anti-expatriate movement" among midwestern regionalists, see Milton M. Reigelman, *The Midland: A Venture in Literary Regionalism* (Iowa City: University of Iowa Press, 1975), 41. Reigelman notes how the regionalists were "so markedly different from the postwar, wasteland world portrayed in much of the better-known fiction of the 1920s." Reigelman, *Midland*, xvi. See also the excellent review by Barry Gross, which refutes the "village revolt" interpretation. Barry Gross, "In Another Country: The Revolt from the Village," *MidAmerica* 4 (1977): 101–111.

13. James H. Shideler, "'Flappers and Philosophers,' and Farmers: Rural-Urban Tensions of the Twenties," *Agricultural History* 47, no. 4 (October 1973): 289 (quoting Harold Stearns); Peter H. Argersinger, "The People's Past: Teaching American Rural History," *History Teacher* 10, no. 3 (May 1977): 405; Wendell Berry, "The Prejudice against Country People," *Progressive* (April 2002); Alfred Haworth Jones, "The Search for a Usable Past in the New Deal Era," *American Quarterly* 23, no. 5 (December 1971): 713; Benjamin Appel, "Easterners and the Middle West," *Prairie Schooner* 5, no. 3 (Summer 1931): 199–204. One literary character admits that midwesterners were "so friendly and decent [that] it shamed her to dislike them," which should serve as a warning that the problem may lie with the character or her creator, not the region. Sanders, *Writing from the Center*, 31. See also Vardis Fisher, "The Western Writer and the Eastern Establishment," *Western American Literature* 1 (Winter 1967): 244–259.

14. Warren I. Susman, *Culture as History: The Transformation of American Society in the Twentieth Century* (Washington, D.C.: Smithsonian Institution Press, 2003), 36.

15. Ronald Weber, *The Midwestern Ascendency in American Writing* (Bloomington: Indiana University Press, 1992), 197.

16. Jon Gjerde, "Middleness and the Middle West," in *The Identity of the American Midwest: Essays on Regional History*, ed. Andrew R. L. Cayton and Susan E. Gray (Bloomington: Indiana University Press, 2001), 190. For views of the Midwest that

contradict the literary "rebels," see Reigelman, *Midland*; John E. Miller, *Memories of Home: Small-Town Boys from the Midwest and the American Dream* (forthcoming from Kansas University Press); Booth Tarkington, "The Middle West," *Harper's Monthly Magazine* (December 1902), 75–83.

17. Zachary Michael Jack, ed., *Iowa: The Definitive Collection* (North Liberty, Iowa: Tall Corn Books, 2009), 7.

18. Warren I. Susman, "History and the American Intellectual: Uses of a Usable Past," *American Quarterly* 16, no. 2 (Summer 1964): 243–263.

19. Richard Hofstadter, *The Progressive Historians: Turner, Beard, Parrington* (New York: Vintage, 1968), 86–87. John Mack Faragher explains how, during the 1920s, an "important component of intellectual radicalism took the form of a kind of inverted frontier thesis, invoking the western past to account for many of the negative aspects of American civilization." John Mack Faragher, "The Frontier Trail: Rethinking Turner and Reimagining the American West," *American Historical Review* 98, no. 1 (February 1993): 109.

20. Hofstadter, *Progressive Historians*, 87; Christopher Lasch, "The Degradation of Work and the Apotheosis of Art," *Harper's* (February 1984), 41.

21. Hofstadter, *Progressive Historians*, 88.

22. James M. Dennis, *Renegade Regionalists: The Modern Independence of Grant Wood, Thomas Hart Benton, and John Steuart Curry* (Madison: University of Wisconsin Press, 1998), 83.

23. Dorothy Ross, "Grand Narrative in American Historical Writing: From Romance to Uncertainty," *American Historical Review* 100, no. 3 (June 1995): 652.

24. Ross, "Grand Narrative," 663–664.

25. Ross, "Grand Narrative," 673; Palmer, "All Coherence Gone?" 134–137.

26. David R. Pichaske, *Rooted: Seven Midwest Writers of Place* (Iowa City: University of Iowa Press, 2006), 3. See also Kerwin Lee Klein, *From History to Theory* (Berkeley: University of California Press, 2011), 90, 166.

27. Pichaske, *Rooted*, 3. For a warning against writing only "from the edge," see Sanders, *Writing from the Center*, 150.

28. Pichaske, *Rooted*, 3; Christopher Lasch, *The Revolt of the Elites and the Betrayal of Democracy* (New York: W. W. Norton, 1995), 185.

29. Pichaske, *Rooted*, 8.

30. Peter Burke, *History and Social Theory*, 2nd ed. (Ithaca, N.Y.: Cornell University Press, 2005), 1; Walter Nugent, "Where Have All the Flowers Gone . . . When Will They Ever Learn?" *Reviews in American History* 37, no. 1 (March 2011): 207–208; John Patrick Diggins, "Language and History," *Reviews in American History* 17, no. 1 (March 1989): 1–9; Margaret MacMillan, *Dangerous Games: The Uses and Abuses of History* (New York: Modern Library, 2009), 37; Gregory Pfitzer, "History Cracked Open: 'New' History's Renunciation of the Past," *Reviews in American History* 31, no. 1 (March 2003): 144; Joyce Appleby, *A Restless Past: History and the American Public* (Lanham, Md.: Rowman & Littlefield, 2005), 141–142; Lasch, *Revolt of the Elites*, 12–13.

31. David Harlan, *The Degradation of American History* (Chicago: University of Chicago Press, 1997), xv, xix; Daniel T. Rogers, *Age of Fracture* (Cambridge, Mass.: Harvard University Press, 2011), 91–107; Bruce Bawer, *The Victims' Revolution: The Rise of Identity Studies and the Closing of the Liberal Mind* (New York: HarperCollins, 2012), xiv.

32. Myra Jehlen, "Beyond Transcendence," in *Ideology and Classic American Literature*, ed. Sacvan Bercovitch and Myra Jehlen (Cambridge: Cambridge University Press, 1986), 5.

33. J. H. Hexter, *On Historians: Reappraisals of Some of the Makers of Modern History* (Cambridge, Mass.: Harvard University Press, 1979), 4.

34. David Hackett Fischer, *Historians' Fallacies: Toward a Logic of Historical Thought* (New York: Harper & Row, 1970), 313–314.

35. Jon K. Lauck, "Dorothea Lange and the Liberal Narrative," *Heritage of the Great Plains* 45, no. 1 (Summer 2012): 18–20.

36. Carl N. Degler, "Remaking American History," *Journal of American History* 67, no. 1 (June 1980): 20.

37. "The Power of Regionalism: A Conversation with David Hackett Fischer," *Humanities* 20, no. 4 (July/August 1999).

38. Andrew R. L. Cayton, "The Anti-Region: Place and Identity in the History of the American Midwest," in Cayton and Gray, *Identity of the American Midwest*, 152.

39. Paula M. Nelson, "State History in Local Perspective," in *The State We're In: Reflections on Minnesota History*, ed. Annette Atkins and Deborah L. Miller (St. Paul: Minnesota Historical Society Press, 2010), 25–30.

40. Alan Brinkley, "The Western Historians: Don't Fence Them In," *New York Times Book Review*, September 20, 1992.

41. Susan E. Gray, "Stories Written in the Blood: Race and Midwestern History," in Cayton and Gray, *Identity of the American Midwest*, 125; Jon K. Lauck, "How South Dakota Sparked the New Western History Wars: A Commentary on Patricia Nelson Limerick," *South Dakota History* 41, no. 3 (Fall 2011): 353–381.

42. Gerald Nash, "The Global Context of the New Western Historians," in *Old West/New West: Quo Vadis?* ed. Gene M. Gressley (Worland, Wyo.: High Plains Publishing, 1994), 149.

43. In a poll of over 1,000 readers of the *Journal of American History*, 67 percent of respondents said that the discipline of American history was too focused on narrow topics, suffered the inhibiting effect of political correctness, suffered from elitism and snobbery, and was too divorced from the concerns of the public at large. Seventy-four percent thought the academy rewarded writing for narrow academic audiences and not a general public, and 65 percent thought that "elite" institutions operated separately from the rest of higher education. A plurality thought that the politics of historians drove their research, and many respondents "felt real pressure to shape what they said in order to satisfy the political tastes of those who gave rewards." David Thelen, "The Practice of American History," *Journal of American History* 81, no. 3 (December 1994): 936–941.

44. On the "crisis in confidence and credibility" within the historical profession, see Joan Hoff, "The Challenges to Traditional Histories," in *The Organization of American Historians and the Writing and Teaching of American History*, ed. Richard S. Kirkendall (New York: Oxford University Press, 2011), 116.

45. George L. Mosse, *Confronting History: A Memoir* (Madison: University of Wisconsin Press, 2000), 172.

46. Mosse, *Confronting History*, 171.

47. Mosse, *Confronting History*, 171.

48. Mosse, *Confronting History*, 5, 167, 139.

49. Mosse, *Confronting History*, 171.

50. Mosse's Western Civilization course in the fall of 1949 saw an enrollment of 830. Stow Persons, "History at Iowa: The Modern Era," 2–5, University of Iowa Libraries.

51. Mosse, *Confronting History*, 6.

52. Mosse, *Confronting History*, 135.

53. Mosse, *Confronting History*, 152–153. Mosse was "discovered" at Iowa by the South Dakotan Merrill Jensen and taken back to Wisconsin. Jensen was born in Iowa and raised in South Dakota. Mosse thought Wisconsin saw "history from the viewpoint of South Dakota (where Merrill Jensen, the colonial historian, grew up), in contrast to the conventional view from New England." Mosse, *Confronting History*, 152, 154. Turner, like Mosse, focused on the broader "forces" that shaped history. See Frederick Jackson Turner, "The Development of American Society," *Alumni Quarterly* (University of Illinois) 2 (1908): 120–121, RS 26/2/801, University of Illinois Archives.

54. Mosse, *Confronting History*, 6.

55. Mosse, *Confronting History*, 128.

56. Mosse, *Confronting History*, 144–147, 163, 166.

57. Mosse, *Confronting History*, 165. For a similar perspective, see Gerald D. Nash, *Creating the West: Historical Interpretations, 1890–1990* (Albuquerque: University of New Mexico Press, 1991).

58. Jon K. Lauck, "The Case for Iowa," *Claremont Review of Books* (Fall 2011): 1–3 (special edition); Jon K. Lauck, "The Historical Case for the Iowa Caucuses," *Fortnightly Review* (Fall 2011).

59. Gordon Wood, "Equality and Social Conflict in the American Revolution," *William and Mary Quarterly* 51, no. 4 (October 1994): 706–707.

60. Wood, "Equality and Social Conflict," 707.

61. Wood, "Equality and Social Conflict," 707, 709.

62. Wood, "Equality and Social Conflict," 707.

63. Frederick Jackson Turner, "Middle Western Pioneer Democracy," in *Rereading Frederick Jackson Turner: "The Significance of the Frontier in American History" and Other Essays*, ed. John Mack Faragher (New Haven, Conn.: Yale University Press, 1998), 162. Turner telegrammed Solon Buck in St. Paul in January to inform him he would travel from Harvard and speak at the dedication and in April informed Buck that his speech would focus on "pioneer democracy." The train ride between Cambridge and St. Paul required five nights in a sleeper car. Turner to Buck, January 10, 1918, Turner to Buck, April 17, 1918, and Turner to Buck, May 17, 1918, all in Collection 307.F.14.3B, Minnesota Historical Society Archives Correspondence, Minnesota Historical Society. On the event, see "Exercises at the Dedication of the Minnesota Historical Building," *Minnesota History Bulletin* 3, no. 7 (August 1920): 415–437.

64. Turner, "Middle Western Pioneer Democracy," 164, 173. On another occasion, Turner remarked that the "Mississippi Valley alone could engulf the combined nations of France, Germany, Italy and Austro-Hungary." Turner, "Development of American Society," 122.

65. Timothy Snyder, *Bloodlands: Europe between Hitler and Stalin* (New York: Basic Books, 2010).

66. Turner, "Middle Western Pioneer Democracy," 160, 162. See also Benjamin Shambaugh's speech, FF remarks at dedication of Minnesota Historical Society

building, Box 9, Shambaugh papers, Special Collections Department, University of Iowa Libraries.

67. Turner, "Middle Western Pioneer Democracy," 160.

68. Turner, "Middle Western Pioneer Democracy," 162. See also Roy F. Nichols, "The Territories: Seedbeds of Democracy," *Nebraska History* 35, no. 3 (September 1954): 171; and John D. Hicks, "Our Pioneer Heritage," *Prairie Schooner* 2, no. 1 (Winter 1928): 23.

EPILOGUE

1. Dean Albertson, "Guy Stanton Ford," *American Scholar* 26, no. 3 (Summer 1957): 350–353.

2. Albertson, "Guy Stanton Ford," 352 (emphasis added).

3. Albertson, "Guy Stanton Ford," 352 (quoting Albertson).

4. Guy Stanton Ford, "A Ranke Letter," *Journal of Modern History* 32, no. 2 (June 1960): 142–144; Albertson, "Guy Stanton Ford," 352.

5. Hiram Haydn, "Guy Stanton Ford, May 9, 1873–December 29, 1962," *American Scholar* 32, no. 3 (Summer 1963): 355 ("gentleness"); Albertson, "Guy Stanton Ford," 350–353.

6. Albertson, "Guy Stanton Ford," 350–353; Guy Stanton Ford, "Some Suggestions to American Historians," *American Historical Review* 43, no. 2 (January 1938): 265. Theodore Blegen praised the University of Minnesota for providing writing fellowships for regional writers and the University of Minnesota Press for making a "place, and a large place, for books interpreting the Upper Midwest." Theodore C. Blegen, *Grassroots History* (Minneapolis: University of Minnesota Press, 1947), 11. John Hicks used the University of Minnesota Press as a model for the creation of the University of Wisconsin Press. Hicks to Buck, October 31, 1935, and Buck to Hicks, November 7, 1935, both in Box 8, Buck Papers, National Archives.

7. Albertson, "Guy Stanton Ford," 350.

8. Guy Stanton Ford to John D. Hicks, August 20, 1945, FF July–December 1945 Correspondence, DB 14, Hicks Papers, Bancroft Library.

9. Benjamin F. Shambaugh, ed., *Proceedings of the Mississippi Valley Historical Association for the Year 1907–1908* (Cedar Rapids, Iowa: Torch Press, 1909), 1:9.

10. Ford to Hicks, August 20, 1945, Hicks Papers, Bancroft Library. For a similar statement of the case, see the note by Indianan John D. Barnhart in *Mississippi Valley History Review* 38, no. 2 (September 1951): 352.

11. Board of Editors Minutes, December 29, 1913, 1, MVHA Correspondence, Alvord Papers, State Historical Society of Missouri.

12. James Madison, "Diverging Trails: Why the Midwest Is Not the West," in *Frontier and Region: Essays in Honor of Martin Ridge*, ed. Robert C. Ritchie and Paul Andrew Hutton (Albuquerque: University of New Mexico Press, 1997), 43. On the cost of the absence of "institutional structures" such as a regional journal, see Andrew R. L. Cayton, "The Anti-Region: Place and Identity in the History of the American Midwest," in *The Identity of the American Midwest: Essays on Regional History*, ed. Andrew R. L. Cayton and Susan E. Gray (Bloomington: Indiana University Press, 2001), 148–149. When midwesterners relinquished the more mainstream standing of the *MVHR* and were forced into the Western History Association, Kerwin Lee Klein argues, the western subfield "slunk off to the dusty edge of the professional

imagination." Kerwin Lee Klein, "Reclaiming the 'F' Word, or Being and Becoming Postwestern," *Pacific Historical Review* 65, no. 2 (May 1996): 214. On the importance of regional magazines and presses to maintaining a regional focus, see Robert L. Dorman, *Revolt of the Provinces: The Regionalist Movement in America, 1920–1945* (Chapel Hill: University of North Carolina Press, 1993), 286.

13. Earle D. Ross, "A Generation of Prairie Historiography," *Mississippi Valley Historical Review* 33, no. 3 (December 1946): 398.

14. Pamela Riney-Kehrberg, "New Directions in Rural History," *Agricultural History* 81, no. 2 (Spring 2007): 157.

15. "Missouri Backs Decision to Close University Press," Associated Press, June 27, 2012; Scott Jaschik, "U. of Missouri Press Survives," *Inside Higher Education*, August 29, 2012.

16. This Google search was conducted on September 12, 2012, and compared results for the search terms "History of the American Midwest," "History of New England," and "History of the American South." The South has been characterized as the "most studied region in the world." John Shelton Reed, *The Enduring South: Subcultural Persistence in Mass Society* (Chapel Hill: University of North Carolina Press, 1972), 1.

17. This review focuses on works written in roughly the past twenty-five years. For a review of an earlier generation of works, see Andrew R. L. Cayton and Peter S. Onuf, *The Midwest and the Nation: Rethinking the History of an American Region* (Bloomington: Indiana University Press, 1990), which was written in conjunction with the 1987 bicentennial of the Constitution and focused on works published since 1950, about the time the Prairie Historians' project began to dissipate.

18. Ross, "Generation of Prairie Historiography," 392–393; Andrew R. L. Cayton and Frederika J. Teute, "On the Connection of Frontiers," in *Contact Points: American Frontiers from the Mohawk Valley to the Mississippi, 1750–1830*, ed. Andrew R. L. Cayton and Frederika J. Teute (Chapel Hill: University of North Carolina Press, 1998), 4, n.5.

19. While Bogue focused most of his regional work on midwestern history, he also taught the broader history of the American West. When Bogue first taught western history at Iowa, he told James Malin that his impatient students were "disappointed that I did not start to punch cattle the first day." Bogue to Malin, November 3, 1952, Mss. Coll. 183, Malin Papers, Kansas State Historical Society.

20. In the 1930s, Merle Curti told John Hicks that he "quite lost my heart to California, and almost decided to stay there. Don't ever go out for a long visit, unless you are prepared to succumb!" Curti to Hicks, May 5, 1937, FF 1937, Carton 13, Hicks Papers, Bancroft Library. Hicks succumbed, but he desperately missed his "home" in the Midwest and almost returned to Wisconsin. Hicks to Frederic Logan Paxson, March 27, 1944, FF January–June Correspondence 1944, DB 10, Hicks Papers, Bancroft Library.

21. Richard White, "Obituary," *Western Historical Quarterly* 24, no. 1 (February 1993): 138.

22. Robert Utley to author, April 16, 2012.

23. Jon K. Lauck, "How South Dakota Sparked the New Western History Wars: A Commentary on Patricia Nelson Limerick," *South Dakota History* 41, no. 3 (Fall 2011): 353–381. Robert D. Johnston concluded that "more than any other writer, Limerick has given shape to the field in both academic and popular forums. She is the

most outspoken advocate of, and tireless proselytizer for, a self-conscious movement known as 'the New Western History.'" Robert D. Johnston, "Beyond 'The West': Regionalism, Liberalism and the Evasion of Politics in the New Western History," *Rethinking History* 2, no. 2 (1998): 242. Richard W. Etulain concluded that "no one has done more than Patricia Nelson Limerick to champion" the New Western History. Richard W. Etulain, *Re-Imagining the Modern West: A Century of Fiction, History, and Art* (Tucson: University of Arizona Press, 1996), 180. Gerald Thompson crowned Limerick as the "queen of the New Western Historians" and the "most prominent" of the group. Gerald Thompson, "The New Western History: A Critical Analysis," *Continuity: A Journal of History* no. 17 (Fall 1993): 7–8.

24. Jon K. Lauck, "The Old Roots of the New History: The Intellectual Origins of Howard Lamar's *Dakota Territory*," *Western Historical Quarterly* 39, no. 3 (Autumn 2008): 261–281. Donald Pisani concluded that the "New Western Historians—like the New Left historians of the 1960s and 1970s—are far more concerned with ideology and the search for a 'usable past' than were earlier western historians." Donald J. Pisani, "Is There Life After Turner? The Continuing Search for the Grand Synthesis and an Autonomous West," *New Mexico Historical Review* 67 (1992): 294. Gerald Thompson saw the New Western Historians as seeking a "usable past for understanding and dealing with present-day problems in the West." Thompson, "New Western History," 6. Limerick calls for a "usable" past in Patricia Nelson Limerick, Clyde A. Milner II, and Charles E. Rankin, eds., *Trails: Toward a New Western History* (Lawrence: University Press of Kansas, 1991), xii.

25. During the high point of these discussions, William Cronon explained that the Midwest "seems to drop out of American history as a discrete unit of analysis if the new western historians are successful in their trans-Mississippi prejudices. Up until the last couple of decades, historians interested in the Midwest found one of their most welcoming homes in the field of western history, with few objections from colleagues whose interests lay beyond the Mississippi. Today, this hospitality seems much more in doubt." William Cronon, February 16, 1996, Western history list-serve discussion.

26. Richard Etulain to author, August 19, 2012.

27. William Cronon remarks, panel discussion on the New Western History, Western History Association annual meeting, October 13, 2011, http://www.western-historyassociation.org/news/2012/02/teaching-the-west-on-c-span/.

28. Cronon's father also noted that the Turner-trained Merle Curti, who served as the Frederick Jackson Turner Professor of History at Wisconsin in an earlier era, directed Roderick Nash's dissertation, "Wilderness and the American Mind" (1965), which became a book of the same title. E. David Cronon, "Merle Curti: An Appraisal and Bibliography of His Writings," *Wisconsin Magazine of History* 54, no. 2 (Winter 1970–1971): 132. Nash began the nation's first course in environmental history at the University of California–Santa Barbara in 1970. Roderick Nash, "American Environmental History: A New Teaching Frontier," *Pacific Historical Review* 41, no. 3 (August 1972): 362.

29. William Cronon, "The West: A Moving Target," *Western Historical Quarterly* 25, no. 4 (Winter 1994): 478.

30. William Cronon, *Nature's Metropolis: Chicago and the Great West* (New York: W. W. Norton, 1992).

31. Lynne Heasley, *A Thousand Pieces of Paradise: Landscape and Property in the*

Kickapoo Valley (Madison: University of Wisconsin Press, 2012); Jeff Alexander, *Pandora's Locks: The Opening of the Great Lakes–St. Lawrence Seaway* (Lansing: Michigan State University Press, 2011); Karl Brooks, "Kansas History as Environmental History," *Kansas History* 29 (Summer 2006): 116–131; John O. Afinson, *The River We Have Wrought: A History of the Upper Mississippi* (Minneapolis: University of Minnesota Press, 2005); Calvin R. Fremling, *Immortal River: The Upper Mississippi in Ancient and Modern Times* (Madison: University of Wisconsin Press, 2005); Rebecca Conard, *Places of Quiet Beauty: Parks, Preserves, and Environmentalism* (Iowa City: University of Iowa Press, 1997); Kim M. Gruenwald, "Space and Place on the Early American Frontier: The Ohio Valley as a Region, 1790–1850," *Ohio Valley History* 4 (Fall 2004): 31–48; Kim M. Gruenwald, *River of Enterprise: The Commercial Origins of Regional Identity in the Ohio Valley, 1790–1850* (Bloomington: Indiana University Press, 2002); Andrew Hurley, *Environmental Inequalities: Class, Race, and Industrial Pollution in Gary, Indiana, 1945–1980* (Chapel Hill: University of North Carolina Press, 1995); Dave Dempsey, *Ruin and Recovery: Michigan's Rise as a Conservation Leader* (Ann Arbor: University of Michigan Press, 2001); James Kates, *Planning a Wilderness: Regenerating the Great Lakes Cutover Region* (Minneapolis: University of Minnesota Press, 2001).

32. Theodore Karamanski, *Northwoods River: The St. Croix Valley in Upper Midwest History* (Madison: University of Wisconsin Press, 2009); Theodore Karamanski, *Time and the River: A History of the St. Croix River Valley* (Washington, D.C.: National Park Service, 2002); Theodore Karamanski, *Deep Woods Frontier: A History of Logging in Northern Michigan* (Detroit: Wayne State University Press, 1989).

33. See, for Iowa examples, Candace Savage, *Prairie: A Natural History* (Vancouver: Greystone Books, 2011); Cornelia F. Mutel, *The Emerald Horizon: The History of Nature in Iowa* (Iowa City: University of Iowa Press, 2007); and Jean C. Prior, *Landforms of Iowa* (Iowa City: University of Iowa Press, 1991).

34. H. Craig Miner, *Next Year Country: Dust to Dust in Western Kansas, 1890–1940* (Lawrence: University Press of Kansas, 2006); Pamela Riney-Kehrberg, *Rooted in Dust: Surviving Drought and Depression in Southwestern Kansas* (Lawrence: University Press of Kansas, 1994). For other treatments of natural disasters on the border of the prairie/plains, see Julie Courtwright, *Prairie Fire: A Great Plains History* (Lawrence: University Press of Kansas, 2011); and Annette Atkins, *Harvest of Grief: Grasshopper Plagues and Public Assistance in Minnesota, 1873–1878* (St. Paul: Minnesota State Historical Society Press, 1984). On the debate among historians over the recent Ken Burns documentary *The Dust Bowl*, see Cody Winchester, "Burns Film Stirs Dust Bowl Debate," *Argus Leader* (Sioux Falls, S.Dak.), December 29, 2012.

35. Cayton, "Anti-Region," 148 ("cultural entity"). While recognizing recent and important works set in the Midwest, Cayton notes that "there is not much sustained effort to articulate an overall sense of region." Andrew R. L. Cayton, "Artery and Border: The Ambiguous Development of the Ohio Valley in the Early Republic," *Ohio Valley History* 1 (Winter 2001): 24.

36. "*Agricultural History* Talks to Hal S. Barron," *Agricultural History* 80, no. 4 (Autumn 2006): 411; Orville Vernon Burton, "Reaping What We Sow: Community and Rural History," *Agricultural History* 76, no. 4 (Autumn 2002): 631–658.

37. Cayton, "Anti-Region," 147. See also Carl Ubbelohde, "History and the Midwest as a Region," *Wisconsin Magazine of History* 78, no. 1 (Autumn 1994): 46.

38. Don Doyle, *The Social Order of a Frontier Community: Jacksonville, Illinois, 1825–1870* (Urbana: University of Illinois Press, 1978).

39. John Mack Faragher, *Sugar Creek: Life on the Illinois Prairie* (New Haven, Conn.: Yale University Press, 1986).

40. Jane Marie Pederson, *Between Memory and Reality: Family and Community in Rural Wisconsin, 1870–1970* (Madison: University of Wisconsin Press, 1992).

41. See Ginette Aley, "Grist, Grit, and Rural Society in the Early Midwest: Insight Gleaned from Grain," *Ohio Valley History* 5 (Summer 2005): 3–20; Susan Sessions Rugh, *Our Common Country: Family Farming, Culture, and Community in the Nineteenth-Century Midwest* (Bloomington: Indiana University Press, 2001); R. Douglas Hurt, "Guide to Reading the Social History of the Ohio Valley, 1780–1830," *Ohio Valley History* 1 (Spring 2001): 29–35; Timothy R. Mahoney, *Provincial Lives: Middle-Class Experience in the Antebellum Middle West* (New York: Cambridge University Press, 1999); Richard O. Davies, *Main Street Blues: The Decline of Small-Town America* (Columbus: Ohio State University Press, 1998); Jon K. Lauck, "'The Silent Artillery of Time': Understanding Social Change in the Rural Midwest," *Great Plains Quarterly* 19, no. 4 (Fall 1999): 245–255; Robert Gough, *Farming the Cutover: A Social History of Northern Wisconsin, 1900–1940* (Lawrence: University Press of Kansas, 1997); Hal S. Barron, *Mixed Harvest: The Second Great Transformation in the Rural North, 1870–1930* (Chapel Hill: University of North Carolina Press, 1997); Richard V. Francaviglia, *Main Street Revisited: Time, Space, and Image Building in Small-Town America* (Iowa City: University of Iowa Press, 1996); and Thomas J. Morain, *Prairie Grass Roots: An Iowa Small Town in the Early Twentieth Century* (Ames: Iowa State University Press, 1988). For an overview, see David B. Danbom, *Born in the Country: A History of Rural America*, 2nd ed. (Baltimore: Johns Hopkins University Press, 2006).

42. Neth also noted that the "Midwest as a region does not have the developed literature that the South and West do." Mary C. Neth, *Preserving the Family Farm: Women, Community and the Foundations of Agribusiness in the Midwest, 1900–1940* (Baltimore: Johns Hopkins University Press, 1995), 334.

43. Betty A. Bergland and Lori Ann Lahlum, eds., *Norwegian American Women: Migration, Communities, and Identities* (St. Paul: Minnesota State Historical Society Press, 2011); Pamela Riney-Kehrberg, *On the Farm: Work, Play, and Coming of Age in the Midwest* (Lawrence: University Press of Kansas, 2005); Linda Schelbitzki, *Contented among Strangers: Rural German-Speaking Women and Their Families in the Nineteenth-Century Midwest* (Urbana: University of Illinois Press, 1996); Carol K. Coburn, *Life at Four Corners: Religion, Gender, and Education in a German-Lutheran Community, 1868–1945* (Lawrence: University Press of Kansas, 1994); Katherine Jellison, *Entitled to Power: Farm Women and Technology, 1913–1963* (Chapel Hill: University of North Carolina Press, 1993); Deborah Fink, *Agrarian Women: Wives and Mothers in Rural Nebraska, 1880–1940* (Chapel Hill: University of North Carolina Press, 1992); Anne B. Webb, "Minnesota Women Homesteaders: 1863–1889," *Journal of Social History* 23, no. 1 (Fall 1989): 115–136; Glenda Riley, *The Female Frontier: A Comparative View of Women on the Prairie and the Plains* (Lawrence: University Press of Kansas, 1988); Lucy Eldersveld Murphy, "Her Own Boss: Businesswomen and Separate Spheres in the Midwest, 1850–1880," *Illinois Historical Journal* 80, no. 3 (1987): 155–176; Deborah Fink, *Open Country, Iowa: Rural Women, Tradition and Change* (Albany: State University of New York Press, 1986); Hal Barron, *Those Who Stayed Behind: Rural Society in Nineteenth-Century New England* (New York: Cambridge University Press, 1984); Glenda Riley, *Frontierswomen: The Iowa Experience*

(Ames: Iowa State University Press, 1981). See generally Ginette Aley, "'Knotted Together Like Roots in the Darkness': Rural Midwestern Women and Region—A Bibliographic Guide," *Agricultural History 77*, no. 3 (Summer 2003): 453–481.

44. Susan Gray, *The Yankee West: Community Life on the Michigan Frontier* (Chapel Hill: University of North Carolina Press, 1996).

45. Odd S. Lovoll, *Norwegians on the Prairie: Ethnicity and the Development of the Country Town* (St. Paul: Minnesota State Historical Society Press, 2007); Anne Gillespie Lewis, *Swedes in Minnesota* (St. Paul: Minnesota State Historical Society Press, 2004); Kathleen Neils Conzen, *Germans in Minnesota* (St. Paul: Minnesota State Historical Society Press, 2003); Jon Gjerde and Carlton C. Qualey, *Norwegians in Minnesota* (St. Paul: Minnesota State Historical Society Press, 2002); Robert P. Swierenga, *Dutch in Chicago: A History of the Hollanders in the Windy City* (Grand Rapids, Mich.: Eerdman's, 2002); Kathleen Neils Conzen, *Making Their Own: Assimilation Theory and the German Peasant Pioneer* (New York: Berg, 1990); Robert C. Ostergren, *A Community Transplanted: The Trans-Atlantic Experience of a Swedish Immigrant Settlement in the Upper Midwest, 1835–1915* (Madison: University of Wisconsin Press, 1988); Walter D. Kamphoefner, *Transplanted Wesfalians: Chain Migration from Germany to a Rural Midwestern Community* (Princeton, N.J.: Princeton University Press, 1987); Jon Gjerde, *From Peasants to Farmers: The Migration from Balestrand, Norway to the Upper Middle West* (New York: Cambridge University Press, 1985). For an older but valuable treatment from a leading figure in immigration history, see Kathleen Neils Conzen, *Immigrant Milwaukee, 1836–1860: Accommodation and Community in a Frontier City* (Cambridge, Mass.: Harvard University Press, 1976).

46. Jon Gjerde, *The Minds of the West: Ethnocultural Evolution in the Rural Middle West, 1830–1917* (Chapel Hill: University of North Carolina Press, 1997). Gjerde told his Cal-Berkeley colleague David A. Hollinger that "in some ways, I've never really left the Middle West." Monica Friedlander, "Jon Gjerde, Dean of the Social Sciences Division, Dies at 55," University of California–Berkeley press release, November 25, 2008. A year before his death, Gjerde was appointed to the Morrison Professorship of American History formerly occupied by John D. Hicks. David A. Hollinger, "In Memoriam: Jon Gjerde, Historian of Immigration and Ethnicity," *Perspectives on History* (April 2009).

47. Leslie A. Schwalm, *Emancipation's Diaspora: Race and Reconstruction in the Upper Midwest* (Chapel Hill: University of North Carolina Press, 2009); Thomas J. Sugrue, *Sweet Land of Liberty: The Forgotten Struggle for Civil Rights in the North* (New York: Random House, 2008); Thomas J. Sugrue, *The Origins of the Urban Crisis: Race and Inequality in Postwar Detroit* (Princeton, N.J.: Princeton University Press, 1996); Darrel E. Bigham, *On Jordan's Banks: Emancipation and Its Aftermath in the Ohio River Valley* (Lexington: University Press of Kentucky, 2005); Bill Silag, ed., *Outside in: African-American History in Iowa, 1838–2000* (Des Moines: State Historical Society of Iowa, 2001); Robert Dykstra, *Bright Radical Star: Black Freedom and White Supremacy on the Hawkeye Frontier* (Cambridge, Mass.: Harvard University Press, 1993); Joel William Trotter Jr., *Black Milwaukee: The Making of an Industrial Proletariat, 1915–1945* (Urbana: University of Illinois Press, 1985).

48. Richard White, *The Middle Ground: Indians, Empires, and Republics in the Great Lakes Region, 1650–1815* (New York: Cambridge University Press, 1991).

49. Richard White to author, October 20, 2012.

50. R. David Edmunds, ed., *Enduring Nations: Native Americans in the Midwest*

(Urbana: University of Illinois Press, 2008); R. David Edmunds, *Tecumseh and the Quest for Indian Leadership* (New York: Pearson, 2006); James H. O'Donnell III, *Ohio's First Peoples* (Athens: Ohio University Press, 2004); Jane T. Merritt, *At the Crossroads: Indians and Empires on a Mid-Atlantic Frontier, 1700–1763* (Chapel Hill: University of North Carolina Press, 2003); Gregory Evans Dowd, *War Under Heaven: Pontiac, the Indian Nations, and the British Empire* (Baltimore: Johns Hopkins University Press, 2002); Daniel K. Richter, *Facing East from Indian Country: A Native History of Early America* (Cambridge, Mass.: Harvard University Press, 2001); Allan Greer, *The Jesuit Relations: Natives and Missionaries in Seventeenth-Century North America* (New York: St. Martin's, 2000); Timothy Shannon, *Indians and Colonists at the Crossroads of Empire: The Albany Congress of 1754* (Ithaca, N.Y.: Cornell University Press, 2000); Stewart Rafert, *The Miami Indians of Indiana: A Persistent People, 1654–1994* (Indianapolis: Indiana Historical Society Press, 1999); Frederick E. Hoxie, Ronald Hoffman, and Peter J. Albert, eds., *Native Americans and the Early Republic* (Charlottesville: University Press of Virginia, 1999); Colin G. Calloway, *The American Revolution in Indian Country: Crisis and Diversity in Native American Communities* (Cambridge: Cambridge University Press, 1995); Gregory Evans Dowd, *A Spirited Resistance: The North American Indian Struggle for Unity, 1745–1815* (Baltimore: Johns Hopkins University Press, 1992); Francis Jennings, *Empire of Fortune: Crowns, Colonies, and Tribes in the Seven Years' War in America* (New York: W. W. Norton, 1988); R. David Edmunds, *The Shawnee Prophet* (Lincoln: University of Nebraska Press, 1985).

51. Jay Gitlin, *The Bourgeois Frontier: French Towns, French Traders, and American Expansion* (New Haven, Conn.: Yale University Press, 2010); Claiborne A. Skinner, *The Upper Country: French Enterprise in the Colonial Great Lakes* (Baltimore: Johns Hopkins University Press, 2008); Colin G. Calloway, *The Scratch of a Pen: 1763 and the Transformation of North America* (New York: Oxford University Press, 2006); Carolyn Podruchny, *Making the Voyageur World: Travelers and Traders in the North American Fur Trade* (Lincoln: University of Nebraska Press, 2006); Alan D. Graf, *Bayonets in the Wilderness: Anthony Wayne's Legion in the Old Northwest* (Norman: University of Oklahoma Press, 2004); Eric Hinderaker and Peter C. Mancall, *At the Edge of Empire: The Backcountry in British North America* (Baltimore: Johns Hopkins University Press, 2003); Cayton and Teute, *Contact Points*; Elizabeth A. Perkins, *Border Life: Experience and Memory in the Revolutionary Ohio Valley* (Chapel Hill: University of North Carolina Press, 1998); Carl J. Ekberg, *French Roots in the Illinois Country: The Mississippi Frontier in Colonial Times* (Urbana: University of Illinois Press, 1998); Eric Hinderaker, *Elusive Empires: Constructing Colonialism in the Ohio Valley, 1673–1800* (Cambridge: Cambridge University Press, 1997); Stephen Aron, *How the West Was Lost: The Transformation of Kentucky from Daniel Boone to Henry Clay* (Baltimore: Johns Hopkins University Press, 1996); John Mack Faragher, *Daniel Boone: The Life and Legend of an American Pioneer* (New York: Henry Holt, 1992); Wiley Sword, "The Contest for the Old Northwest, 1790–1795: An Overview," *Northwest Ohio Quarterly* 64, no. 1 (Winter 1992): 3–20; Peter S. Onuf, *Statehood and Union: A History of the Northwest Ordinance* (Bloomington: Indiana University Press, 1987).

52. Andrew R. L. Cayton and Stuart D. Hobbs, eds., *The Center of a Great Empire: The Ohio Country in the Early Republic* (Athens: Ohio University Press, 2005); Andrew R. L. Cayton, *Ohio: A History of a People* (Columbia: Ohio State University

Press, 2002); Cayton, "Artery and Border," 19–26; Andrew R. L. Cayton, *Frontier Indiana* (Indianapolis: Indiana University Press, 1996); R. Douglas Hurt, *The Ohio Frontier: Crucible of the Old Northwest, 1720–1830* (Bloomington: Indiana University Press, 1996); Michael N. McConnell, *A Country Between: The Upper Ohio Valley and Its Peoples, 1724–1774* (Lincoln: University of Nebraska Press, 1992); Kenneth J. Winkle, *The Politics of Community: Migration and Politics in Antebellum Ohio* (Cambridge: Cambridge University Press, 1988); Andrew R. L. Cayton, *The Frontier Republic: Ideology and Politics in the Ohio Country, 1780–1825* (Kent, Ohio: Kent State University Press, 1986).

53. Nicole Etcheson, *A Generation at War: The Civil War Era in a Northern Community* (Lawrence: University Press of Kansas, 2011); Nicole Etcheson, *Bleeding Kansas: Contested Liberty in the Civil War Era* (Lawrence: University Press of Kansas, 2006); Nicole Etcheson, *The Emerging Midwest: Upland Southerners and the Political Culture of the Old Northwest, 1787–1861* (Bloomington: Indiana University Press, 1996).

54. Jon K. Lauck, *Prairie Republic: The Political Culture of Dakota Territory, 1879–1889* (Norman: University of Oklahoma Press, 2010).

55. Jon K. Lauck, John E. Miller, and Don Simmons, eds., *The Plains Political Tradition: Essays on South Dakota Political Culture* (Pierre: South Dakota State Historical Society Press, 2011); Jon K. Lauck, John Miller, and Edward Hogan, "The Contours of South Dakota Political Culture," *South Dakota History* 34, no. 2 (Summer 2004): 157–178; Robert Cook, *Baptism of Fire: The Republican Party in Iowa, 1838–1878* (Ames: Iowa State University Press, 1993).

56. Jeffrey Ostler, *Prairie Populism: The Fate of Agrarian Radicalism in Kansas, Nebraska, and Iowa, 1880–1892* (Lawrence: University Press of Kansas, 1993); Thomas A. Woods, *Knights of the Plow: Oliver H. Kelley and the Origins of the Grange in Republican Ideology* (Ames: Iowa State University Press, 1991).

57. David B. Danbom, *Going It Alone: Fargo Grapples with the Great Depression* (St. Paul: Minnesota Historical Society Press, 2005); Michael Johnston Grant, *Down and Out on the Family Farm: Rural Rehabilitation in the Great Plains, 1929–1945* (Lincoln: University of Nebraska Press, 2002); Peter Fearon, *Kansas in the Great Depression: Work Relief, the Dole, and Rehabilitation* (Columbia: University of Missouri Press, 1997); Paula M. Nelson, *The Prairie Winnows Out Its Own: The West River Country of South Dakota in the Years of Depression and Dust* (Iowa City: University of Iowa Press, 1996); Michael W. Schuyler, "New Deal Farm Policy in the Middle West: A Retrospective View," *Journal of the West* 33 (1994): 52–63; Catherine McNicol Stock, *Main Street in Crisis: The Great Depression and the Old Middle Class on the Northern Plains* (Chapel Hill: University of North Carolina Press, 1992).

58. Deborah Kay Fitzgerald, *Every Farm a Factory: The Industrial Ideal in American Agriculture* (New Haven, Conn.: Yale University Press, 2010); J. L. Anderson, *Industrializing the Corn Belt: Agriculture, Technology, and Environment, 1945–1972* (DeKalb: Northern Illinois University Press, 2008); Richard F. Nation, *At Home in the Hoosier Hills: Agriculture, Politics, and Religion in Southern Indiana, 1810–1870* (Bloomington: Indiana University Press, 2005); Dennis Nordin and Roy V. Scott, eds., *From Prairie Farmer to Entrepreneur: The Transformation of Midwestern Agriculture* (Bloomington: Indiana University Press, 2005); Jon K. Lauck, *American Agriculture and the Problem of Monopoly: The Political Economy of Grain Belt Farming, 1953–1980* (Lincoln: University of Nebraska Press, 2000); Thomas B. Colbert, "Iowa

Farmers and Mechanical Corn Pickers, 1900–1952," *Agricultural History* 74, no. 2 (2000): 530–544; Steven Keillor, *Cooperative Commonwealth: Co-ops in Rural Minnesota, 1859–1939* (St. Paul: Minnesota Historical Society Press, 2000); H. Craig Miner, *Harvesting the High Plains: John Kriss and the Business of Wheat Farming, 1920–1950* (Lawrence: University Press of Kansas, 1998); Deborah Kay Fitzgerald, *The Business of Breeding: Hybrid Corn in Illinois, 1890–1940* (Ithaca, N.Y.: Cornell University Press, 1990); J. Sanford Rikoon, *Threshing the Midwest, 1820–1940: A Study of Traditional Culture and Technological Change* (Bloomington: Indiana University Press, 1988).

59. William B. Friedricks, *Covering Iowa: The History of the Des Moines Register and Tribune Company, 1849–1985* (Ames: Iowa State University Press, 2000); William B. Friedricks, *In for the Long Haul: The Life of John Ruan* (Ames: Iowa State University Press, 2003); Kurt E. Leichtle, "Power in the Heartland: Tractor Manufacturers in the Midwest," *Agricultural History* 69, no. 2 (1995): 314–325.

60. David Blanke, *Sowing the American Dream: How Consumer Culture Took Root in the Rural Midwest* (Athens: Ohio University Press, 2000). See also Barron, *Mixed Harvest*; and Ronald R. Kline, *Consumers in the Country: Technology and Social Change in Rural America* (Baltimore: Johns Hopkins University Press, 2002).

61. Jim Norris, *North for the Harvest: Mexican Workers, Growers, and the Sugar Beet Industry* (St. Paul: Minnesota Historical Society Press, 2009); Tobias Higbie, *Indispensable Outcasts: Hobo Workers and Community in the American Midwest, 1880–1930* (Urbana: University of Illinois Press, 2003); Deborah Fink, *Cutting into the Meatpacking Line: Workers and Change in the Rural Midwest* (Chapel Hill: University of North Carolina Press, 1998); Daniel Nelson, *Farm and Factory: Workers in the Midwest 1880–1990* (Bloomington: Indiana University Press, 1995); Donald D. Stull, Michael J. Broadway, and David Griffith, eds., *Any Way You Cut It: Meat Processing and Small-Town America* (Lawrence: University Press of Kansas, 1995); Lizabeth Cohen, *Making a New Deal: Industrial Workers in Chicago, 1919–1939* (New York: Cambridge University Press, 1990).

62. Kathleen Mapes, *Sweet Tyranny: Migrant Labor, Industrial Agriculture, and Imperial Politics* (Urbana: University of Illinois Press, 2009); David M. Lewis-Colman, *Race against Liberalism: Black Workers and the UAW in Detroit* (Urbana: University of Illinois Press, 2008); John F. Lyons, *Teachers and Reform: Chicago Public Education, 1929–1970* (Urbana: University of Illinois Press, 2008); Rosemary Feurer, *Radical Unionism in the Midwest, 1900–1950* (Urbana: University of Illinois Press, 2006); Warren J. Wilson, *Struggling with "Iowa's Pride": Labor Relations in the Rural Midwest* (Iowa City: University of Iowa Press, 2000); Dionicio Nodin Valdes, *Barrios Notenos: St. Paul and Midwestern Mexican Communities in the Twentieth Century* (Austin: University of Texas Press, 2000); Kimberley L. Phillips, *Alabama North: African-American Migrants, Community, and Working-Class Activism in Cleveland, 1915–45* (Urbana: University of Illinois Press, 1999); Rick Halpern, *Down on the Killing Floor: Black and White Workers in Chicago's Packinghouses, 1904–54* (Urbana: University of Illinois Press, 1997); Roger Horowitz, *"Negro and White, Unite and Fight!": A Social History of Industrial Unionism in Meatpacking, 1930–90* (Urbana: University of Illinois Press, 1997); Marvin L. Bergman and Shelton Stromquist, eds., *Unionizing the Jungles: Labor and Community in the Twentieth-Century Meatpacking Industry* (Iowa City: University of Iowa Press, 1997); Shelton Stromquist, *A Generation of Boomers: The Pattern of Railroad Labor Conflict in Nineteenth-Century America* (Urbana: University of Illinois Press, 1993); Shelton Stromquist, ed., *Solidarity*

and *Survival: An Oral History of Iowa Labor in the Twentieth Century* (Iowa City: University of Iowa Press, 1993); Zaragosa Vargas, *Proletarians of the North: A History of Mexican Industrial Workers in Detroit and the Midwest, 1917–1933* (Berkeley: University of California Press, 1993); James R. Barrett, *Work and Community in the Jungle: Chicago's Packinghouse Workers, 1894–1922* (Urbana: University of Illinois Press, 1990); Richard Jules Oestreicher, *Solidarity and Fragmentation: Working People and Class Consciousness in Detroit, 1875–1900* (Urbana: University of Illinois Press, 1990).

63. Adam Arenson, *The Great Heart of the Republic: St. Louis and the Cultural Civil War* (Cambridge, Mass.: Harvard University Press, 2011); Lawrence H. Larsen, Harl A. Dalstrom, Kay Calame Dalstrom, and Barbara J. Cottrell Larson, *Upstream Metropolis: An Urban Biography of Omaha and Council Bluffs* (Lincoln, Neb.: Bison Books, 2007); David Blanke, "Buckeye Legacies: Aspects of Urban Community in Ohio and the Ohio River Valley," *Journal of Urban History* 29, no. 3 (March 2003): 310–321; Mary Lethert Wingerd, *Claiming the City: Politics, Faith, and the Power of Place in St. Paul* (Ithaca, N.Y.: Cornell University Press, 2003); Donald L. Miller, *City of the Century: The Epic of Chicago and the Making of America* (New York: Simon & Schuster, 1997); Jon C. Teaford, *Cities of the Heartland: The Rise and Fall of the Industrial Midwest* (Bloomington: Indiana University Press, 1993); Sherry Lee Linkon and John Russo, *Steeltown U.S.A.: Work and Memory in Youngstown* (Lawrence: University Press of Kansas, 2003); Jeffrey Adler, *Yankee Merchants and the Making of the Urban West: The Rise and Fall of Antebellum St. Louis* (New York: Cambridge University Press, 1991); Cronon, *Nature's Metropolis*; Timothy Mahoney, *River Towns in the Great West: The Structure of Provincial Urbanization in the American Midwest, 1820–1870* (New York: Cambridge University Press, 1990).

64. Cayton and Onuf, *Midwest and the Nation*; Cayton and Gray, *Identity of the American Midwest*; Andrew R. L. Cayton, Richard Sisson, and Chris Zacher, eds., *The American Midwest: An Interpretive Encyclopedia* (Bloomington: Indiana University Press, 2006); Cayton and Teute, *Contact Points*.

65. Cayton and Gray, *Identity of the American Midwest*.

66. James H. Madison, *Heartland: Comparative Histories of the Midwestern States* (Bloomington: Indiana University Press, 1988).

67. David C. Brown, *Beyond the Frontier: The Midwestern Voice in American History Writing* (Chicago: University of Chicago Press, 2009); Michael C. Steiner, "Frontier to Region: Frederick Jackson Turner and the New Western History," *Pacific Historical Review* 64, no. 4 (November 1995): 479–501; Michael C. Steiner, "The Significance of Turner's Sectional Thesis," *Western Historical Quarterly* 10, no. 4 (October 1979): 437–466. On Brown, see Jon K. Lauck, "The 'Interior Tradition' in American History," *Annals of Iowa* 69, no. 1 (Winter 2010): 82–93.

68. Joseph A. Amato and David R. Pichaske, *Southwest Minnesota: A Place of Many Places* (Marshall, Minn.: Crossings Press, 2007); David R. Pichaske, *Rooted: Seven Midwest Writers of Place* (Iowa City: University of Iowa Press, 2006); Richard O. Davies, Joseph A. Amato, and David R. Pichaske, eds., *A Place Called Home: Writings on the Midwestern Small Town* (St. Paul: Minnesota Historical Society, 2003); Joseph A. Amato, *Rethinking Home: A Case for Writing Local History* (Berkeley: University of California Press, 2002); David R. Pichaske and Joseph A. Amato, eds., *Southwest Minnesota: The Land and the People* (Marshall, Minn.: Crossings Press, 2000); Joseph A. Amato, John Meyer, John Radzilowski, Donata DeBruyckere, and

Anthony Amato, *To Call It Home: The New Immigrants of Southwestern Minnesota* (Marshall, Minn.: Crossings Press, 1996).

69. Miller notes that small towns and the Midwest "have received less than their fair share of attention in recent decades." The small town has "lost its centrality in the American imagination," and the "Middle West, for a time considered to be the heartland and center of American life, has lost its prominent position in American thought, as the two coasts and the Southern rim have attracted the bulk of internal migration and become the repository of most of the nation's industrial, financial, political, and cultural influence." John E. Miller, review of Richard O. Davies, Joseph A. Amato, and David R. Pichaske, *A Place Called Home*, *Minnesota History* 58, no. 8 (Winter 2003–2004): 417. John E. Miller, *Memories of Home: Small-Town Boys from the Midwest and the American Dream* (forthcoming from Kansas University Press).

70. Justin Wolff, *Thomas Hart Benton: A Life* (New York: Farrar, Straus & Giroux, 2012); Kenneth H. Wheeler, *Cultivating Regionalism: Higher Education and the Making of the American Midwest* (DeKalb: Northern Illinois University Press, 2011); Wayne A. Wiegand, *Main Street Public Library: Community Places and Reading Spaces in the Rural Heartland, 1876–1956* (Iowa City: University of Iowa Press, 2011); Jennifer Marie Holly Wells, "The Construction of Midwestern Literary Regionalism in Sinclair Lewis's and Louise Erdrich's Novels: Regional Influences on Carol Kennicott and Fleur Pillager" (Ph.D. diss., Drew University, 2009); Anita Clair Fellman, *Little House, Long Shadow: Laura Ingalls Wilder's Impact on American Culture* (Columbia: University of Missouri Press, 2008); William Barillas, *The Midwestern Pastoral: Place and Landscape in Literature of the American Heartland* (Athens: Ohio University Press, 2006); Timothy B. Spears, *Chicago Dreaming: Midwesterners and the City, 1871–1919* (Chicago: University of Chicago Press, 2005); Keith Newlin, *Hamlin Garland: A Life* (Lincoln: University of Nebraska Press, 2008); James R. Kieselburg II, "Midwestern Images of Labor: Wisconsin Artists and Their Portrayal of Industry," *Journal of the Society for Industrial Archeology* 34, nos. 1–2 (2008): 135–148; Edward Watts, *American Colony: Regionalism and the Roots of Midwestern Culture* (Athens: Ohio University Press, 2002); John E. Miller, "Midwestern Regionalism during the 1930s: A Democratic Art with Continuing Appeal," *Mid-America* 83, no. 2 (Summer 2001): 71–93; Wendy J. Katz, "Creating a Western Heart: Art and Reform in Cincinnati's Antebellum Associations," *Ohio Valley History* 1 (Fall 2001): 2–20; Christine Pawley, *Reading on the Middle Border: The Culture of Print in Osage, Iowa, 1860–1900* (Amherst: University of Massachusetts Press, 2001); David R. Reynolds, *There Goes the Neighborhood: Rural School Consolidation at the Grass Roots in Early Twentieth-Century Iowa* (Iowa City: University of Iowa Press, 1999); John E. Miller, *Becoming Laura Ingalls Wilder: The Woman behind the Legend* (Columbia: University of Missouri Press, 1998); James M. Dennis, *Renegade Regionalists: The Modern Independence of Grant Wood, Thomas Hart Benton, and John Steuart Curry* (Madison: University of Wisconsin Press, 1998); E. Bradford Burns, *Kinship with the Land: Regionalist Thought in Iowa, 1894–1942* (Iowa City: University of Iowa Press, 1996); Paul Theobald, *Call School: Rural Education in the Midwest to 1918* (Carbondale: Southern Illinois University Press, 1995); John E. Miller, *Laura Ingalls Wilder's Little Town: Where History and Literature Meet* (Lawrence: University Press of Kansas, 1994); William Holtz, *The Ghost in the Little House: A Biography of Rose Wilder Lane* (Columbia: University of Missouri Press, 1993); Nan Wood Graham, *My Brother, Grant Wood* (Iowa City: State Historical Society of Iowa, 1993); Ronald

Weber, *The Midwestern Ascendancy in American Writing* (Bloomington: Indiana University Press, 1992); Wayne Fuller, *The Old Country School: The Story of Rural Education in the Middle West* (Chicago: University of Chicago Press, 1982).

71. James Shortridge, *The Middle West: Its Meaning in American Culture* (Lawrence: University Press of Kansas, 1989); John C. Hudson, *Making the Corn Belt: A Geographical History of Middle Western Agriculture* (Bloomington: Indiana University Press, 1994); John C. Hudson, *Plains Country Towns* (Minneapolis: University of Minnesota Press, 1985).

72. Jane Adams, ed., *Fighting for the Farm: Rural America Transformed* (Philadelphia: University of Pennsylvania Press, 2002); Kathryn Marie Dudley, *Debt and Dispossession: Farm Loss in America's Heartland* (Chicago: University of Chicago Press, 2000); Jane Adams, *The Transformation of Rural Life: Southern Illinois, 1890–1990* (Chapel Hill: University of North Carolina Press, 1994); Sonya Salamon, *Prairie Patrimony: Family, Farming, and Community in the Midwest* (Chapel Hill: University of North Carolina Press, 1992).

73. Robert Wuthnow, *Red State Religion: Faith and Politics in America's Heartland* (Princeton, N.J.: Princeton University Press, 2011); Robert Wuthnow, *Remaking the Heartland: Middle America since the 1950s* (Princeton, N.J.: Princeton University Press, 2010); Patrick J. Carr and Maria J. Kefalas, *Hollowing Out the Middle: The Rural Brain Drain and What It Means for America* (Boston: Beacon Press, 2009); Jess Gilbert, "Rural Sociology and Democratic Planning in the Third New Deal," *Agricultural History* 82, no. 4 (Fall 2008): 422–438; Jess Gilbert, "Eastern Urban Liberals and Midwestern Agrarian Intellectuals: Two Group Portraits of Progressives in the New Deal Department of Agriculture," *Agricultural History* 74, no. 2 (Spring 2000): 162–180; Jess Gilbert, "Wisconsin Economists and New Deal Agricultural Policy: The Legacy of Progressive Professors," *Wisconsin Magazine of History* 80 (Summer 1997): 280–312.

74. Martin Bruce King, "Interpreting the Consequences of Midwestern Agricultural Industrialization," *Journal of Economic Issues* 34, no. 2 (June 2000): 425–434; Mary Eschelbach Gregson, "Rural Response to Increased Demand: Crop Choice in the Midwest, 1860–1880," *Journal of Economic History* 53, no. 2 (1993): 332–345.

75. Nick Reding, *Methland: The Death and Life of an American Small Town* (New York: Bloomsbury USA, 2010); Richard E. Wood, *Survival of Rural America: Small Victories and Bitter Harvests* (Lawrence: University Press of Kansas, 2010); Dale Maharidge and Michael Williamson, *Denison, Iowa: Searching for the Soul of America through the Secrets of a Midwest Town* (New York: Free Press, 2008); Richard Longworth, *Caught in the Middle: America's Heartland in the Age of Globalism* (New York: Bloomsbury USA, 2009).

76. Denis Boyles, *Superior, Nebraska: The Commonsense Values of America's Heartland* (New York: Doubleday, 2007); Thomas Frank, *What's the Matter with Kansas? How Conservatives Won the Heart of America* (New York: Holt, 2005).

77. Andrew R. L. Cayton to author, September 6, 2012.

INDEX

abolition, 106n128
academic politics, 56–57, 59, 63–65
African Americans: attitudes toward, 54–55, 106n128; as focus of historians, 54; in Midwest, 27–28
The Age of Reform (Hofstadter), 57
agrarianism, 6–7, 25–26, 45
agricultural history, 45–47, 55, 88, 89
Agricultural History (journal), 46–47, 65, 85
Agricultural History Society (AHS), 46
AHA. *See* American Historical Association
AHS (Agricultural History Society), 46
Algonquin tribes, 27
Allen, William, 126n233
Alvord, Clarence A.: approach to history/research, 40, 49, 64–65, 67, 68–69; areas of study, 56; on Midwest people/experience, 39; and *MVHR*, 33, 60, 66; professional activities of, 32, 35, 37, 62
Amato, Joe, 89
American Archivist, 35–36, 65
American Bureau of Industrial Research, 55
An American Colony (Watts), 22
American exceptionalism, 18, 25, 42–43, 76, 78
American Historical Association (AHA), 32, 46, 68, 108–109n17
American Indians: as focus of

historians, 55–56, 88; in Midwest, 14; in Seven Years War, 27
American Revolution: buildup to, 14–15, 41; historiography of, 88–89; Midwest role in, 15, 41, 81; political institutions stemming from, 16–17, 22–23, 41, 81
Ames, Fisher, 17
Anderson, David D., 122n193
Annals of Iowa, 5
anti-semitism, 56
Appel, Livia, 129–130n2
Appleby, Joyce, 18
archival research, 64–65
Atherton, Lewis, 68
"Atlantic History" (Games), 117n116
audience for historiography, 33, 65–66, 80

backcountry: in colonial history, 14–15, 41; defined, 97–98n7; vs. frontier, 97–98n7; political atmosphere in, 15, 21; settlers of, 15, 18, 81
Bancroft, Frederic, 108–109n17
Barnhart, John D.: approach to history/research, 41; areas of study, 45–47, 121n186; background of, 33–34, 58; on Midwest people/experience, 39; professional activities of, 43, 63; on Turner, 38
Beard, Charles A., 61–62, 68, 69
Beard, Mary R., 69
Becker, Carl, 68, 140n186

Bemis, Samuel Flagg, 118n129

Bergman, Marv, 5

Beyond the Frontier (Brown), 30–31, 56, 89

bias. *See* interpretation, scholarly; objectivity; prejudice

Billington, Ray Allen, 86, 128n261, 140n196

Blanke, David, 89

Blegen, Theodore: approach to history/research, 38, 49; areas of study, 114n68; background of, 36, 58, 59; professional activities of, 67, 125n218

Bloodlands (Snyder), 81

Bogue, Allan: approach to history/research, 36, 43, 60, 66, 69; areas of study, 46–47, 85, 147n19; background of, 35, 54, 64, 123n203; influence of, 87; professional activities of, 50, 65, 67, 140n196

Bogue, Margaret Beattie, 54, 123n204

Bolton, Herbert, 85

Brown, David, 30–31, 56, 89

Buck, Solon Justus: approach to history/research, 36, 65, 66; areas of study, 45; background of, 33; professional activities of, 35, 44

Buley, R. Carlyle: approach to history/research, 43, 67–68; areas of study, 50; background of, 35, 55, 62; on Midwest people/experience, 39; on predecessors, 51–52; professional activities of, 67

capitalism, 25–27, 76

Carstensen, Vernon, 35, 49, 61, 63, 85–86

Carter, Clarence E., 110n34

Catapano, Joan, 92n12

categories of analysis in historical study, 6–7, 87–89

Cayton, Andrew, 78, 87, 88–89, 90

Chicago, 26–27

church attendance/activities, 59–60

civic participation: in Midwest, 16, 21, 24, 39; of Prairie Historians, 58. *See also* democracy

civil rights movement, 55, 131n15

Civil War, 18–20, 24, 27–28, 106n128

Clark, George Rogers, 15

colonial history, 14–15, 18, 41, 88–89

common law, 16

Commons, John, 55

Confronting History (Mosse), 79–80

Connelley, William, 34

constitutionalism, 44

consumer culture, 89

cosmopolitanism vs. regionalism, 94–95n41

"counternarratives," 76

Craven, Avery, 71, 74, 141n202

Cronon, William, 4, 86–87, 148n25

cultural influences: of East, 3, 15, 21–23, 41–42, 48, 50, 71; language and, 77; of North, 4, 39; regionalism and, 22, 77–78; of South, 17, 24

Cumings, Bruce, 24–25

Curti, Merle: approach to history/research, 42; background of, 60, 61, 64; professional activities of, 63, 148n28; on Turner, 38, 43

Dale, Edward, 132n27

democracy: backcountry influence on, 16, 17–18, 41, 99n27; fostered by capitalist enterprises, 26; influence of oppression on, 80–81; linked to egalitarianism, 39; as theme in American exceptionalism, 43–44

determinism, 47–48

Dick, Everett: areas of study, 49–50; background of, 35, 64; professional activities of, 67, 127n245

diversity: in historical perspectives, 70–71; in Midwest, 27–28; social/political effects of, 24, 39, 79, 81–82

Doig, Ivan, 126n232

Dominion from Sea to Sea (Cumings), 24–25

Draper, Lyman, 34

Dykstra, Robert, 54

East: cultural dominance of, 3, 15, 21–23, 41–42, 48, 50, 71; as focus of historians, 29, 31–32, 50, 68, 85; political orientation, 62

ecology, 48

IOWA AND THE MIDWEST EXPERIENCE